Handbook of Public Services Management

Handbook of Public Services Management

Christopher Pollitt and Stephen Harrison

Copyright © Christopher Pollitt and Stephen Harrison 1992

First published 1992

Blackwell Publishers
108 Cowley Road
Oxford OX4 1JF
UK

Three Cambridge Center
Cambridge, Massachusetts 02142
USA

British Library Cataloguing in Publication Data
A CIP catalogue record for this book is available from the British Library.

Library of Congress Cataloging-in-Publication Data
Handbook of public services management / [edited by] Christopher
    Pollitt and Stephen Harrison.
        p.   cm.
    Includes bibliographical references (p.   ) and index.
    ISBN 0-631-16961-X
    1. Administrative agencies—Great Britain—Management.
I. Pollitt, Christopher.   II. Harrison, Stephen. 1947–
JN425.H36   1992   91-38282
354.4104—dc20   CIP

Typeset in 10/12 pt Plantin
by Best-set Typesetter Ltd., Hong Kong
Printed in Great Britain by T.J. Press Ltd, Padstow, Cornwall.

This book is printed on acid-free paper

Contents

Figures

Tables

Contributors

John Bourn is the Comptroller and Auditor General, and head of the National Audit Office. Previously he held a series of senior appointments in the Ministry of Defence and the Northern Ireland Office.

Rodney Brooke was Chair of Bradford Health Authority and is now the Secretary for the Association of Metropolitan Authorities.

David Burningham is Senior Lecturer in Economics at Brunel University.

Alan Butler is Senior Lecturer in Social Work at the University of Leeds.

Brian Edwards is Regional General Manager of Trent Regional Health Authority.

Andrew Gray is a Senior Lecturer in Accountancy at the University of Kent.

Stephen Harrison is Senior Lecturer in Policy Studies at the Nuffield Institute for Health Services Studies, University of Leeds. Previously he was an NHS Personnel Officer.

Mary Henkel is Lecturer in Government at Brunel University.

Bill Jenkins is Senior Lecturer in Politics at the University of Kent.

Kate Jenkins is Director of Personnel for the Royal Mail. She was previously head of the Prime Minister's Efficiency Unit, and an author of the 1988 *Next Steps* report.

Rosalind Levacic is Senior Lecturer in Educational Policy and Management at the Open University.

Andrew F. Long is Senior Lecturer in Research Methods at the Nuffield Institute for Health Services Studies, University of Leeds.

Jean Neale is Special Projects Officer, Leeds Social Services.

Christopher Pollitt is Professor of Government at Brunel University, having previously held a variety of academic and civil-service posts.

Graeme Salaman is Senior Lecturer in Sociology at the Open University.

John Sizer is Professor of Financial Management at Loughborough University.

Christine Stewart is the Finance Officer of the Prison Service.

David Symes is a Lecturer in Informed Management at the Nuffield Institute for Health Services Studies, University of Leeds.

C. J. Train is Director General of the Prison Service.

Norman Tutt is Director of Leeds Social Services and Professor of Applied Social Studies at Lancaster.

William Warburton is Assistant Director, Planning and Monitoring Division, Leeds Social Services.

Norman Warner is Director of Social Services for Kent County Council. Previously he was a senior civil servant at the Department of Health and Social Security.

Brian Wilcox is Chief Adviser at the Education Department, Sheffield City Council. He has also held a visiting professorship at Sheffield University.

Roy Wilkie is Professor of Management at Strathclyde University.

Gerald Wistow is Senior Lecturer in Health and Social Care Management at the Nuffield Institute for Health Services Studies, University of Leeds.

Preface

Public services are indispensable to the social, economic and political health of the United Kingdom – and, indeed of every other liberal democratic state. How these services are managed is therefore a topic of profound significance. In this book we seek not only to illuminate this topic (though that is one of our objectives) but also to offer guidelines, suggestions and models which are of practical help.

In one sense the managers of our public services are not short of advice. Indeed, it could be argued that there has arisen a surfeit of glossy conference folders, five-minute managers' booklets, consultancy reports and the like. Few middle- or senior-management offices are without some of these languishing on the bookshelf. Also, at the academic end, there is beginning to be quite a copious literature, analysing the surge of managerial reform which has spilled over the public-service sector since the late 1970s. We believe, however, that there is an important space between these two kinds of publication, and that this book will fit into that niche.

The aim of the *Handbook of Public Services Management* is to be close enough to the experience and vocabulary of actual management practice to be of practical use. Yet at the same time we intend it to be sufficiently detached to provide an analytical tool-kit that will enable readers to pare away the fine detail of their local circumstances, penetrate the rhetoric of this year's fashionable technique or buzz-word, and grasp the enduring conceptual core of the issues confronting them. It is not a student primer, and neither is it meant to be a formulaic 'how to do it' text of the evangelical school of management. The essence of senior management often lies in tackling problems for which there is no 'one best way', or certainly not one which can be reduced to a few slogans or check-lists. Nevertheless, our belief is that there *are* certain common and recurring issues and dilemmas which face senior managers right across the public services, and these are much more likely to yield to careful reflection and analysis than to a simple cookbook approach. We identify and explain these issues in the following introduction.

In keeping with the aim of the *Handbook* we have sought contributions from persons with a wide range of relevant experiences. Half our authors are accomplished managers from a range of public-service backgrounds. The other half are senior academics (many of whom have themselves been practitioners at various stages in their careers) with specialist expertise in the study of public-sector policies and organizations. All our contributors agreed to write within a broad framework which the editors laid down beforehand. What follows, therefore, is not a collection of conference papers or personal testimonies, but a focused group of chapters assembled under a set of common rules and guidelines. It is further integrated by some short reflective passages which the editors have inserted at the end of each major section. Our hope is that, taken together, these features make for a kind of book which has hitherto been much needed but little in evidence. But this, of course, is no more than the editors, as 'managers' of the book, pointing to the high quality of the inputs and the diligence of the processing. The readers, as always, will be the final judges of the outcome.

Our thanks are due to Linda Clark, who typed the final manuscript, and to the staff of the Nuffield Institute Library.

SH
Slaithwaite
CJP
Eaglescliffe
April 1991

Introduction

Christopher Pollitt and Stephen Harrison

This book is based on the belief that managing public services is different. In our view these differences are not just matters for abstract hypothesizing, but are manifest in the everyday work of the managers concerned. Furthermore they are recognized as being of great significance by many of the service providers themselves. On the whole the impact of the differences appears to increase with the seniority of the manager concerned, so their significance is at its maximum at the levels of permanent secretary, chief executive, general manager, chief constable and so on. But the impact is certainly not exclusive to such peak positions: rather it needs to be appreciated and understood by managers at all levels, and certainly by those who aspire to the top three or four levels in their respective hierarchies. Therefore, as editors seeking original contributions, we decided to opt for a roughly half-and-half mixture between academic experts and senior managers themselves.

Our assertion of the distinctiveness of public services would not be accepted by all managers, or even by all public-service managers. There are a variety of views on this issue, ranging from the extreme generic management position (all management is basically the same) to the 'public services are unique' position – or even to the assertion that the police force, health service (etc.) is unique (Gunn, 1987). Because this question of similarity/distinctiveness is a controversial one – and fundamental to the organization of this book – we need to explain and justify our line.

The book is focused on aspects of public services management which we argue are significantly different from the classic model of private-sector corporate management (upon which many general management texts are still based). The classic model proceeds on the assumption that clear corporate objectives can be identified and prioritized, and that management then has the task of devising and implementing programmes of activity to achieve those objectives. All this takes place in a competitive environment which offers sharp sanctions to the inefficient. Unless otherwise specified, that classic model is the yardstick for comparison. Against that yardstick public services are distinctive because of:

1 The existence of accountability to elected political representatives.
2 The frequent lack of both consensus and precision concerning the overall goals and priorities of the service.
3 The complexity of the organizational networks in which the managers' own organization must work.
4 The occasional absence or rarity of competing organizations. Obviously this is not a *necessary* feature of the public-service environment, and has diminished in salience with the rise of market and quasi-market processes since the mid-1980s. We will argue, however, that it is often still significant.
5 The fact that providing more of a public service often increases the providing unit's revenue only marginally, or not at all. Again, in some services this is changing, but in a distinctively public-sector manner.
6 The way in which a central feature of most public services is the face-to-face 'processing' of large numbers of people (citizens), and the conduct of transactions with them which are far more complex (and less standardized) than buying and selling (e.g. in schools, hospitals, social security, policing, social services).
7 The prominence, in most such services, of professional groups of service deliverers who are more or less resistant to classic 'line management' relationships, and who work partly according to standards which are formulated nationally – often by a professional body rather than by the employer – and are only vestigially within the control of local management.
8 Their distinctive legal context.

Each of these eight key differences will bear some preliminary discussion (see also Pollitt, 1990a). We are certainly not claiming that each one is equally salient in each and every public service. Elected representatives, for example, are much 'closer to the action' in the personal social services than in the National Health Service. Professionalism has been a more prominent and pervasive issue in the NHS than in the police force. Taken together, however, these eight features shape both the management behaviour and the management culture of every major public service, and do so to a degree that is quite foreign to other kinds of organization such as, say, Sainsbury's, Ford or ICI. This does not make public-service management *totally* different (we are not supporters of the uniqueness hypothesis), but it does imply that many of the prescriptions of generic management will require considerable adaption before they will fit in this distinctive context.

Accountability to Elected Representatives

Believers in generic management sometimes liken this feature of public services to accountability to a company board of directors. But politicians are not at all like boards of directors. Their powers, interests and motives are all likely to diverge markedly from the model of the company board. Only occasionally do they bring with them any detailed knowledge of the particular services for which they assume political responsibility. They operate with – indeed often seek – a degree of exposure in the mass media which most boards of directors would regard as a public-relations disaster. They conduct themselves in ways which reflect the incessant fact of party political competition – as though a board had to operate with rival, alternative boards constantly looking for flaws in its performance. These sensitivities to current tendencies in public opinion and to the policies of rival would-be office holders help explain the short time horizons and attention spans which politicians frequently display. As Harold Wilson said, 'A week is a long time in politics.' 'Statesmen' (or women) is the term which is reserved for those politicians who manage to retain some longer term vision and consistency despite these conditions. They are in a minority.

Also, it is important to appreciate the distinction between *managerial* accountability and *political* accountability (Day and Klein, 1987, pp. 26–7). *Political* accountability is a concept with a long and colourful history. The English Civil War was at least partly a struggle over the proper extent of political accountability. More recently the concept has come to play a key role in the liberal democratic perspective on the relationship between the state and society. In this perspective politicians are viewed as representatives who are answerable to the citizenry. They are obliged to give account, demonstrating that their actions have been reasonable, fair, honest, prompt and so on. In other words political accountability involves a *justification* of decisions and actions, and the justification is usually couched in terms of the values which are currently supposed to characterize stewardship of the citizens' interests. In practice, since these values are very general, and often do not all point in the same direction, there is usually considerable scope for argument as to the justifiability of a particular course of action.

By contrast, *managerial* accountability is a more recent and restricted notion. It is 'about making those with delegated authority answerable for carrying out agreed tasks according to agreed criteria of performance' (Day and Klein, 1987, p. 27). The criteria typically used in the assessment of managerial performance include economy (input minimization), efficiency (input/output ratios) and effectiveness (congruence between outcomes and objectives) – the famous 'three Es' which sum to value for money (VFM). Our contributors will be mainly concerned with this species of accountability, but they recognize the special problems which arise in public-service management because of the possible tension between the different criteria applied to the performances of elected representatives and senior officials – who must nevertheless work together on a close and regular basis.

Overall Goals and Priorities

Politicians tend to find the task of setting clear objectives harder than the boards of private companies (not that this is easy for the latter). Again, the exposed and competitive nature of political activity accentuates the difficulties. Articulating a manageable number of clear priorities sounds very sensible in the management textbooks, but to a politician the identification of clear priorities may lead to loss of support among those groups who do *not* see themselves as benefiting from those programmes which have been given pride of place. For the politician, therefore, it is often easier to say that almost *everything* is important and to remain vague about exactly which groups occupy which slots in the queue for service. A classic example of this occurred during the 1980s when the number of 'priorities' within the NHS grew to nearly 50. Each time a new health problem achieved sufficient notoriety it was added to the department's list. AIDS, waiting lists and other matters of political salience were added to the existing 'priorities' which had been carried over from the seventies (moving patients out of long-stay institutions into the community, mental handicap services, etc.) This 'priority shyness' among politicians, though widespread, does vary. Generally speaking, the more secure the governing party (be it in central or local government), the more clearly stated may be its objectives and priorities. Hence, as Mrs Thatcher's political hold strengthened through the elections of 1983 and 1987, so her administration's policies for the public services became more focused and radical.

It is not only politicians who find the formulation of objectives a difficult and sometimes disagreeable task. Senior officials and managers may be no better equipped to resolve those conflicts over objectives which are rooted in competing value systems among the community at large. Thus (for example) popular opinion is, and long has been, divided over whether the prime purpose of imprisonment is punishment or rehabilitation. Or again, is university education supposed to produce inventions and trained persons to feed the needs of the economy or to broaden and train minds in a more general way, producing individuals who are 'cultured', tolerant and critical yet appreciative of the history and traditions of the society in which they live? For a decade or more the former (vocational) view has clearly enjoyed the upper hand in government pronouncements, but it is quite possible to argue that the high reputation of British higher education abroad owes more to the latter (liberal) tradition. In this situation vice-chancellors and other senior university officers have shown little appetite for meaningful statements of objectives. One recent survey of university goal and mission statements concluded that 'In the matter of goals we are not sophisticated at all: I fear, in fact, that in some respects we are still in the bronze age' (Allen, 1988, p. 3).

Clearly these tendencies raise some major questions about the role of public-service managers. How can they manage in the (frequent) absence of clear, stable, ordered objectives? If they cannot secure sufficiently firm objectives by seeking them in the public pronouncements of elected representatives, is there anywhere else from whence they can be sought? How, in this situation, can operational targets be generated for middle and junior management? These will be among the issues tackled by our contributors later in this *Handbook*.

The Complexity of Organizational Networks

Complexity, of course, is a matter of degree, and the assertion that the networks of public-service organizations are more complex than those of most private-sector firms is no more than a statement of tendency. Private-sector firms do have a variety of 'stakeholders' – shareholders (if they are a quoted company), bankers, suppliers, clients, etc. – and there may certainly be particular firms whose relationships are more complex than those of Toy Town police force or Rural Rides Social Services Department. Nevertheless many business people, coming into public-service management, express surprise (and sometimes dismay) at the number and variety of significant organizational relationships with which they have to contend. Take, for example, a district general manager in the NHS. At minimum he or she must deal with the regional general manager, the District Health Authority, the Community Health Council, the managers of local provider units, the local representatives of the British Medical Association, the Royal College of Nursing, the National Union of Public Employees and the Confederation of Health Service Employees, local councillors and the local MP, the local Social Services Department and the local press.

Such complexity implies that certain managerial skills – those to do with managing multiple (and frequently conflicting) relationships – are of particular importance, especially in the upper reaches of public-service management. The nature of such skills, the tactical principles involved, and best way of acquiring or learning about them, will all feature in subsequent sections of the present text (see also Beneviste, 1989, pp. 156–94).

The Absence or Rarity of Competing Organizations

Again, most standard management texts assume that the manager is managing a firm which is in competition with other firms. For many public-service organizations (though far fewer than in the recent past) overt competition is not a problem. A police force does not face rival forces offering the same services on its 'patch', and neither does the prison service. The consequences of this state of affairs may be quite pervasive. Some research work seems to show that the degree of competition an organization faces may have a much greater influence on its performance than its ownership status, where the latter is measured along a continuum running from government departments to owner/manager private firms (Dunsire et al., 1988).

This is, however, an area of rapid change among UK public services. Forms of competition or quasi-competition have been introduced in many parts of the public sector. Thus far there appear to be three basic types. First, there is quasi-competition through performance measurement schemes. Thus sets of performance indicators (PIs) are put together which show, in 'league table' format, how apparently similar units within the same service are 'scoring' (Pollitt, 1986a and 1990b). PIs have been introduced to the NHS, the police, the prison service, personal social services, education (primary, secondary and tertiary) and the courts. Second, and more recently, there have been attempts to create direct competition, but still within the public sector. This has involved, for example, the creation of city technology colleges and the provisions of the 1988 Education Reform Act permitting schools to 'opt out' from local authority control. In the health sector the 1989 White Paper (Cm. 555) encourages larger hospitals to assume the status of self-governing trusts and introduces new financing arrangements which are intended to stimulate all hospitals to compete for patients. In higher education universities and polytechnics have, in a variety of ways, been pressed to compete over student numbers and research. Third, there is competition between public and private service providers. This too has grown, especially in the health, education and social-care sectors where tax and other provisions have been altered so as to encourage citizens to consider privately-provided alternatives.

All these developments are of profound concern to public-service managers. What is the appropriate relationship between public and private providers? ('Partnership' may be an attractive political slogan, but exactly how can this work in practice?) Which forms of direct competition between units within a public service produce which mixtures of problems and benefits? Can real competition be stimulated, or will most local 'markets' for health care or education soon degenerate into *de facto* monopolies or oligopolies? Can broad service planning be combined with such competition, or are the two fundamentally irreconcilable? Can PI systems be designed so that they register quality and effectiveness, or will they continue to reflect a lop-sided concern with economy and efficiency? All these questions will be addressed in the chapters which follow.

The Relationship between Provision, Need, Demand and Revenue

Marketed goods and services have money prices, and the more of them are bought, the more the income of the supplying organization is increased. Only if the service/good is priced below marginal cost can increasing sales spell financial trouble. Most public services are not marketed in this way – and even where a price is charged it typically represents only a fraction of the full cost of producing the service, or is subject to so many exemptions that a significant proportion of service users are receiving it free. Indeed, increased demand is frequently an embarrassment rather than a benefit for public service managers, who may know that their revenues are fixed (at least in the short term) by cash limit, and that a larger than expected volume of services will therefore have to be supplied from a static resource base.

What is more, economic analysis long ago suggested that, where goods or services are supplied free at the point of access, demand is indeed likely to be high, and that the problem of 'excess demand' will be endemic (Charles and Webb, 1986, chapter 6). Hence the necessity for some form of overt or covert rationing, to substitute for the market's covert rationing by price. Such rationing may be sought through more or less complex eligibility criteria, through granting professionals the authority to decide who really 'needs' a service and who doesn't, or by 'deterrents' such as queues or the attachment of social stigma to the receipt of the service. Most of these ways of combating 'excess demand' necessitate considerable managerial involvement. Finding politically and socially acceptable ways of rationing services – ways that are seen as fair as well as efficient – is therefore another distinctive task for public-service managers, and not one which is likely to make them especially popular. It is a task the prominence of which is increasing as market-like mechanisms are introduced in health and social care, schools, higher education and other public services.

Processing People

The public services 'process' people – very large numbers of them, and mainly at first hand rather than remotely. In 1988 the NHS dealt with roughly eight million in-patients and state schools enlightened nine million students. Whilst it is true that millions also entered the portals of Marks and Spencer or Boots the transactions most of them concluded in those stores were far less complex than the transactions which make up the daily lives of doctors, nurses and teachers. Most of the visitors to the retail chains went there to purchase highly standardized items at nationally standardized prices. In public services, however, the service can usually be standardized only to a limited degree – one history class is not identical to another and neither are all hysterectomies or cases of schizophrenia. Even in the more bureaucratized world of social security, the immense variations in claimants' personal circumstances are constantly throwing up new precedents and 'case law'.

Lack of standardization of 'product' is, however, only the beginning of the distinctiveness of public services as people-processing organizations. As 'people processors' they are highly labour-intensive organizations, with consequences for (a) costs; (b) vulnerability to external forces such as demographic shifts, government pay policies, etc.; (c) the ways in which they can improve organizational performance; and (d) the speed at which they can change.

Another very striking feature of these services is that the final outcomes (effects) of their provision are often extremely hard to discern, or, at least, hard to separate from the effects of many other factors simultaneously acting on their consumers. Would the patient have got better/died anyway? How much of Mrs Higgins's improvement was due to the physician's skill, how much to good nursing, how much to the loving attentions the patient's illness called forth from her hitherto neglectful family, how much to the change in diet which the illness finally brought about? Did little Johnny learn to read when he did because of school lessons, or would he have picked it up fairly soon anyway, from parents and peers? What is the 'outcome' of all the history that is studied in secondary schools? What are the 'outcomes' of the probation service, and how different would be the career trajectories of offenders if it did not exist? On the whole there is not much questioning of the utility of a Marks and Spencer jacket or a bar of Boots' soap – if you don't want one, you shouldn't buy one. Public services are not remotely in this position. Their final utility, as well as their efficiency, is frequently under scrutiny. Their 'production function' may be unknown. Their provision is sometimes compulsory (for the consumer) rather than voluntary. Their objectives (as we noted above) are often vague or contested.

Finally, in the public services the fashionable vocabulary of 'consumerism' has distinct limitations (Pollitt, 1988). Those who are processed by public services are never only 'consumers', they are also always *citizens* (Rhodes, 1987). This places them, potentially at least, in a relationship with the providers which has no real counterpart in the private sector. Historically, the concept of citizenship has been closely bound up with notions of representation and participation which are foreign to the world of the supermarket or chain store. *Democratic* citizenship, what is more, is intimately linked to notions of equality which have nothing to do with the ability to pay. It is true that such considerations are not normally at the forefront of the doctor–patient or teacher–child transaction, but they are potentially, or latently present. In times of stress and dissatisfaction they may emerge, often embryonically, in the form of statements such as 'I'm a taxpayer too you know' or 'my child deserves a decent education.'

Thus the people-processing aspects of public-service management compel us to ask many practical questions about what is necessary in order to 'get closer to the public' with respect to a wide range of complex and non-standardized transactions (Local Government Training Board, 1987). In addition, however, there are subtle questions – both practical and philosophical – concerning what is due to the consumers who are sometimes obliged to consume services which are not to their liking, and who are always not *merely* consumers but also citizens.

Professionalism and Line Management

The seventh significant difference is the unusual prominence and autonomy of professionals delivering services. While it is obviously true that many professionals are employed by commercial firms or other private-sector organizations they seldom achieve, in these contexts, the same salience. It would be unusual, to say the least, for middle-rank ICI chemists to come out with public statements accusing company policy of being wrong and local management of being high-handed or misguided. Yet in the NHS consultants not infrequently go to the local press with such disgruntlements. As one NHS director of finance said to us during research fieldwork: 'It's like having production managers who aren't responsible to the general manager' (Harrison et al., 1992).

It might reasonably be pointed out that the medical profession is something of a special case, in that, for a variety of historical and political reasons, it has secured an unusually high degree of autonomy. Yet other public services have also operated in ways which afford their professionals considerable latitude and protection from the more direct forms of managerial intervention. Until invaded by Conservative Secretaries of State during the 1980s, the schoolteachers had their 'secret garden' of the curriculum and were usually not subject to any formal and regular appraisal of their work. Much the same applied to academic staff in the universities and polytechnics, though there too the eighties witnessed growing pressure from central government to strengthen the hands of management, give priority to some types of course over others and institute new systems of appraisal. In the sphere of law and order the autonomy of chief constables and the relative impotence of police authorities (at least on some issues) has been a focus for considerable controversy, both academic and political (Morgan and Swift, 1987). During the 1970s (though less so during the eighties) there were a number of episodes in which social or community workers 'sided' with their clients against at least some of the policies of their employing authorities. Even during the 1980s, as was seen during the Cleveland child sex-abuse saga, social workers retained the capacity to conduct highly interventionist and controversial policies with only limited political or managerial direction. Finally it should be allowed that social security is something of an exception to the general salience of professionalism. It is the most bureaucratized, routinized and therefore 'clericalized' of the major public services and does not boast a strong group of professional service deliverers.

The general prominence and autonomy of professionals within most public services represents a strong challenge to generic notions of 'management'. In contrast to the pro-active managers of the generic textbooks – hugely energetic leaders who set targets, allocate resources, motivate, reward success, discipline failure and monitor performance – the reality of management in some public services has been much more concerned with diplomatic and administrative functions – persuading and pleading with the professionals, tidying up after them and attempting, with some difficulty, to involve them in service planning and the implementation of those plans (see, e.g. Harrison, 1988). Under the pressures of the 1980s this situation began to change, but the overall outcome is by no means yet clear. Managing with professionals therefore remains as a crucial issue for this *Handbook*.

The Legal Context

Most public services are creatures of statute law. Their operations are constrained by statutory obligations of a kind which are not present in company law and which are therefore absent from most discussions of management couched in terms of commercial or industrial models. For example, a public authority or corporation may be statutorily obliged to offer a particular service or provision despite the fact that, by contemporary accounting criteria, that service is 'uneconomic'. Management is not as free as in large corporations to redefine its 'mission', moving out of this business and into that.

The legal context may also have significant consequences for 'customer relations'. Some statutes conferring powers on public authorities set up special grievance procedures or even 'watchdog' consumer bodies. There are Community Health Councils, ombudspersons, various types of tribunal and so on. In both education and social care failures to proceed 'correctly' have resulted in policy decisions being overturned by the courts. Since the collapse of the relative political consensus of 1950–75 challenges to the legality of new public service arrangements and procedures seem to have become more frequent. Commercial and industrial managements do, of course, have their own legal constraints and problems. These are, however, substantially different from those faced by most public-service managers.

The Eight Differences: Summary

Each of the eight differences introduced in the preceding paragraphs has a major impact on the possible strategies and tactics open to public service managers. Taken together they create, for most public services most of the time, a quite distinctive ethos or 'culture' (for other analyses tending to this same conclusion see Ackroyd et al., 1989 and Harrow and Willcocks, 1990). The 'excellence' which is sometimes visible in this or that unit or department or organization may not be obtainable through the faithful application of the nostrums of generic management or, at least, these prescriptions may need to be heavily modified (for the most famous example of generic prescription, see Peters and Waterman, 1982). Something more attuned to the special world of public services is required. We have therefore divided the remaining chapters into four sections, each corresponding to what we see as a major area or choice for those who would manage the public services. These are:

1 Evaluation: if the goals of public-service organizations are rarely clear or consensual (the second key difference discussed above) then it follows that the question of how to evaluate organizational performance will be problematic.
2 The control strategies available to professionals and to managers: this arises directly from our observations that (the seventh difference) many

groups of public-service employees are resistant to control through classical chain-of-command hierarchies, and (the sixth difference) that this resistance can be buttressed by the role of public-service organizations as deliverers of personal or individualized services.

3 New approaches to resource management: if, as we note above (fifth difference) public-service organizations lack the usual commercial connections between levels of product produced and revenue obtained, and (fourth difference) often lack effective competitors, special arrangements may be necessary to ensure that managers and others do not disregard the financial consequences of their decisions and actions. Alternatively, in those localities and services where quasi-markets *are* working, how can traditional budgetary arrangements be adapted to meet the challenge of competition?

4 Strategic management: accountability to elected politicians can result in short time horizons and attention spans (first difference). If, therefore, organizational stability and continuity are to be obtained, managers must in some sense strive to operate *in spite* of such considerations. Such concerns lead directly to issues of organizational design (third difference).

Our contributors discuss these four areas in considerable detail, and analyse their impacts on particular public services. We conclude this introduction with a more general discussion of each issue.

Evaluating Public Services

Discourse about the evaluation of organizational performance is beset by rhetoric; terms such as 'quality', 'excellence' and 'efficiency' are often employed indiscriminately, as terms of general approbation. As the late George Woodcock is reputed to have said, 'We're all against sin, aren't we?' And sometimes somewhat impoverished notions of performance are given rather grand designations; one recent official document defined 'effectiveness' as the extent to which a policy is actually implemented!

Although we are unable to impose our own semantics on this discourse, we are able to set out some basic terms within which our contributing authors can discuss specific developments. *Inputs* are the resources, including staff, equipment, materials and buildings, which are employed in an organization. The lowest common denominator in which such inputs can be expressed, is of course, money. *Economy* is the minimization of inputs. *Outputs* are the services or activities or processes being provided in the public-service organizations which are the focus of this book: what is done to or for clients. These include performing operations, giving lessons, home visiting and so on. *Outcomes* or *impacts* are the effects of those services (etc.) upon clients: improvements (or not) in their educational status, health status, financial status or whatever. A programme or service is more or less *effective* to the extent that it results in an improvement in this status *which would not otherwise have occurred*.

Two other crucial performance terms are derived from combinations of the above. *Efficiency* is the ratio of the inputs to outputs. On this definition (which corresponds to the economist's concept of X-efficiency: see Leibenstein, 1966), improvements in efficiency are only to be valued insofar as the output is valued. It is possible to kill people efficiently or spread litter efficiently. *Cost-effectiveness*, by contrast, relates to what are by definition desired outcomes, being the cost per unit of such an outcome, e.g. the cost per person with eyesight restored or per examination passed or per elderly person enabled to stay at home rather than go into institutional care. Finally, *equity* is the extent to which equal needs are equally met; it will readily be seen that the possible operationalizations of this concept are large in number, since a wide range of proxies for need (age, social class, geography, 'diagnosis', and so on) can be employed, and the currency in which the receipt of services is measured could consist of inputs, processes outputs or outcomes.

Prevailing opinions about appropriate definitions of public-service organizational performance have changed somewhat over time, though until the mid-1970s it was largely taken for granted that increasing inputs was desirable *per se*, a view apparently then shared by both governments and service providers. Following the introduction in the late 1970s of cash limit (as opposed to volume) financing to much of the public sector, interest developed in controlling the growth of inputs (economy) and in relating them more closely to processes and outputs (efficiency). It is only more recently that widespread attempts to measure effectiveness have developed, and it is not always easy to tell how much of this is principally rhetorical.

A feature of the late 1980s and early nineties has been the emergence of a strong rhetoric around the notion of improving the *quality* of public services. This reached an apogee in mid-1991 when the Prime Minister personally identified himself with a *Citizen's Charter* which had as its first aim to 'work for better quality in every public service' (Cm. 1559, 1991). What precisely constitutes 'quality' has been the focus of an intense and untidy debate (e.g. Pfeffer and Coote, 1991). 'Quality' can evidently refer to inputs, processes, outputs or outcomes – as a term it has been used even more promiscuously during the 1990s than 'efficiency' was in the 1980s. One popular short definition is that quality is fitness for purpose. From management's point of view one of the most important features of this fashion is that most of the quality literature stresses the primacy of *user* or *consumer* judgements. Thus it is incumbent on managers and professionals to set, declare and justify clear *standards* for key aspects of service (e.g. waiting or response times, complaints procedures, provision of information) and then to subject themselves to users' judgements of whether or not these standards have been met.

It is clear that the public services are all at present engaged in exercises aimed at measuring and improving their performance, however defined. The most pervasive form which such attempts have taken is that of performance indicators, developed, *inter alia*, in social security (MacPherson, 1987), health (Pollitt, 1985), education (Pollitt, 1990c) and crime (Carter, 1988). As these commentators note, such indicators are at present still often narrow in their conceptualization of performance (Pollitt, 1990b). This reflects in part the greater availability of information about processes/outputs than about outcomes, in part the conceptual difficulties in defining outcome in people-processing organizations, and perhaps also the potentially threatening nature of information about effectiveness.

The growing salience of evaluation has also been evident in the creation of new evaluative institutions, and the modification of existing ones (Henkel, 1991). As the first five chapters demonstrate, *both* appropriate performance criteria *and* potent evaluative units are required if evaluation is to be genuinely useful rather than merely ritualistic or self-serving.

Professions and Management

Almost by definition, professionalism and management are opposed concepts. Management is 'getting things done through people' or 'planning, organizing, controlling, and evaluating'. Academic definitions of professionalism are diverse, but the main perspectives all stress a certain autonomy. To put it bluntly, management is getting others to do what one wants whilst professionalism is using one's own judgement.

This is not meant to imply that professional–managerial conflict need be unproductive or unmanageable. Managers might not seek to control professionals, preferring instead to adopt a reactive, facilitating role (for an example, see Harrison, 1988, chapter 3). There may be degrees of professionalism whereby more or less autonomy may be demanded. And there is always the possibility that the two groups will have sufficient common interests for conflict to be avoidable. Nevertheless, public service professionals are often resistant to classical management techniques. Add to this the increasing financial pressures on public-service institutions which have resulted from demographic changes and other sources of rising demand, plus macroeconomic policies which stress the containment of public expenditure, and it is hardly surprising that tension and conflict have been endemic for a decade or more.

If differences in relative power are important determinants of the outcomes of such conflict, what control strategies are available to managers? One possibility would be to employ chain-of-command techniques, if necessary supported by incentives and/or sanctions based on management, rather than professional criteria. Such an exercise of the 'first dimension' of power (Lukes, 1974) is implied in, for instance, recent proposals to change the basis of medical staff distinction awards so that management criteria are added to the previous professional requirements and managers are added to the committees making the awards. However, there are a number of obstacles to such an approach.

First, many public services purport to be personalized, to respond to the needs of individual clients. Since such needs are conventionally seen as infinite, and since professional time and effort is finite, it is left to professionals to ration services through their daily decisions about how to categorize clients. Thus the decisions of such 'street-level bureaucrats' (Lipsky, 1980) become, in aggregate, the service policy of the agency that employs them. Second, and closely related, such professional freedom actually functions partly to insulate managers from blame, whether from clients or elsewhere. Third, line management of professionals requires an intellectual grasp of the relevant work which is unlikely to be found outside the profession itself. Taken together, therefore, these obstacles suggest that successful employment of the chain-of-command model may depend on the employment of numbers of the professionals themselves as managers. This is already well established in some public services (e.g. headteachers as managers of schools) but other services, such as the NHS, are moving away from such a model.

A second possible control strategy for managers is to seek to control the premises and information upon which professionals make their decisions: in effect structuring what is, and is not, on their agendas. This would be an exercise of Lukes's second dimension of power. In practice, this means the formalization of professional work by such means as national curricula for education or standardized treatment protocols for health workers. As with the chain-of-command strategy, a successful formalization strategy is likely to require the involvement of professionals as managers.

The third control strategy is for managers to seek to change the way in which professionals see their role. As Peters and Waterman (1982) note in their best-selling *In Search of Excellence*, it may be more reliable to control subordinates by manipulating the organizational climate or culture so that they 'internalize', or *choose* to behave in the ways preferred by management, than to employ direct supervision or extensive proceduralization. Such an approach, which corresponds to Lukes's third dimension of power, would have the further advantage of flexibility: it would allow unpredicted situations to be dealt with within the specified organizational culture but without the need for formalization. In public-service organizations, manipulation of the content of professional education offers an important means of cultural change; management education for doctors (National Health Service Training Authority, 1986) and the inclusion of business criteria in further education courses (Manpower Services Commission, 1987) are examples of such an approach. This strategy may, of course, be reinforced by changes in broader aspects of organization structure, such as increased business representation on the Universities Funding Council or by moves to introduce competition into public services (see below).

Strategic Management

The notion of strategic management springs from the idea that organizations should be seen as existing within, and affected by, an external environment. Such an approach is common to a range of otherwise rather diverse theories, including systems, contingency, resource dependence and Marxist models (see, for instance, Pfeffer, 1982). Strategic management is the way in which an organization's managers attempt to position their institution within this environment. The precise operationalization of the concept of environment of course varies between theoretical approaches, but it seems to fall into two broad categories: first, those that focus on concrete actors and institutions as the environment, and, second, those that focus on forces deriving from changes in macro-level phenomena such as economics and demography.

Approaches of the first kind are concerned with other organizations and institutions with which the focal organization transacts (see, for instance, Pfeffer and Salancik, 1978). Such transactions may themselves be contractual, such as those with suppliers and customers, or may be symbolic or hierarchical, as with auditors or hierarchically superior institutions. The latter category of symbolic and hierarchical transactions is likely to be especially important for public-service agencies, because it is partly through these that the legitimacy of their activities is confirmed. It is evident that government's demands are often conflicting and a number of incidents (such as the resignation in 1986 of Mr Victor Paige as chief executive of the National Health Service: Davies 1986) suggest that immediate political considerations are likely to lead to continued government incursions into the detailed work of public-service organizations.

One way in which managers might avoid becoming the passive victims of immediate political concerns, or, perhaps worse, being caught between these and the demands of other actors in the environment, is actively to manage the way in which their organization appears to the outside world. In such a 'marketing' approach, the choice, manipulation and presentation of information is likely to be a key strategy, as is the use of symbolic actions such as changes in top personnel (Pfeffer and Salancik, 1978).

The second approach is to conceptualize the organizational environment in terms of shifts in economic trends, demography, technology and markets. Demographic trends have considerable importance for public-service organizations; a combination of improving life expectancy and a declining birth rate has resulted in a population containing a increasing proportion of elderly people and a declining proportion of young adults (*Social Trends*, 1988). Such changes have obvious potential impacts on welfare state expenditure, since the elderly not only need to be supported in terms of social security but are much greater consumers of services such as health care and social services (DHSS, 1983). Changes in the relative size of the working population have implications for the taxation base and hence potentially for welfare state funding, though of course the falling birth rate has also meant falling school rolls and (potentially at least) lower teenage entries to higher and further education. This also affects the potential recruitment to welfare-state professions, such as nursing, where entry is typically in the late teens.

Technological developments (not just 'hardware', but more general techniques for delivering services) are in many cases specific to particular public service sectors, and may be more or less expensive, more or less substitutes for labour (public services are typically highly labour-intensive), and more or less subject to managerial control of their adoption and diffusion. Other technology, especially that concerned with computerized information systems, is more generally applicable, and in recent years has been diffused quite widely in the public services. Indeed, information technology is essential underpinning for many of the budgetary and evaluatory reforms discussed below. One consequent choice for managers is whether to employ this new technology merely to improve the efficiency of bureaucratic processes, whether to see it as a potential means of enhanced control over the workforce, or whether to seize the opportunity to enhance the information accessible to the citizens who use public services (Pollitt, 1986b).

Finally, economic policy: during the 1980s government macroeconomic policy has been much concerned to reduce the proportion of gross domestic product occupied by, initially, the public sector borrowing requirement and, subsequently, general government expenditure (Thain and Wright, 1990b). The effect of trying to minimize these ratios has been to place great financial strain on those parts of public expenditure which can be controlled via cash limits. This has been especially true at times when public expenditure has seemed to be growing beyond plans, leading (as with the 'Lawson cuts' of 1983) to sudden government modification of financial allocations. For public services managers, financial unpredictability is enhanced by continuing underfunding of public sector pay awards by a government not only concerned with its own expenditure, but with its role as an exemplar to industry of the need to link pay to productivity.

Whichever of the two main conceptualizations of the environment is adopted one common management response is institutional redesign. The notion of 'fitting' an organization's structure to its environment, originating in academic research, has become commonplace among practising managers. To conclude our discussion of strategic management it may therefore be useful briefly to revisit some of the key concepts in this field.

Child's classic account of the variables of organizational design has five elements (Child, 1977). *Specialization* is the division of labour between jobs, and greater specialization may take the form either of narrower compass accompanied by greater intellectual depth (as typified by professional specialization) or of narrow compass accompanied by greater routinization (as typified by factory production-line work). By contrast, *grouping* is the division of labour between departments within an organization. This may be accomplished along several possible lines, of which the most frequently encountered are function (i.e. by profession or occupation), geography, or by product (i.e. by service or client group). *Configuration* is, as it were, the shape of the organizational pyramid; a high ratio of tiers of management to total employees will exhibit short average spans of control and a tall hierarchical pyramid, whereas a low ratio of tiers to employees entails wider spans of control and a flat pyramid. *Integration* arrangements within an organization are the devices, such as teams, committees, plans and procedures, which co-ordinate the work of the various divisions of labour. Finally, an organization is more or less *decentralized* to the extent that significant decision-making discretion is available at lower hierarchical levels.

Although, for some years, greater decentralization has been seen as a desideratum for public service organizations, attention in their design has in practice focused on the other variables. Design prescriptions have not been consistent across different services; for instance, the NHS has tended to display increasing professional (and managerial) specialization (Harrison, 1988, chapter 2), whereas there has been more than one attempt to create generic social workers (Howe, 1986). But there has been less variation in grouping (where the functional principle has been dominant) and integration (where much attention has been devoted to the development of multidisciplinary teamwork).

More recently, however, more concrete steps have been taken towards decentralization, partly in an attempt to generate greater responsiveness to local customers. Frequently this has been linked to a shift towards greater prominence of the geographical principle in grouping. The creation of area teams or offices in such local authority services as social work and housing exemplifies this shift, as does the introduction of local management of schools (LMS). Another prominent example of decentralization has been the carving-out of independent agencies from Whitehall departments, following the 'Next Steps' report (Efficiency Unit, 1988).

How far such changes can be seen as representing 'real' decentralization depends upon more than the level in the hierarchy at which decisions are ostensibly taken. The crucial variables are the extent of discretion allowed (i.e. how wide a range of alternatives is allowed to the relevant actor) and the means and criteria by which the exercise of delegation is judged. As Hickson and Macmillan (1981) note, centralization and decentralization are alternative modes of control, the latter typically being accompanied by greater degrees of formalization. A recent example of this was the Treasury's delegation of running costs responsibilities to departments (Thain and Wright, 1990a). In other words, procedural rules are typically employed to limit the discretion available to actors, in what amounts to a more general application of Lukes's second dimension of power.

The Shape of the Book

The remainder of the book is organized within the four areas we have already identified and discussed, i.e.:

- Evaluating public services
- Controlling public service professionals
- New approaches to resource management
- Strategic management

The contributions in each section come from a mixture of academic experts and distinguished practitioners. They cover a wide range of public-service organizations. They draw on both generic ideas of good management and more particular concepts and practices developed to address the special features of this or that service or organization. They deal with the currently fashionable matters of market processes, contracts, consumerism and cultural change, but they also tackle more long-standing questions of public accountability, professionalism and the identification of need.

Each contributor has attempted to offer some pointers for successful management in the future. They have done this not in the kind of narrowly prescriptive way that is doomed to rapid obsolescence but by identifying key questions for managers to pose and/or by identifying the basic components of effective systems for coping with the turbulent public-service environment of the 1990s. Finally, at the end of each of the four main sections the editors offer some brief reflections on what has gone before. We hope that, taken together, these features will make the *Handbook* a genuinely useful companion for those charged with the difficult, distinctive and enormously consequential task of managing our public services.

References

Ackroyd, S., Hughes, J.A. and Southill, K. (1989) Public services and their management, *Journal of Manpower Studies*, 26, 603–617.

Allen, M. (1988) *The Goals of Universities*. Milton Keynes: Society for Research into Higher Education and Open University Press.

Beneviste, G. (1989) *Mastering the Politics of Planning*. San Francisco: Jossey-Bass.

Carter, N. (1988) Performance indicators in the criminal justice system. In *Crime UK*, Hermitage: Policy Journals, 87–91.

Charles, S. and Webb, A. (1986) *The Economic Approach to Social Policy*. Brighton: Wheatsheaf.

Child, J. (1977) *Organisation: a guide to problems and practice*. London: Harper and Row.

Cm. 555 (1989) *Working for Patients*. London: HMSO.

Cm. 1599 (1991) *The Citizen's Charter*. London: HMSO.

Davies, P. (1986) The day the chairman left, *Health Service Journal*, 12 June, 784.

Day, P. and Klein, R. (1987) *Accountabilities: five public services*. London: Tavistock.

Department of Health and Social Security (1983) *Health Care and its Costs*. London: HMSO.

Dunsire, A., Hartley, K., Parker, D. and Dimitriou, B. (1988) Organisational status and performance: a conceptual framework for testing public choice theories, *Public Administration*, 66, 363–88.

Efficiency Unit (1988) *Improving Management in Government: the next steps* (the Ibbs Report). London: Cabinet Office.

Gunn, L. (1987) Perspectives on public management. In J. Kooiman and K. A. Eliassen (eds), *Managing Public Organisations: lessons from contemporary European experience*, London: Sage, 33–46.

Harrison, S. (1988) *Managing the National Health Service: shifting the frontier?* London: Chapman and Hall.

Harrison, S., Hunter, J., Marnoch, G. and Pollitt, C. (1992) *Just Managing: power and culture in the NHS*. London: Macmillan.

Harrison, S. and Long, A. F. (1989) Concepts of performance in medical care organisations, *Journal of Management in Medicine*, 3, 176–92.

Harrow, J. and Willcocks, L. (1990) Public services management: activities, initiatives and limits to learning, *Journal of Management Studies*, 27, 281–304.

Henkel, M. (1991) *Government, Evaluation and Change.* London: Jessica Kingsley.

Hickson, D. J. and McMillan, C. J. (eds) (1981) *Organisation and Nation: the Aston Programme IV.* Farnborough: Gower.

Hill, D. (1988) Local management in Cambridgeshire schools. In M. Brenton and C. Ungerson (eds), *Yearbook of Social Policy 1987–8,* London: Longman, 47–57.

Howe, D. (1986) *Social Workers and their Practice in Welfare Bureaucracies.* Aldershot: Gower.

Leibenstein, H. (1966) Allocative efficiency vs. X-efficiency, *American Economic Review,* 56, 392–405.

Levacic, R. (1988) Schools and the management of public money, *Public Money and Management,* 8, 53–6.

Lipsky, M. (1980) *Street-level Bureaucracy.* New York: Russell Sage Foundation.

Local Government Training Board (1987) *Getting Closer to the Public.* Luton: LGTB.

Lukes, S. (1974) *Power: a radical view.* London: Macmillan.

MacPherson, S. (1987) Department of Health and Social Security. In J. Gretton and A. Harrison (eds), *Reshaping Central Government,* Hermitage: Policy Journals, 131–44.

Manpower Services Commission (1987) *Enterprise in Higher Education.* London: MSC.

Metcalfe, L. and Richards, S. (1990) *Improving Public Management.* Second edition. London: Sage.

Morgan, R. and Swift, P. (1987) The future of police authorities, *Public Administration,* 65, 259–76.

National Health Service Training Authority (1986) *Developing the Role of Doctors in the Management of the National Health Service: a discussion document.* Bristol: NHS.

Peters, T. J. and Waterman, R. H. (1982) *In Search of Excellence: lessons from America's best-run companies.* New York: Harper and Row.

Pfeffer, J. (1982) *Organisations and Organisation Theory.* Boston, Mass.: Pitman.

Pfeffer, J. and Salancik, G. R. (1978) *The External Control of Organisations: a resource dependence perspective.* New York: Harper and Row.

Pfeffer, N. and Coote, A. (1991) *Is Quality Good for You?* London: Institute for Public Policy Research.

Pollitt, C. (1985) Measuring performance: a new system for the National Health Service, *Policy and Politics,* 13, 1–15.

— (1986a) Beyond the managerial model: the case for broadening performance assessment in the government and the public services, *Financial Accountability and Management,* 2, 155–70.

— (1986b) Democracy and bureaucracy. In D. Held and C. Pollitt (eds), *New Forms of Democracy,* London: Sage, 158–91.

— (1988) Bringing consumers into performance measurement: concepts, consequences and constraints, *Policy and Politics,* 16, 77–88.

— (1990a) *Managerialism and the Public Services: the Anglo-American experience.* Oxford: Blackwell.

— (1990b) Performance indicators, root and branch. In M. Cave, M. Kogan and

R. Smith (eds), *Output and Peformance Measurement in Government: the state of the art*, London: Jessica Kingsley, 167–78.

— (1990c) Measuring university performance: never mind the quality, never mind the width, *Higher Education Quarterly*, 44, 60–81.

— (1991) Resources. In Block 2A of *B887 Managing Public Services*. Milton Keynes: Open University.

Pollitt, C., Harrison, S., Hunter, D. J. and Marnoch, G. (1988) The reluctant managers: clinicians and budgets in the NHS, *Financial Accountability and Management*, 4, 213–33.

Rhodes, R. (1987) Developing the public service orientation – or let's add a soupçon of political theory, *Local Government Studies*, 13, 63–73.

Social Trends, 18 (1988).

Thain, C. and Wright, M. (1990a) Running costs control in UK central government, *Financial Accountability and Management*, 6, 115–31.

— (1990b) Coping with difficulty: the Treasury and public expenditure 1976–1989, *Policy and Politics*, 18, 1–15.

Part I

Evaluating Public Services

Part 1

Evaluating the Performance of Central Government

John Bourn

Introduction

The evaluation of governmental activities is of crucial importance to a democracy. Indeed, the crucial idea of democracy is that the government should be accountable, and answerable to the people, for the policies that they adopt and for the manner in which they implement them.

How are the people to evaluate the performance of central government? This essay will examine an answer to this question which focuses on three subsidiary questions as follows:

- By what criteria is it decided whether a public service is performing poorly, adequately or well?
- Who sets these criteria, and how?
- Is there a divergence between these criteria and the criteria which the organisation is actually applying?

By What Criteria is it Decided Whether the Public Service is Performing Poorly, Adequately or Well?

At least five different answers to this question may be distinguished. They may be described as the following, in this book, the determinate and the manageable. The various criteria are examined all here is. They are all important and significant. But these various governments cannot influence the detailed performance of public authorities for the purposes they are charged to achieve. The reasons for this are indicated in the history as described in further detail in this book.

The managerial approach to public management may occur in quite dependent answers, including the identification of objectives, the framing of alternative services, and which is a large group and different governments.

1

Evaluating the Performance of Central Government

John Bourn

Introduction

The evaluation of governmental activities is of crucial importance to a democracy. Indeed, the central idea of democracy is that the government should be *accountable* and *responsible* to the people for the policies that they adopt and for the manner in which they implement them.

How are the people to evaluate the performance of central government? This essay will attempt an answer to this question by breaking it down into three subsidiary questions as follows:

- By what criteria is it decided whether a public service is performing poorly, adequately or well?
- Who sets these criteria and how?
- Is there a divergence between these criteria and the *de facto* criteria by which the organizations actually operate?

By What Criteria is it Decided Whether a Public Service is Performing Poorly, Adequately or Well?

At least five different answers to this question may be distinguished. They may be described as the political, the legal, the procedural, the responsive and the managerial. The first four are outlined in box 1. They are all important and significant. But none of them provides the means for evaluating the detailed performance of public authorities against the purposes they are charged to achieve. The managerial approach aims to do this, and is described in further detail in this essay.

The managerial approach conceives management as a series of interdependent activities including the formulation of objectives, the examination of alternative ways of achieving them, and their implementation by

Box 1
Criteria of Performance

Political

Elected representatives forming the government are responsible to Parliament and the people for the policy and administration of government services. The electorate has an opportunity at least every five years to give its verdict on the performance of the government at a general election; and this exposure to the popular will constitutes an incentive to the government and reassurance to the people that government services will be provided well.

Legal

The law can lay down the desired standards of public service; conformity to the law will then constitute a guarantee of good performance.

Procedural

Detailed procedures can be laid down for the activities of public authorities. Checks can be made to ensure that they are observed and thus ensure that the work of government conforms to defined standards.

Responsive

Decisions made by central government may be improved by more open government, allowing the general public greater access to the work of government and involving more people in policy formulation and implementation.

---

programmes of executive action conducted within organizations designed, staffed and directed to the particular tasks in hand.

According to the managerial approach, evaluation should be directed towards assessing the degree to which objectives have been achieved, measuring the extent and causes of any shortfall and guiding management towards successful remedial action. This can be depicted diagrammatically, as in figure 1.1.

Such a system has four essential elements:

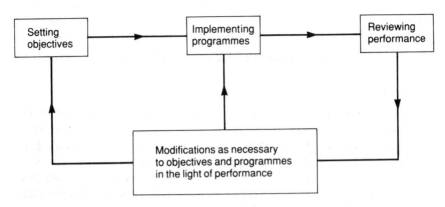

FIGURE 1.1

The managerial approach to the evaluation of performance

1 *Specific objectives.* The targets and objectives of an organization must be clearly specified in such a way that the degree and quality of their achievement can be measured. This is a crucial feature; unless it is clear what an organization is trying to do, there will be no means of deciding whether it has been successful or not.

2 *A reporting system.* Any control system must also include a system for reporting. This system must provide useful, practical and timely information, and do so in a form that enables the manager to pinpoint deviations from the planned line of progress.

3 *Interpretation and evaluation.* The results of the reporting system will provide the manager with a range of information about progress. This information will take many forms. It is important that the information is processed into easily assimilated forms so that the manager is able to use it to interpret and evaluate the economy, efficiency and effectiveness of the project.

    These measures – the 'three Es' – are the basic components of the concept of 'value for money'. *Economy* means minimizing the cost of resources used for an activity having regard to appropriate quality. *Efficiency* concerns the relationship between the inputs of resources and outputs of services. *Effectiveness* measures the extent to which objectives have been achieved and the relationship between the intended impact and the actual impact of an activity.

    The relationship between inputs and outputs and the place of economy, efficiency and effectiveness are shown in figure 1.2.

4 *Corrective action.* The final element of evaluation is taking corrective action. When interpretation and evaluation of the information yielded

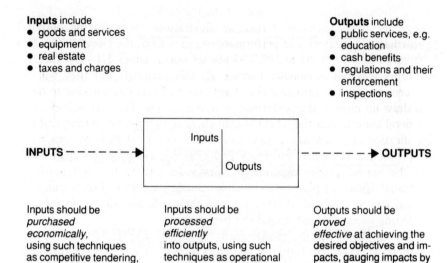

Inputs include
- goods and services
- equipment
- real estate
- taxes and charges

Outputs include
- public services, e.g. education
- cash benefits
- regulations and their enforcement
- inspections

INPUTS – – – – – – ▸   Inputs | Outputs   – – – – – ▸ **OUTPUTS**

Inputs should be *purchased economically,* using such techniques as competitive tendering, quality specification and negotiating discounts

Inputs should be *processed efficiently* into outputs, using such techniques as operational research; organization and methods studies; work study; job design and job evaluation

Outputs should be *proved effective* at achieving the desired objectives and impacts, gauging impacts by such techniques as statistical surveys of consumer satisfaction

FIGURE 1.2

The relationship between inputs and outputs and the place of economy, efficiency and effectiveness in government programmes

by the system of reporting shows that the specified targets and objectives are not being met, then the manager must be armed with the requisite authority to put matters right and to work towards the achievement of goals. If this is not possible then the manager should use the control system to make clear to superiors that the objectives and targets of the organization are unrealistic and require amendment.

The criteria embodied in the five approaches that we have examined above all have an important place in the evaluation of the performance of public services.

Who sets these criteria and how?

The criteria set under the managerial approach are determined by the government of the day in setting out the objectives, outputs and performance measures of government programmes. They are principally to be found in the departmental volumes of the Public Expenditure White Paper. They take many different forms: as illustrations, some of the outputs, performance indicators and performance targets from the *Government's Expenditure Plans 1990–91 to 1992–93* are set out in tables 1.1–1.4. Clearly, ministers will not personally prepare all this material; but they will be concerned to set the principal objectives and civil servants working to them will draw up most of the performance measures. The Treasury will exercise a general control over the whole annual exercise of objective setting and the specification of performance measures in the context of their responsibility for promoting economy, efficiency and effectiveness in government work and the annual public expenditure survey leading to the determination of annual spending plans and revenue raising measures. But within this general control, individual ministers and their officials will be responsible for setting objectives and appraising performance.

This emphasis on the management approach was underlined by the Financial Management Initiative launched in 1982. The aim was to promote the introduction in all departments of a system where managers would have:

1 a clear view of their objectives and means to assess and, wherever possible, measure outputs or performance in relation to those objectives;
2 well-defined responsibilities for making the best use of resources including a critical scrutiny of output and value for money; and
3 the information (particularly about costs), the training and access to expert advice that they need to exercise their responsibilities effectively, (Cmnd. 8616, 1982, paragraph 13).

And in 1988 this statement of management philosophy was buttressed by a report proposing a fundamental restructuring of central government that would facilitate the more effective application of the FMI principles. This was a report by the Efficiency Unit in the Cabinet Office, then led by Sir Robin Ibbs, on *Improving Management in Government: the next steps*. It pointed out that each department has different functions, and proposed that the work of each should be 'organised in a way that focuses on the job to be done; the systems and structures must enhance the effective delivery of policies and services' by setting up agencies in each department to be responsible for major executive functions. Each would be headed by a chief executive, who would be responsible for securing designated objectives within a defined budget and in accordance with defined standards capable of performance measurement. These proposals were adopted. By 1990 there were plans to establish over 80 agencies, which would employ three-quarters of the civil service.

TABLE 1.1

Youth training expenditure, coverage and performance indicators

	1987–8 outturn	1988–9 outturn	1989–90 estimated outturn	1990–1 plans	1991–2 plans	1992–3 plans
Expenditure (£ million)	1,008	1,002	1,010	907	808	763
16- and 17-year-old school leavers entering the labour market (thousands)	557	525	497	465	442	425
Numbers joining YTS/YT (thousands)	328	315	281	260	240	217
Percentage of leavers gaining a qualification	29	42	50	60	75	85
Percentage of leavers going into jobs, further education or training	76	82	83	84	85	85
Gross public cost/trainee week	50	49	50	42	37	33

'It is in the interests of both employers and young people that, through the Training and Enterprise Councils employers should progressively take over from Government the ownership and development of youth training so as to help ensure its relevance to the needs of industry and commerce in the 1990s and progressively raise the level of qualifications of young entrants to the workforce. It is therefore planned that Exchequer funding of Youth Training will gradually reduce.' The figures in table 1.1 reflect 'demographic change, the greater cost effectiveness of Youth Training compared with YTS, and a substantial increase in contributions by employers'.

Source: Government Expenditure Plans 1990–1 to 1992–3, chapter 6 – Department of Employment (Cm. 1006 p. 8).

TABLE 1.2

Highlands and Islands Development Board: output and performance indicators

	1984–5 outturn	1985–6 outturn	1986–7 outturn	1987–8 outturn	1988–9 outturn	1989–90 plans	1989–90 forecast outturn	1990–1 plans	1991–2 plans	1992–3 plans
A Overview										
1 Total gross expenditure (£ million)	42.1	39.7	35.5	37.9	42.0	46.9	46.9	46.7	51.2	54.5
2 Total net expenditure (£ million)	34.7	30.5	26.4	26.2	31.5	34.4	34.4	31.9	36.3	39.2
3 Total receipts (£ million)	7.4	9.2	9.1	11.7	10.5	12.5	12.5	14.8	14.9	15.3
4 Total running costs (£ million)	4.4	4.9	5.3	5.6	6.0	6.3	6.3	6.5	6.6	6.7
B Premises provision										
1 Total stock owned at 31 March (thousand sq metres)	104.3	120.6	123.3	123.6	132.2	147.6	137.4	143.9	147.4	150.0
2 Area of total completions during year (thousand sq metres)	7.0	18.6	2.8	6.1	11.5	14.9	13.2	12.5	12.4	12.4
3 Vacant space (percentage of total stock)	17.7	16.9	10.5	4.5	2.5	3.8	3.8	5.0	5.0	5.0

TABLE 1.2

Highlands and Islands Development Board: output and performance indicators (continued)

	1984–5 outturn	1985–6 outturn	1986–7 outturn	1987–8 outturn	1988–9 outturn	1989–90		1990–1 plans	1991–2 plans	1992–3 plans
						plans	forecast outturn			
C Equity investment										
1 New investments during year:										
i No of companies	13	9	16	9	10	10	10	10	10	10
ii Value of investments (£ thousand)	0.9	0.2	0.4	0.4	0.4	0.4	0.4	0.4	0.4	0.4
2 Total companies in Board's share portfolio (at 31 March)	85	87	86	92	91	77	77	75	73	71
D Grants and loans										
1 Total value of approvals (£ million)	21.1	19.8	19.2	14.3	25.3	19.1	19.1	19.1	19.1	19.1
2 Associated jobs	2,040	2,800	2,380	2,680	3,340	2,500	2,500	2,500	2,500	2,500
3 Private sector leverage	1.96	3.25	3.01	2.95	2.15	2.88	2.72	2.72	2.72	2.72

'The Highlands and Islands Development Board (HIDB) aims to encourage economic and social development in the Highlands and Islands of Scotland by stimulating initiative and enterprise among the residents of the area and assisting in the creation of a visible and self-sustaining economy and society. Its main functions are the provision of financial and other assistance to business and factory building; provision of advisory services; and social development.' Key indicators of the HIDB's activities and performance are given in table 1.2. The Government has announced that the functions of the HIDB will be amalgamated with those of the Training Agency in Scotland to form a new body, Highlands and Islands Enterprise, with effect from 1 April 1991.

Source: Government Expenditure Plans 1990–1 to 1992–3, chapter 15 – Scotland (Cm. 1015, p. 15).

TABLE 1.3

Gypsy sites grant: expenditure and outputs

	1987–8 outturn	1988–9 outturn	1989–90 estimated outturn	1990–1 plans	1991–2 plans	1992–3 plans
Expenditure (£ million)	4.4	5.8	7.0	8.0	9.0	10.0
Cost of programme of new pitches (£ million)	3.4	4.5	5.5	6.6	7.5	8.4
Number of new pitches created	251	251	275	290	310	330
Cost of programme of improvements (£ million)	1.0	1.3	1.5	1.4	1.5	1.6

'Gypsy Sites Grant is paid to local authorities to meet the capital costs of constructing new gypsy caravan sites and improvements to, or upgrading of, existing gypsy sites. The grant is paid at the rate of 100 per cent to encourage authorities to fulfil their obligations, under the provisions of Part II of the Caravan Sites Act 1968, to make adequate provision of gypsies residing in, or resorting to, their areas. At present, approximately 65 per cent of the country's gypsy population is accommodated on authorised sites, of which about two thirds are on local authority sites and one third on private sites. The Government's intention is to encourage authorities to accommodate the balance (4,500 caravans approximately) as speedily as possible and, to this end, is increasing pressure on authorities to fulfil their duty.'

Source: Government Expenditure Plans 1990–1 to 1992–3, chapter 8 – Environment (Cm. 1008, p. 41).

TABLE 1.4

Prison Service: resources, accommodation and inmate population

	1984–5 outturn	1985–6 outturn	1986–7 outturn	1987–8 outturn	1988–9 outturn	1989–90 estimated outturn	1990–1 plans	1991–2 plans	1992–3 plans
Expenditure (£ million)									
(a) Capital	74	105	110	108	151	339	474	350	280
(b) Current	528	550	586	667	751	767	829	920	990
(c) Total	602	655	696	775	902	1,106	1,303	1,270	1,270
Inmates	43,500	46,700	47,400	49,300	49,800	49,800	51,600	53,000	54,600
Number of staff	27,380	27,610	28,180	29,000	30,900	32,800	34,180	36,337	38,606
Certified normal accommodation	39,101	41,198	41,864	44,050	45,050	45,690	47,020	51,200	55,690
Inmate hours per officer hour	8.7	9.3	9.3	9.8	11.1	11.0	11.4	11.4	11.7
Real operating cost per inmate (£ per year)	14,872	13,745	13,970	14,163	14,011	14,391	14,643	15,327	15,637

'The Government's policy aim is to provide suitable facilities for all those whom the courts remand in custody or sentence to imprisonment. This task is entrusted to the Prison Service, which has the following statement of purpose: "Her Majesty's Prison Service serves the public by keeping in custody those committed by the courts. Our duty is to look after them with humanity and to help them to lead law abiding and useful lives in custody and after release."'

'Expenditure on the Prison Service covers the capital and current costs of prison establishments and the pay costs and general administrative expenditure of of Prison Service Headquarters and the Parole Board. For 1989–90 the forecast outturn expenditure on the Prison Service is £1,106 million (which includes higher than forecast receipts of £30 million from the discount sale of quarters) compared with a planned total of £1,140 million. [Table 1.4] provides information about actual and planned or projected levels of expenditure and increases in manpower, prison places and inmate numbers over the period 1984–85 to 1992–93. In 1988–89 the operating costs of Prison Service Headquarters were £64 million (approximately 8.5 per cent of the total operating costs). The operating costs of the prison establishment and regional offices were £687 million.'

'Indicators of performance are the number of inmate hours (hours in custody) per hour worked by prison officers and the operating cost per inmate. [Table 1.4] shows that for 1988–89 the number of inmate hours per prison officer hour (Principal Officer, Senior Officer and Officer, formerly Grades VI, VII and VIII respectively) was 11.1 compared to the estimated outturn in last year's public expenditure White Paper (Cm 611) of 11.3.'

The real operating cost per inmate in 1988–89 was £14,011 compared with an estimated outturn of £13,820: this difference is accounted for by the fact that although the inmate population was less than had been expected, the total operating costs did not decrease by an equivalent factor as only a small percentage of such costs is directly affected by fluctuations in the inmate population. More generally, as the Prison Service moves towards the goal of eliminating overcrowding and matching prison accommodation to the prison population, the operating cost per inmate will increase in real terms, as [Table 1.4] indicates, notwithstanding increasing efficiency in the deployment of staff.'

Source: Government Expenditure Plans 1990–1 to 1992–3, chapter 9 – Home Office (Cm. 1009 paragraphs 34–7).

Is There a Divergence Between these Criteria and the *De Facto* Criteria by which the Organizations Actually Operate?

The final question in this essay concerns the possibility that the overt criteria presented by the five approaches that we have distinguished may be less important than the *de facto* criteria by which organizations actually operate. Why might this be so? There are two possible answers, which we shall examine in turn:

- public servants may have personal objectives which transcend their obedience to the criteria laid down for public-service performance;
- the criteria may be obscure, incapable of yielding precise standards, or otherwise problematic, and so public servants must in fact be guided by other norms.

The first answer is, in fact, derived from the claim that public servants are, like other people, 'economic men' concerned to maximize their income, and that they will best do this by securing the promotions and advancement that will come from maximizing the rate of growth of their budgets and the size of their departments and the scale of services they provide. The bureaucrats' monopoly of relevant information facilitates this strategy (Niskanen, 1973; see also McLean, 1987).

This argument has to meet the claim that many successful bureaucrats' careers develop without their controlling large budgets; that most public servants disavow adherence to purely 'economic' motives; and that many seem moved instead by professional standards, as engineers, lawyers and other specialists. Of course, it is possible to reformulate the argument to take account of wider ranges of circumstances, such as the possibility that departments with different kinds of responsibilities and activities will offer different opportunities for different kinds of bureaucratic advancement (Dunleavy 1989a, b). And in the last analysis, it is hard to deny that public servants will show some substantial concern in their behaviour for personal progress and a rising level of income. Against this lies the argument that the personal utility maximizing bureaucrat will have to cope with competition from other utility maximizers, including other bureaucrats, interest groups and politicians, and that a balance of motives and forces is the likely outcome rather than the supremacy of a single bureaucratic will.

The second answer is linked with the idea that the criteria – especially those of the managerial approach – do not in fact give adequate guidance to the public servant in the determination of his action or the evaluation of its performance. This is expressed by Greenwood and Wilson (1989, pp. 133–4) as follows:

One Treasury review . . . candidly admitted, 'What has been achieved so far amounts to an impressive array of intermediate indicators . . . there are, as yet, relatively few links . . . between inputs and outputs which show managers how changes in resources and priorities can lead to changes in output . . . Performance measures still impact only slightly on resource allocation decisions.' Certainly the measurement of *programme* expenditure has lagged far behind that of *administrative* expenditure . . . while 'little progress' has also apparently been made with integrating performance measurement with the public expenditure survey and parliamentary supply procedures . . . Particularly striking [was] the failure to find, or agree on, measures or acceptable proxies of final output . . . Some used [were] ambiguous, misleading or open to manipulation by managers.

This latter difficulty, possible manipulation by managers, is found with practically all performance indicators, with gaming often being practised both to meet targets and to downgrade aspects of performance not specifically measured.

A further charge is that, being introduced in an era of expenditure restraint, performance measurement has focused largely on measuring and minimizing inputs (costs and manpower) with 'little evidence of genuine assessment beyond the establishment of a few input indicators', and that we are witnessing 'the ascendancy of economy and efficiency over effectiveness and efficacy'. The emphasis is upon input cost minimization, with wider questions of quality, customer satisfaction and policy outcomes being largely ignored. Similarly, Plowden (1985, p. 407) complains that the focus is 'almost entirely on the costs of governmental activities rather than on their quality'. How far, he asks, 'are the relatively simple techniques relating to the facts about costs and outputs – numbers of staff, numbers of applications dealt with – capable of being developed to deal with far more complex questions about outcomes: what did this activity actually achieve, in terms of modernizing British industry . . . improving the nation's health, or educating it for the 21st Century?'

Pollitt (1986, p. 168) draws attention to one further problem: namely that performance measurement in the public sector is 'at root a . . . political question'. Performance criteria are often 'value-laden' and raise 'perennially awkward, political question[s]'. There is also 'the problem of how to aggregate different judgements of performance' which presents 'formidable difficulties of principle and practice'. In 1985 a Financial Management Unit report admitted that as a policy-analysis tool the FMI left 'scope for very considerable further improvement'. It particularly noted the setting of imprecise goals, hidden assumptions underlying policies, and a failure to test the link between policy and impacts on the outside world. A further point is that departmental officials (and client groups) might feel threatened by the policy implications of performance measurement, as might 'a Cabinet of ministers committed to a party programme and to ways of winning the next general election'.

This quotation exemplifies the difficulties of analysing the performance of public authorities. Yet it would be wrong to conclude that it is impossible to analyse the performance of public authorities and make suggestions for their improvement (see Jackson, 1988 for some suggested criteria). The work of such bodies as the Treasury, the Efficiency Unit and the National Audit Office may not constitute the last and final word; but this does not rule out the possibility of their proposals and suggestions securing at least incremental improvements in the quality of public services by the government departments and other organizations responsible for their provision, especially by greater sensitivity to the factors outlined above and, for example, not confusing ouputs with impacts, or intermediate with final measures.

In 1988/9, for example, the government accepted 229 out of 240 recommendations made by the Public Accounts Committee. The Committee's recommendations arose from their examination of 242 conclusions and suggestions made by the National Audit Office (1989a). These are analysed in box 2.

The National Audit Office was established in 1983; it was a reconstitution of the Exchequer and Audit Department, whose responsibilities for auditing government accounts it assumed, together with newly conferred duties to evaluate the implementation of government programmes. The NAO takes government objectives as a starting-point, and then examines government spending for value for money. The head of the Office, the Comptroller and Auditor General, has the statutory authority to 'carry out examinations into the economy, efficiency and effectiveness with which a department . . . has used its resources in discharging its functions' (National Audit Act, 1983, section 6). The purpose of these investigations is to provide assurance or, where necessary, instigate change or encourage existing changes. In its reports the National Audit Office will draw conclusions and make recommendations which are presented to Parliament and considered by the Public Accounts Committee which makes recommendations to the Government after hearings to which the head civil servant of the departments concerned is summoned. The remit of the NAO is not to comment on the merit of policy objectives but to assess how those objectives have been implemented and to draw lessons which can be applied across the board of central government spending.

The criteria for selecting particular areas of study will depend on factors such as the size of the resources involved, the apparent strengths and weaknesses of control and management systems, and whether it is a poten-

Box 2
242 Value-For-Money Conclusions and Suggestions

Accountability weaknesses 25

Inadequate accountability for expenditure to Parliament and to government departments (6)
Inadequate external control and monitoring by government departments (11)
Inadequate internal controls (8)

Effectiveness in doubt 49

Inadequate justification of need or measurement of performance (25)
Duplication of effort or lack of co-ordination (7)
Failure to achieve objectives (17)

Poor Financial Planning 33

Objectives not stated, policy unclear, targets ill-defined (9)
Priorities not worked out (3)
Inadequate financial management information (21)

Poor Financial Management:

Lack of Commercial Insight 54

Under-recovery of costs, failure to economize (23)
Costly delays (3)
Weak contract procedures, inadequate incentives (28)

Poor Control and Management 80

Manpower (22)
Assets (33)
Projects (15)
Resources (10)

Poor Accounting 1

tial area of risk to value for money. Some examples of NAO reports illustrate the range and depth of the investigations:

- *The Reliability and Maintainability of Defence Equipment* (National Audit Office, 1989b)
- *Coronary Heart Disease* (National Audit Office, 1989c)
- *Road Safety* (National Audit Office, 1988a)
- *Urban Development Corporations* (National Audit Office, 1988b)
- *Assistance to Small Firms* (National Audit Office, 1988c)

Furthermore, patient examination of public services may reveal patterns of activity across a wide range of functions wherein improvements may be made. In the reports of the National Audit Office over the last few years, some major themes have emerged which illustrate how departments tend to make much the same mistakes time after time.

First is a *weakness in the management of assets*. It seems very difficult for public services to look at assets from a proper financial viewpoint and to attend to their acquisition, the management of the output to be obtained from them and ultimately their disposal in a way that recognizes the significance of the investment the community has put into them. Too often, they seem to appear as a 'free good' – something that exists and is used, but to which no special thought is given as to its value and management.

The NAO has conducted several studies into estate management in central government. These discovered a failure to appreciate the value of land and buildings; there was no clear maintenance strategy which therefore led to deterioration and a drop in value. Sites were left undeveloped and buildings empty. And there were many examples, including the National Health Service (National Audit Office, 1988d) and the Metropolitan Police (National Audit Office, 1989d) of surplus holdings whose value had not been realized, denying the taxpayer substantial capital sums.

Failure to apply commercial insight has proved to be another weakness in the expenditure of central government funds. Government departments necessarily have to place contracts, sometimes very large ones, with private-sector suppliers. They are committing taxpayers' money and have a duty to ensure that the best value for money is obtained. Yet in many cases, in spite of the fact that government departments have been letting contracts for many years, there is a lack of professionalism on the part of civil servants which has ultimately led to greater costs. The public sector should be negotiating from a position of strength and maximizing the benefits on offer. For example, spending on defence is a considerable item on the public-sector bill and by implication offers the greatest opportunities and risks. Many contract specifications have been worded too loosely. And contractors' proposals are not always thoroughly analysed during tender assessments. This creates difficulties in enforcing contracts and measuring performance. Ideally – and improvements are being made on these lines – product testing should be included in a contractor's activities and 'milestone' payments at specified stages of development and production should be introduced, as well as incentive payments.

Another important subject is *project management*. In any project it is important that the programme is developed at the right pace, the results come in on time and within budget, and that it achieves the planned benefits. Too often, however, in both public and private sectors, problems occur because projects start before being properly thought out; staff changes at awkward times; and projects are altered during implementation, with costly implications for time and money.

Project management skills are also being tested by the introduction of information technology. The Department of Social Security, for instance, is introducing an operational strategy which is believed to be the largest programme of computerization in Europe. The strategy is due to be fully implemented within the original time-scale of 12 years. But one of the negative aspects of this project is that there has been extensive use of overtime and external consultants because of slippage earlier on. The estimate of costs has risen and the estimated savings have fallen since they were first calculated because the financial viability of the strategy as a whole was not properly monitored during the initial stages. Between 1982, when the first broad estimates were made, and 1988 the estimated costs of the strategy from commencement to 1998–9 rose from £713 million to £1,749 million in real terms (an increase of 145 per cent) while net savings fell from £915 million to £414 million in real terms (a fall of 55 per cent). Because of the size of the project the Department has learnt from its mistakes and applied the lessons at a later stage (National Audit Office, 1989e).

Expenditure on day-to-day activities can be just as much an area of risk as project management and requires substantial monitoring and control. So many organizations, in industry and commerce as well as the public sector, fall into the trap of losing their sense of purpose in the succession of day-to-day routines which fail to capture the interest and commitment of the staff. Systems need to be in place to measure progress and detect weaknesses, especially in the selection, training and development of staff, which can often be overlooked when inspecting the basic figures of inputs, outputs and impacts. Furthermore, systems of performance should themselves instantiate, encourage and support the behaviour necessary to achieve the outcomes desired. In short, performance measures should not stand outside judgement on administrative behaviour. They should instead become a motivating force and encouragement of that behaviour; though as yet they seldom do fulfil this potential.

These are all examples of where performance falls short across many areas of government work; it is important to analyse the reasons for this. They often lie in the complexity of government operations, which has at least three dimensions – intellectual (in terms of understanding exactly what is required and how to achieve it), social (in terms of securing complicated chains of commitment, obedience and agreement to carry out tasks), and administrative (in terms of bringing together organizations or other co-operative arrangements which facilitate the construction of these chains of interdependence) (this point is well made in Moran, 1986). And while it is certainly too much to expect that the world of public action will ever be as simple as the 'rational policy analyst' hopes it will be if his theories are to work, we may nevertheless hope to make progress in the depth and scale of our understanding and consequently in our actions.

Conclusion

To sum up; departments do face a daunting task in evaluating performance. Progress has been made in setting targets and objectives and managers are increasingly being made more accountable for their success or failure. But they must not lose sight of their ultimate purpose, which is to make an effective impact upon the real world.

Although the goal of the public sector is to be effective, there are a number of problems concerning this concept. We have to understand these if we are to make progress with the evaluation of government work, particularly if we are to avoid unrealistic expectations of its likely achievements in its present stage of development. The problems include:

1 *Relationships between inputs, outputs and impacts.* The first point concerns the relationship between inputs, outputs and impacts. The transformation of inputs into outputs requires specialist help or knowledge. Thus teachers spend time and apply their professional skill in deciding how to put together a good lesson, and surgeons debate the optional organization and team for supporting a complex operation. The translation of outputs into impacts also requires a specialist contribution. For example, translating the output of the number of operations performed into their impact on health requires medical judgement; the translation of the educational outputs of numbers of students passing courses into the

impact of the students on the society and economy which they enter demands a contribution from such experts as sociologists and economists; and a study of the quality with which roads, bridges, schools and offices are constructed requires the civil engineers to say whether the physical output, which can be measured in such terms as miles or cubic capacity, is of a sufficient quality to secure the desired impact. In short, the transformation of inputs into outputs and the translation of outputs into impacts nearly always seems to require some professional input. And those transmutations will always be problematic, since we will always be able to find professional doctors, engineers and other experts who take contrary or different views on any question; this is inevitable, since the frameworks of thought and analysis of the various professional and expert groups are always subject to revision.

2 *Relationships between costs and benefits.* Secondly, when we have specified what impact we are concerned with the question arises as to whether the benefits which it brings outweigh the costs which are associated with obtaining it. Cost-benefit analysis is relevant at two levels – at the level of policy itself, where it is an important constituent of policy evaluations, and at the level of policy instruments. Here it could in principle provide, for each possible and/or actual instrument, an account of the input achievable and/or achieved, to what benefit and at what cost. It would thus facilitate comparisons between instruments that produce high benefits at high costs and those producing lower benefits at lower costs; and it would thus facilitate comparisons at the margin.

Cost-benefit analysis can also bring out the cost and benefits of the unintended effects – or 'externalities' as the economist would put it – of the employment of particular policy instruments. Thus building a dam across a river might have the negative effect of destroying the local fishing industry and the positive effect of preserving stocks of scarce fish. Should we investigate externalities such as these? For example, we may examine the cost of treating heart disease and the economic losses from the illness. But should we take into account the fact that the savings from healthier hearts would lead to extra long-term expenditure on geriatric medicine, as healthy centenarians require increasing care?

But, of course, just as with the professionals noted above, cost-benefit analysts have to build into their studies various assumptions; for example, for a new motorway, assumptions concerning the value of time saved for the different kinds of travellers who may use it. And these assumptions are themselves always problematic and arguable.

3 *Relationships between analysis and power.* The 'impact' of a programme is not simply to be gauged in financial and quantitative terms; it also often has significant implications for the balance and distribution of power

and reward in the community and in the audited organization. Certain sections of society may get a tougher or better deal than the government says, in its objectives, that it intends to bestow. And there may be various unintended effects, or externalities which confer benefits on certain groups (e.g. owners of large farms) denied to others (e.g. owners of small farms). Evaluations of government work which bring out such points may therefore contribute to the debate about the balance of power and opportunity in society in ways that the analysts did not expect. Their work may become part of a political manifesto whether they intend this or not.

4 *Relationships between 'insiders' and 'outsiders'*. Finally, and in extension of what is said above, we need to pay attention to the obvious fact that there will be different views of the analyses made between those who stand outside the organization concerned, and the government administrators and programme supporters who will be ingenious in devising reasons why apparently negative findings about policy impacts should be rejected. Wilson made this point, in an amusingly informal way, by formulating two 'laws' which he claimed would cover all cases of social science research on policy impact. 'Wilson's first law: all policy interventions in social problems produce the intended effect – if the research is carried out by those implementing the policy or their friends. Wilson's second law: no policy intervention in social problems produces the intended effect – if the research is carried out by independent third parties, especially those sceptical of the policy.' And he goes on to say that, 'Studies that conform to the first law will accept an agency's own data about what it is doing and with what effect; and minimise the search for other variables that might account for the effect observed. Studies that conform to the second law will gather data independently of the agency; adopt a short time frame that either minimises the chance for the desired effect to appear or, if it does appear, permits one to argue that the results are "temporary" and probably due to the operation of the "Hawthorne" effect (i.e. the reaction of the subjects to the fact that they are part of an experiment); and maximises the search for other variables that might explain the effects observed' (Wilson, 1973). These 'laws', of course, only state in a graphic way the very obvious point that there can be no such thing as an objective appraisal of whether a programme has a positive or a negative impact.

Clearly then, evaluating the performance of central government presents a number of challenges. But the methods discussed above all contribute to accountable and responsible management within the public sector, and a fuller understanding of their features and capacities can help to diminish false expectations and nourish what realistic possibilities they have to offer.

References

Cmnd. 8616 (1982) *Efficiency and Effectiveness in the Civil Service: government observations on the third report from the Treasury and Civil Service Select Committee* (HC 236). London: HMSO.

Dunleavy, P. (1989a) The architecture of the British central state: part 1: framework for analysis, *Public Administration*, 67, 249–75.

— (1989b) The architecture of the British central state: part 2: empirical findings, *Public Administration*, 67, 391–417.

Efficiency Unit (1988) *Improving Management in Government: the next steps* (the Ibbs Report). London: Cabinet Office.

Greenwood, J. and Wilson, D. (1989) *Public Administration in Britain*. Second edition. London: Unwin Hyman.

House of Commons Debates (1990) 2 April, columns 386–8.

Jackson, P. (1988) The management of performance in the public sector, *Public Money and Management*, 8, 11–16.

McLean, I. (1987) *Public Choice*. Oxford: Blackwell.

Moran, M. (1986) *The Politics of Banking*. Second edition. London: Macmillan.

National Audit Act (1983) Section 6.

National Audit Office (1988a) *Department of Transport, Scottish Development Department and Welsh Office: road safety* (HCP 517, 1987–88). London: HMSO.

— (1988b) *Department of the Environment: urban development corporations* (HCP 492, 1987–88). London: HMSO.

— (1988c) *Department of Employment, Training Commission: assistance to small firms* (HCP 655, 1987–88). London: HMSO.

— (1988d) *Estate Management in the National Health Service* (HCP 405, 1987–88). London: HMSO.

— (1989a) Annual report.

— (1989b) *Ministry of Defence: reliability and maintainability of defence equipment* (HCP 173, 1988–89). London: HMSO.

— (1989c) *National Health Service: coronary heart disease* (HCP 208, 1988–89). London: HMSO.

— (1989d) *Home Office: control and management of the Metropolitan Police estate* (HCP 455, 1988–89). London: HMSO.

— (1989e) *Department of Social Security: operational strategy* (HCP 111, 1988–89). London: HMSO.

Niskanen, W. A. (1973) *Bureaucracy: servant or master?* London: Institute of Economic Affairs.

Plowden, W. (1985) What prospects for the civil service? *Public Administration*, 63, 393–414.

Pollitt, C. (1986) Beyond the managerial model: the case for broadening performance assessment in government and the public services, *Financial Accountability
and Management*, 2, 155–70.

Wilson, J. Q. (1973) On Pettigrew and armor, *Public Interest*, 31, 132–4.

2

Assessing the Performance of Schools

Brian Wilcox

Current Interest in Assessing School Performance

Assessing the performance of schools has been a growing preoccupation of governments since the mid-1970s – not only in this country but throughout the world. The passing of the Education Reform Act (1988) has emphasized the centrality of the strategic planning function which local education authorities (LEAs) are to assume. Assessing the performance of schools (and other aspects of educational provision) will be an important condition of making strategic planning a reality.

Interest in assessing school performance is associated with several issues. Firstly, it is an expression of the need to make schools publicly accountable. This in turn is a consequence of the increasing disquiet felt about the achievements of education – often manifested in a concern about 'standards' – that has marked the previous 20 years of educational development. Secondly, a major feature of the Government's educational policy – underlined particularly by the Education Reform Act (ERA) – has been to increase 'people power' and the exercise of educational choice. The intention has been to re-orient the educational system in terms of a 'consumer' and 'educational market' model. The proponents of the model would argue that consumers, if they are to make rational educational choices, e.g. between schools, must have access to appropriate information. Information on schools should crucially include details of their performance. Thirdly, the decision to delegate the control of financial budgets and major management responsibilities to schools is based on the assumption that these will give headteachers the freedom to improve the opportunities offered and the results achieved. Fourthly, the introduction of a centrally determined national curriculum is a major means by which the government seeks to diminish what is seen as excessive curricular diversity, to ensure the availability of a basic curriculum entitlement to all pupils, and to improve educational performance.

The process of assessing the performance of schools is to be accomplished by regular monitoring and evaluation carried out by the LEA. This represents a marked departure from the situation which has pertained in many LEAs, at least until recently. In the past, the systematic assessment of school performance has seldom been seriously addressed. The ability to assess schools must rest upon the existence of a broad consensus about the purposes of education and how these might be translated into practice. In the absence of such a consensus the notion of school performance remains at best an obscure concept. The lack of detailed consensus has been the characteristic of the English education system. Indeed some might even argue that it has been a positive strength.

The Role of HMI and Local Inspectorates

The traditional arbiter of school performance has been Her Majesty's Inspectorate (HMI: see Lawton and Gordon, 1987). HMI can be said to have been reporting, in some way or other, on this issue throughout its 150 years of existence. By means of inspection, HMI communicates its judgements on individual schools to those responsible for them (headteachers, governors and the LEA). The findings of inspections also provide the basis for advice to those at national level responsible for the education service, i.e. the Secretary of State for Education and Science and civil servants in the Department of Education (DES). It is only since 1983 that inspection reports have been publicly available. Only comparatively recently then has it been possible for the wider public to discern the nature of the implicit criteria which HMI uses in formulating its judgements about individual schools. Even today the criteria which HMI employs are not made explicit and generally disseminated.

Increasingly since the mid-1970s HMI has extended the range of inspection activities beyond that of the familiar 'full inspection' to include short inspections dealing with *some* aspects of a school's activities and concerns, surveys of national samples of schools, as well as inspection visits of half a day or so made by individual inspectors to the schools within their 'districts'. Thus the range and comprehensiveness of the information which HMI collects has been increased and much is now stored centrally on computer. The information can be retrieved for use in providing evaluative accounts of different aspects of education across the country as a whole. HMI has also published a wide range of pamphlets on different aspects of curricular and educational provision which constitute accounts of 'good practice'. Until the advent of the ERA the government has generally shied away from the task of formulating precise performance targets for schools.

As a result the criteria of effective school performance have largely been implicit – at best inferred from the plethora of guidance on education provided by HMI (and the DES).

The education service has of course been administered and managed locally through the agency of the LEAs. In the past LEAs have had a considerable measure of autonomy for running the education service in their areas. In turn schools have had substantial freedom to determine how they should organize the curriculum. Budgets, staffing and administrative practices, however, have been centrally controlled by the LEA. Typically LEAs have shown little interest in the past in defining explicit criteria for effective school performance or making widely known any assessments which they might have made of it. Few LEAs until recently have had developed inspection policies despite being empowered by the 1944 Education Act to carry out inspections. Although all LEAs have had advisers, even in some cases specifically designated as 'inspectors', there is little evidence of the development of sustained, coherent and co-ordinated strategies for evaluating the performance of schools. Studies of advisers have tended to reveal the amazingly diverse range of their activities. Advisers vary in what they do from one LEA to the next and even within the same LEA. Inspection has been very much a minority activity and any kind of systematic monitoring and evaluation rare (Stillman and Grant, 1989).

Other Approaches to Assessing Performance

In the late seventies early eighties a number of LEAs espoused the cause of self-evaluation, perhaps better termed school-based review, as an alternative to inspection. They either sought to implement LEA-wide schemes or encouraged their schools to devise their own. The general effect of this initiative was disappointing (Clift et al., 1987). Although in some cases school-based review was influential in carrying through programmes of change, it did not take hold in the vast majority of schools and seldom, if ever, functioned as an appropriate instrument of accountability.

Perhaps the only common, sustained and systematic attempt by LEAs to assess performance has been for secondary schools in terms of examination achievement. This provides a set of quantitative measures which the public and politicians seem to value. Examination success is, of course, only a partial indication of a school's performance. Even then examination results do not speak unambiguously for themselves. Good examination performance may indicate more about the quality of the pupil intake than about the effectiveness of the teaching and learning provided. More work has been done on the use and interpretation of examination results as indicators of school performance than on any other aspect. Attempts to present examination results fairly, so that variations of pupil intake are controlled, continue to exercise the imagination of a small number of influential researchers using statistical techniques of analysis and interpretation.

Despite the general lack of *explicit* criteria for assessing school performance and systematic ways of carrying this out, most LEAs would claim to know how their schools were performing. The evidence on which such a claim is based would be varied. It would typically be stored in the 'heads' of advisers, officers and possibly committee members. The validity and reliability of that evidence is largely unknown. Whilst professional knowledge of this kind is wholly appropriate, to be effective it has to be pooled and subjected to collective scrutiny. Most LEAs will probably 'know' the quality of their headteachers because of the frequent contact made with them by advisers and officers. Their knowledge of the quality of the teaching and learning going on in the schools may be much less certain and comprehensive.

The Situation Prior to the Education Reform Act

Several developments in recent years, however, have pushed LEAs in the direction of making their criteria of effective schooling more precise. These include the requirement to publish a curriculum policy statement and participation in the technical vocational education initiative (TVEI). TVEI, at least for secondary schools, has required LEAs to specify in some detail the direction in which the development of the curriculum is expected to go. TVEI is a major example of a series of categorically funded initiatives which the government has introduced over the last few years to ensure that LEAs and schools implement curriculum and staff developments consistent with government intentions.

Categorical funding is a strategy which requires LEAs to bid for funds against specifically targeted intentions. It has made the implementation of change much more predictable than hitherto. In the past the predominant model of innovation was to attempt to change teachers' knowledge and attitudes in the hope that behavioural change would follow. Categorical funding effectively turns the model on its head. It ensures, by means of financial 'carrots', that behaviours occur and then finds that the attitudes follow! TVEI provides an excellent example of the success of the strategy. When initially proposed TVEI was met with scepticism, if not downright hostility. Now every LEA is involved – invariably as enthusiastic converts.

I conclude this section with the observation that where criteria for effective school performance exist they have been largely implicit and undisclosed. Although some possible indicators of performance have been collected, most notably examination results, these have generally been disconnected exercises and seldom brought together on an institution by institution basis. LEAs have traditionally had a loosely coupled relationship with their schools in which notions of individual professionalism have applied to those working within education departments, as officers and advisers, no less than those in the schools. The result has been that an LEA's criteria of school effectiveness, like other aspects of policy and practice, have often been the aggregate of the activities of individual advisers and officers. The way in which the latter have typically worked in the past is close to that of the 'street-level bureaucrats' mentioned in the introduction to this book.

The Co-ordination of LEA Evaluation Programmes Post the ERA

It is the arrival of the Education Reform Act which has, as noted at the beginning of this chapter, not only put the assessment of school performance firmly in place on the accountability agenda but has also created the apparatus – the local management of schools (LMS), the national curriculum, the possibilities of schools opting out of LEA control, and the use of performance indicators – to make it a reality.

It is now increasingly recognized that LEAs need to develop a co-ordinated monitoring and evaluation strategy which is authority wide and which includes the regular assessment of school performance as an important component. There will be three major elements of such a strategy: an enhanced monitoring and inspection role by advisers, increasingly now being designated as 'inspectors'; involvement of institutions in self-evaluation; and the use of performance indicators. Each of these elements can be regarded as a source of information. The range of information produced will need to be systematically recorded, analysed and converted into a variety of formal reports and statements on educational provision. It is very likely that local inspectors, as well as constituting a major information source in their own right, will play an influential role in the functions of analysing, interpreting and reporting information. The latter will occur both formally and informally to several different audiences – officers, members, headteachers and staff, governors, etc.

Because of the variety of educational provision which could in principle be assessed – of which schools and other educational institutions form a major part – it will be necessary for LEAs to develop evaluation programmes annually on a rolling basis. This in turn will necessitate the formulation of specific evaluation priorities that are related to those of the education service as a whole. Strategies of sampling will be required to ensure that an adequate number of institutional evaluations are carried out each year to give reliable information on trends and issues across the LEA.

The effective co-ordination of such an enterprise poses a formidable challenge. Nevertheless it is already apparent that many LEAs are responding by major reorganizations of their education departments and reviews of existing ways of working. The information handling task which an enhanced evaluation strategy demands will be substantial and will require the imaginative use of information technology. These issues have been faced by HMI in recent years. HMI now has an inspection programme which is planned in advance on a term by term basis. Details of many of the 'notes of visit', questionnaires, and *aides-mémoire* completed on inspections are now stored in a sophisticated computer system. Similar systems will almost certainly become commonplace in many LEAs.

Components of an LEA Evaluation Strategy

I shall now consider in turn the three components of an LEA-wide evaluation strategy. I will indicate how each can be developed to overcome some of the inherent weaknesses and disadvantages.

Inspection

Inspection is the most familiar method of assessing schools. As mentioned already, inspection, particularly as practised by HMI, incorporates a range of types ('inspection in all its forms' to use an oft quoted description). These may be speedier and less labour-intensive than the traditional full inspection. Many LEAs are following suit by developing programmes where full inspections are relatively infrequent and where departmental reviews, regular monitoring visits and the like are more the norm. Inspection is, of course, a form of external evaluation (Wilcox, 1989). Somewhat surprisingly, however, inspection has tended to be neglected in the now voluminous literature of educational evaluation. Whilst descriptions of the organization of inspection and the process of reporting (particularly in the HMI style) are available there is virtually nothing formally documented about the details of the methods used. Particularly obscure is the process by which the notes of inspectors made 'on the hoof' during the frenetic round of classroom visits are transformed into the individual and collective judgements which finally appear in the formal report.

As inspection becomes more commonplace – no longer the almost exclusive preserve of HMI – it is likely that teachers and the general public will demand to know more about the methods used and the criteria for the judgements made. An acceptance of what inspectors say about schools and teaching as being 'true' can no longer rest largely on the formal authority of the inspector's role. The methods used must be open to scrutiny. Indeed, the importance of making inspection criteria explicit is already recognized and many LEA inspectorates are involved in attempting this task, sometimes in collaboration with teachers.

Inspection utilizes methods which are not dissimilar to those employed by qualitative researchers. Indeed, a better understanding of such methods by inspectors could provide the basis for a sounder methodology for inspection than currently exists. Inspection does however differ in several significant ways from qualitative research as commonly understood. These differences limit the extent to which qualitative methods can simply be taken 'off the shelf' and transposed to the practice of inspectors. One of the most marked differences is that inspection is carried out and completed within a time-span which is dramatically shorter than most qualitative researchers experience. During an inspection information is typically collected, analysed, interpreted and fed back to the institution within a period of five days or less. This ultra 'condensed fieldwork' approach has few parallels in the literature of qualitative research. As a consequence qualitative methods such as interviews, naturalistic observation, etc. must be significantly modified if they are to be accommodated within such tight time-scales.

Inspection – as an example of what I call 'time constrained evaluation' – is worthy of more detailed study than it has customarily received. This is because working under conditions of severe time constraint is likely to be the characteristic of practitioners other than inspectors who may be involved in evaluations as part of their normal responsibilities. Teachers taking part in school-based reviews are an example. Inspection then is likely to become much more methodologically sophisticated than it is at present. Moreover, as the nature of the methodology of inspection becomes clearer it will prompt the need for more systematic ways of training inspectors. Thus the credibility of inspections in the future may largely rest on demonstrating that inspectors have been trained to use a range of appropriate techniques and methods. For example, if inspection criteria are to be publicly disclosed then it will also be necessary to confirm that inspectors are able to employ them with an acceptable degree of consistency.

School-based Reviews

Inspection by itself will be unable to deliver the substantial evaluation programme that LEAs are now being expected to provide. It will be necessary for the evaluation task to be shared between the LEA and its schools. Schools, in other words, will need to develop procedures for regularly assessing their own performance. As already indicated, earlier attempts by LEAs to encourage school-based review or school self-evaluation were generally disappointing. There are several reasons why this time round the experience is likely to be more successful. Firstly, the fact of LMS requires an annual review by schools of their performance as a key process in the setting of an annual budget. In other words a major part of the ERA apparatus (LMS) makes it certain that performance will need to be reviewed in some way.

One of the recent requirements of schools is that they should formulate annual curriculum development plans setting out, inter alia, how they intend to implement the national curriculum. Some schools have extended this notion to include a general development plan embracing all the main aspects of a school's concerns. A recent project being carried out by David Hargreaves and his team in Cambridge (Hargreaves and Hopkins, 1989) has outlined a rationale and a methodology for school development plans which are likely to be influential. They envisage a developmental cycle involving four processes: *audit* – where a school reviews its strengths and weaknesses; *plan construction* – which involves the selection of development priorities and their conversion into specific targets; *implementation* of the proposed priorities and targets; and *evaluation* – where the success of the implementation is checked. They recommend that the annual plan should concentrate on three or four major priorities. Plans would be constructed in detail for the year ahead with longer-term priorities for the following two to three years being described in outline only.

The merit of the Cambridge recommendations is that they focus self-evaluation (the audit and evaluation components of the cycle) on to very specific priorities, targets and success criteria. The approach is therefore likely to overcome both the unrealistic comprehensiveness and the general vagueness of purpose which characterized some of the earlier efforts in self-evaluation. The Cambridge model also treats the processes of implementation and evaluation as interlaced. Evaluation is an ongoing process in which regular progress checks are made *in the course of* implementation and success checks conducted at the end of the developmental work on a target. Finally at the conclusion of the planning cycle *stock taking* occurs. This involves reviewing all the reports on the priorities and constitutes the most formal evaluation activity of the school year.

The use of a planning model of the kind outlined will require a major shift of teacher attitudes and the acquisition of new skills. Not least amongst the latter will be developing ways of deciding what will count as evidence in relation to success criteria and constructing quick but reliable methods for collecting it. LEA inspectors might contribute to development plans in several ways. Inspection reports on visits made during the year by inspectors (individually and collectively) as part of the LEA inspection cycle would provide an important source of evidence on which to draw in reviewing progress in implementing the plan. Inspectors might also have a 'moderating' or 'accrediting' function in the review process. They could also play an important part in training school staff in planning and evaluation methods.

Performance Indicators

The third component of future LEA evaluation programmes involves the use of performance indicators (PIs). Several attempts have been made over the last 20 or so years to introduce PIs into the education service. They did not take hold. There are, however, good reasons for believing that now they are well on the way to becoming an operational reality. Firstly, PIs are a logical consequence of the kind of planning model which schools are being encouraged to adopt. An emphasis on priorities and targets naturally leads to an attempt to formulate related PIs. In the most general sense a PI is a quantitative measure of a specific management or planning objective. Secondly, several comprehensive lists of PIs have recently been produced. The DES in conjunction with a group of LEAs and one of their head-teachers have published a set which represents the outcome of collaborative work over a year or so (DES, 1989). The Training Agency has developed a set of PIs which it is expected that LEAs involved in TVEI Extension will use (Training Agency, 1990). So PIs are already beginning to penetrate the school system as a means for assessing performance.

PIs are often categorized into *input* indicators – what we work with, *process* indicators – how we work; and *output* indicators – what has happened at the end. In the past PIs have largely been of the input variety with relatively few of the process and output kind. I have already noted the use of examination results. These have usually been collapsed into a single indicator such as the number of GCE (now GCSE) passes (grades A to C) per fifth-year pupil on roll. Other PIs which have been proposed include staying-on rates, attendance figures, proportions going into employment. The advent of the national curriculum is likely to extend the range of available indicators of learning outcomes. This is because pupils will be assessed at ages 7, 11, 14 and 16 on a range of standardized assessment tasks (SATs) for the subjects of the national curriculum. It should be possible therefore in future to compare the aggregated SAT scores of pupils at 14 (or 16) with those obtained at 11. This will enable a better assessment to be made than at present of the specific contribution which a school makes to pupil learning – the so-called *added value*. In a similar way SAT scores at

7 will be used as measures of pupil intake to the junior school and related to those achieved four years later at 11.

We are likely to see the emergence of a wider range of output measures over the next few years. It is being increasingly recognized that the perceptions of the 'clients' for education (pupils, students, parents, employers) should be collected on a regular basis. Some promising developments in the further education sector, arising out of the current interest in the marketing of educational courses, are relevant. For example, the responsive college project (Theodossin and Thompson, 1987) has demonstrated how simple and easily completed questionnaires can be used to assess the views of students (and their employers) to the courses provided. Analysis of the questionnaire returns allows the isolation of a number of client satisfaction indicators related to the course, its content and teaching derived from individual ratings on a five-point scale.

Another potential source from which PIs may be derived is from information collected through direct observation of the working of a school. The practice of HMI is instructive. In recent years HMI has been supplementing the descriptive judgements that it makes of some aspects of educational provision by the use of rating scales. This enables a number of separate judgements to be aggregated and expressed in terms of the percentages falling in particular categories. For example statements like '81.6 per cent of assessments of overall work in schools of all types visited were judged satisfactory or better' are now commonplace in HMI reports. Similar assessments are also given for other aspects of provision. These types of quantification are forms of performance indicator. They are likely to be developed locally through the activities of LEA inspectors.

Another important reason why PIs are likely to become influential in assessing school performance is the development and application of advanced statistical techniques to model and interpret them. These have been important in two principal ways. Techniques such as multi-level modelling (Gray et al., 1990) enable schools to be compared (e.g. in terms of their public examination results) so that differences in pupils' background or prior attainment can be controlled and estimates made of the extent to which differences in pupils' performance can be attributed to the school. Another technique, data envelopment analysis (DEA: see Jesson et al. 1987), has been used to relate the multiple outputs of schools to their multiple inputs. A major advantage claimed for the technique is that it allows individual 'units' (e.g. schools, LEAs) to be compared in terms of efficiency when facing different circumstances and resource inputs. As distinct from a 'league table' analysis DEA gives some indication of where improvements might be sought. It is highly likely that statistical techniques of these kinds will continue to be developed. In due course then LEAs may have access to a range of techniques capable of manipulating a variety of indicators to model the differential levels of performance across their schools.

Concluding Comment

Thus the task of assessing the performance of schools is at an interesting stage of development. If it is to be tackled seriously and effectively it will need to be done in partnership between the LEA and its schools. An essential prerequisite is that there should be a broad consensus on the detailed criteria by which schools and their programmes are to be judged. Those criteria should be equally applicable whether the assessment is carried out externally by inspectors or internally by school staff. The detailed criteria should also be operationally related to the more general indicators of performance that it will be necessary to use at the LEA level. Greater agreement about criteria and indicators is also likely to lead to a more rigorous methodology of both inspection and school-based review. The integration of inspectorial and institutional evaluation into a comprehensive, credible and fair system for assessing school performance is a creative challenge which faces all LEAs. Success in achieving this will in no small measure determine the viability of the new strategic planning function of LEAs and thereby their continued existence through the 1990s as a separate organizational tier of education.

References

Clift, P. S., Nuttall, D. L. and McCormick, R. (1987) *Studies in School Self-Evaluation*. London: Fulmer Press.

Department of Education and Science (1989) *School Indicators for Internal Management: an aide-mémoire*. London: DES.

Gray, J., Jesson, D. and Sime, N. (1990) *Estimating Differences in the Examination Performances of Secondary Schools in Six LEAs: a multi-level approach to school effectiveness*. Sheffield University: QQSE Research Group, Education Research Centre.

Hargreaves, D. H. and Hopkins, D. (1989) *Planning for School Development*. London: DES.

Jesson, D., Mayston, D. and Smith, P. (1987) Performance assessment in the education sector, *Oxford Review of Education*, 13, 249–66.

Lawton, D. and Gordon, P. (1987) *HMI*. London: Routledge and Kegan Paul.

Stillman, A. B. and Grant, M. (1989) *The LEA Adviser–a changing role*. Windsor: NFER–Nelson.

Theodossin, E. and Thompson, C. (1987) Performance indicators: theory and practice, *Coombe Lodge Reports*, 20, 1–68.

Training Agency (1990) *TVEI Programme Performance Indicators*. London: Training Agency.

Wilcox, B. (1989) Inspection and its contribution to practical evaluation, *Educational Research*, 31, 163–75.

3

Evaluating Health Services: from Value for Money to the Valuing of Health Services

Andrew F. Long

To evaluate an activity means to come to a judgement about its worth or value. *Evaluation* of health services is intertwined with the notion of the quality of services provided to patients ('quality assurance') and with the process of *performance review* (reviewing the extent to which specific targets are being achieved). In a narrower usage, the focus lies on evaluating a particular health intervention (for example, a new treatment or way of providing a service). Questions arise over what criteria should be used to assess success or failure and who decides what the criteria should be. Evaluation is not a value-free activity, nor is it a straightforward technical process. There is too much at stake and open to interpretation.

The question of whether any evaluation can be truly independent is moot. One possibility is to adopt the approach of pluralistic evaluation (Smith and Cantley, 1985). In this approach evaluation entails establishing the extent to which each actor or set of actors achieves his/her/their objectives.

Quality assurance and performance review, whilst similar concepts, are not identical. The former can be defined as the activity of evaluating health care. It is sometimes interpreted more narrowly to relate only to 'medical' care (as, for example, in *medical audit*). While the activity of evaluation necessarily involves the contrast of the programme's aims and objectives with the actual outcomes, performance review is more narrow in its approach. Targets of performance are established (not necessarily in terms of outcome) these usually being set by the political masters and funders. These then serve as the criteria against which the health services are reviewed.

Concepts and Criteria of Evaluation

The most widely known framework for evaluating health services is Donabedian's (1980) model of structure–process–outcome. *Structure* refers to the physical and organizational setting, and available resources for providing health care to (prospective) patients. In other vocabularies it represents the *input* to health services. *Process* involves what is done to the health consumer by way of advice (for example, in health promotion activities), diagnosis, treatment and after-care. *Outcome* relates to the changes, if any, in the health status of the client. All three dimensions are supposed to be interrelated, although the precise character of the inter-relationship is often hard to pin down. Structural characteristics affect the process of care, and both affect the outcome of care. None of the three elements alone represents quality. Each provides an approach to explore the presence or absence of quality.

Focusing on structure (or inputs) provides a starting-point for reviewing health services performance. This dimension is a facilitator of high quality health care services. A link to the concept of *economy* can be noted (the minimization of financial input). Without a 'favourable' set of inputs (money, manpower, equipment and buildings) 'lower' quality care is a likely consequence, although the contrary does not follow – high costs/inputs do not ensure 'high' quality.

The characterization of quality as 'lower' or 'high' indicates a value judgement and a comparative reference point. For example, lower might be interpreted in terms of lower than expected from the point of view of the consumer or lower in terms of professionally defined standards.

Examining the process of health services provision provides a sounder yet still partial insight and approach to evaluation. 'Good practice' protocols (care plans, appropriate diagnostic procedures and so on) can be explicated from the health practitioners, to form standards and points of reference to contrast with actual (clinical) practice. In theory, these could take into account a consumer viewpoint. For example, procedures with high specificity and sensitivity might be identified, or issues of patient anxiety and pain management addressed, or the protocol might explicitly link to a measure of outcome (even a negative outcome), like recognizing that a certain percentage of cases will have a particular side effect.

To achieve high quality processes 'adequate' inputs must be provided. This underlines the fact that 'good practice' care is definable only in relation to a given level of input. If the standards are established 'under ideal conditions' (for example, as in a nursing work-load system such as GRASP) then they cannot be used as criteria for quality if conditions were not in fact ideal. Similarly, standards outlining the 'right' process of diagnosis and care imply necessary inputs. While the exposition of standards of care provides a valuable avenue for process evaluation, its link to structure must not be forgotten. However, if the protocols involve a reference to expected changes in patient health status (as yet rare) then they become powerful means for evaluation, integrating the three dimensions of the Donabedian model.

Appraising outcomes provides the single best dimension for evaluating health services. Favourable changes in the health status of patients (be it recovery to complete health following an episode of ill health or accident, or modifying behaviour as a result of health promotion advice, thus reducing risk status) must surely be the implicit, if not explicit, objective of health services. However, outcome review is not a straightforward technical activity. Pressures over inputs – limited resources, difficulties in staff recruitment, controls over manpower numbers, inflexibility in manpower utilization and so on – encourage a managerial culture emphasizing economy and efficiency rather than an outcome perspective. But even within the health practitioner–patient relationship the outcome approach is fraught with difficulty. For how is the health status of an individual to be assessed? How can one determine if the change or lack of change observed in patient health status is 'due to the health services' and not something else? If changes in health status are observed, then not only must there be a prior basis for assuming a possible relationship between the change in health status and health intervention (the issue of *causal validity*), but also other possible factors which might otherwise explain the change in health status must be absent (the issue of *attributional validity*). Health services can only be accountable for variations in levels of health caused by variables capable of being controlled or manipulated by the health care system.

Structure and process are often used as proxies for outcome, but this assumes that the relationship between them is known. In general terms, structure and process incorporate the potential for quality, while outcome is the expressed quality of a particular service that is experienced by an individual patient or population (Bainton, 1986). However, Donabedian's framework is not the only available approach. Indeed, other concepts, and thus criteria, are at the forefront of discussion in the United Kingdom. In particular there are the notions of effectiveness, efficiency and acceptability.

A service has to be capable of producing the desired effects (*efficacy*). But while it may have proven efficacy, its full potential may not be realized in every-day practice because of structural limitations of resources, organizational setting, manpower and the like. It is thus necessary to ascertain the *effectiveness* of the service in that context.

Effectiveness is defined as the extent to which a policy, intervention or resource group achieves its intended effect. To assess effectiveness involves identifying the objectives of the programme, drawing up indicators to see the extent to which they are being met and comparing the end-state achieved with that desired. Such a description rests easily within the notion of quality assurance (whose steps are the same). The criterion of effectiveness is equivalent to a focus on outcome in Donabedian's framework.

The sole pursuit of this criterion would be to ignore other relevant issues. The *efficiency* of the service also needs to be reviewed. As the ratio of inputs or resources (structure) to outputs decreases, so greater efficiency occurs. Output is used here in the general sense of the number of units of service provided. Inputs can be expressed in terms of specific resources or by using monetary value as a lowest common denominator: for example, deaths and discharges per bed or cost per case.

Yet another criterion for evaluating health services is that of the *acceptability* of the service to the providers, the funders and the consumers. For the providers, the centre of attention will lie on the general working environment. There is an obvious link with structure in the form of acceptable facilities, for example. For the consumer, interest lies in the whole health system: in particular, the structural characteristics (facilities in the health system in terms of buildings and equipment) and the care and attitude of the providers. The patient also has a prima-facie interest in health outcome, but this may be more implicit than explicit, with the individual assuming or expecting everything possible is being done for him/her.

Another relevant criterion is that of *equity*. This is concerned with the distribution of the service to individual patients (the link to justice) and to the wider population. It also involves the principle of equal *accessibility* for those in equal *need*. The notion is linked to the concept of *adequacy* which relates available services to the needs of the population. Equity addresses the question of 'what sort of health service is being provided to whom, and what ought to be provided?' It is of central interest to debates over quality.

These four criteria together with Donabedian's framework provide a perspective for assessing health services' quality. No single criterion provides an adequate approach to addressing the quality issue. Indeed, choice of one single dimension unduly narrows the evaluation perspective. But there is an element of competition in the various criteria. The dimension of equity clashes with that of efficiency. For example, increased equity may be achieved by increasing available inputs with little noticeable increase in output, thus reducing efficiency. The operation of market forces in health care also competes with equity. How much equity to achieve is one of the many covert value judgements made in service provision. Sole pursuit of the criterion of efficiency can be problematic – maximizing outputs, say, in the form of poor patient care, or 'playing the system' by reducing length of stay and increasing throughput, with meagre resources in the community to cope with the early discharges (but in someone else's budget, and thus compromising someone else's efficiency and effectiveness). Further, an exclusive concern with the patient's health outcome may lead to hyper-expensive care and defensive medicine (with one eye to the potential threat of litigation). The notion of trade-offs is central. But who sets the criteria, and who judges the balance?

Whose Criteria in Practice?

Politicians, members, managers, health practitioners, and the consumers have differing interests in the evaluation process. For the health prac-titioners, standards of process often predominate, along with the issue of efficiency in the managerial role and their search for additional funds. For the consumer, the issue of acceptability and the efficacy of care are the main criteria. In contrast, the funders and management are most concerned with cost containment and the way the financial allocations are spent. The rhetoric of *value for money* is highlighted along with efficiency. It is apparent that no one set of actors has a major stake in all dimensions of health services' quality.

Equity is partly determined by the way resources are allocated. Under the method devised in the 1970s by the Resource Allocation Working Party (RAWP) the allocation method weighted the regional population, in a crude way, to take account of variations in need. *Working for Patients* (Cm. 555, 1989) will change this procedure. Variations in admission rates for conditions are evident across the country, not just in the incidence and prevalence of the condition, but in terms of social class, income, employ-ment status and poverty.

The activities of performance review and quality assurance are under-taken either by management (at each tier), by health professionals, or by semi-independent evaluators such as the Management Advisory Service or the National Audit Office. The motivations of the varying parties involved are potentially different. For the health practitioner, interest lies primarily in reviewing the quality of the service being given to the patient. A secondary consideration is to ensure that any managerial targets are attained, particularly in the area of cost containment. At the managerial level, the overriding motive is to control and account for allocated resources.

The consumer voice is likely to be least influential. Managers and health practitioners have begun to seek systematic information on patient sat-isfaction. For example, the clinical accountability service planning and evaluation (CASPE) project at Bloomsbury has tried to develop a routine, computer-read system for monitoring patient satisfaction, as a part of a management information system (Kerruish, Wickings and Tarrant, 1988). The approach has, however, not been without its critics (Carr-Hill, Dixon and Thompson 1989a and 1989b), raising *inter alia* questions of the validity and reliability of the data collected. Wickings and colleagues' (1989) response is that the system works. Another available questionnaire in this area is that of Moores and Thompson (1986).

But opinions on care in hospital are only one aspect of the consumer viewpoint on acceptability. The consumer has self-interest in the accessibility and availability of services and facilities, and in the outcome of care. This latter aspect is poorly expressed by British consumers (in contrast to their American counterparts – Aaron and Schwartz, 1984), patients being trusting and passive in their contacts with health practitioners. It is interesting to observe that this passivity is reinforced with the general practitioner's role as the patient's advocate in identifying 'best buys' of hospital treatment under the government White Paper (Cm. 249, 1987) for the family practitioner services. Consumer views need to be canvassed and heed taken of them.

The funders, including the Minister of Health and Parliament ultimately, set performance targets for achievement by the health authorities, and the health authorities for those lower down the hierarchy. Such targets are based at least in part on performance indicators (PIs). These were introduced into the NHS 'to help to assess service efficiency' (DHSS, 1983). Over time the indicators have increased from 123 to 418. However, their predominant focus has lain on resource input and cost (in total 193 indicators), and process (165), mainly reflecting clinical practice. Only five indicators relate to outcome, and three of these to mortality in the first year of life (Smith, 1990).

A survey of managers (Jenkins et al., 1988) suggests that few managers are making use of them extensively and where they do it is either to identify problem areas or to provide supporting evidence for policy decisions. But besides their predominant emphasis on process and efficiency, use of PIs 'focuses attention on the chosen indicator to the exclusion of less easily quantified aspects' (Smith, 1990, p. 69). Further, the implication of the PI philosophy is that outliers should be examined, and thus that managers should be striving for median behaviour.

A reliance on performance indicators, themselves efficiency dominated, reinforces a cost containment approach, to the detriment of evaluating the effectiveness of what is being done. Such an emphasis leads to conflicting and perverse results in practice (Mullen, 1983; Green and Harrison, 1989). It should be noted that 'a start has also been made on the complex task of developing outcome measures to help in assessing the effectiveness of clinical care' (Treasury, 1989, p. 13), but given the political climate and resulting managerial culture it must be doubtful whether outcome and thus effectiveness considerations can be seriously pursued. A potential exception is the use of the quality adjusted life year notion (QALY) – for example, its use within the North Western Regional Health Authority (Gudex, 1986). But, as the National Audit Office comments, the QALY 'has yet to achieve widespread recognition as a valid technique . . . [and] the information required . . . has not been readily available' (1988, p. 17).

Other measures such as 'avoidable' deaths (Charlton et al., 1983 and 1986 – an outcome indicator) and waiting-list times (another process indicator) form further parts of the armoury of information to help managers assess the quality of their services. However, avoidable deaths count for a very small proportion of all deaths, and use mortality as a measure of outcome (Long, 1985). Yet another criterion is the notion of *value for money* (for example, through the pursuit of 'good' clinical and management practices, cost improvement schemes, income generation, and competitive tendering). Yet again, this criterion involves a concern with efficiency, but with the potential implication of cost effectiveness.

Another point of reference for the evaluation of health services is statements of the objectives of the NHS. For example, the expenditure plans of the government state:

> The NHS aims to improve and promote health and to provide necessary treatment for illness and care while making the best possible use of available resources. In meeting these objectives the NHS needs to:
>
> – take advantage of advances in clinical treatment and diagnosis;
> – improve its response to the consumer;
> – give increasing prominence to the promotion of good health and the prevention of illness. (Treasury, 1989, p. 4)

The effectiveness of a service is very difficult, if not impossible, to assess without very explicit objectives. It would seem idle to presume that the basic objective of the NHS was anything other than 'to improve and promote health'. But what in practice does this mean? And how can this explicit objective be used to explore the effectiveness of service provision, in the hospital, community and primary health care context? There is a need for more specific, operational targets to be derived from these objectives. In particular, targets need to be focused on desired changes in the health status of the individual patients and impact on the population: that is, to move to an *outcome* orientation for evaluation.

The Management Advisory Service provides a semi-independent evaluation service. Their own stated criteria are as follows: prepare a profile of the service to be reviewed; clarify the objectives of the service; examine its appropriateness in relation to demand and need; assess the effectiveness of the service; review its management in terms of direction, co-ordination and control (Hanson and Mowbray, 1988). Whether their actual studies are able to manifest this approach so explicitly is another matter. An external, independent evaluator may become caught up in the local political context as well as needing to take account of the wider arena.

The Way Forward

Evaluating health care services needs to be an ongoing activity. It often has an affinity to the process of action research. In this model, research is depicted as a cycle involving the stages of planning, acting, observing and reflecting, before planning again. Evaluating the quality of the service provided ought to be the task of every health practitioner and manager. Criteria need to be broad.

Two ideas in the 1989 White Paper, *Working for Patients* (Cm. 555), point towards desirable extensions to the somewhat narrow, efficiency based approach to evaluation hitherto evident in the NHS. Firstly, there is the proposal that all doctors (and not just consultants) should be participating in 'regular and systematic' medical audit, with a target date of April 1991. Secondly, there is the introduction of competition into the provision of health services. Their possible implications for future approaches to health services evaluation are worthy of elaboration.

Medical audit refers to the review by doctors of the quality of care they provide. The audit cycle – observe practice, set standards, improve practice and observe practice again – has been popularized *inter alia* by the report of the Royal College of Physicians (1989). In 1988 medical audit was rare among British doctors; in 1990 frequent reports on audit in practice were evident, indicative of wide interest in medical circles in areas such as surgery (Ellis et al., 1990) and physicians in a district general hospital (Gabbay et al., 1990).

In practice medical audit has usually been oriented towards the process dimension of quality, looking at what care should have been (under good practice criteria, for example) and what actually occurred. In the sense that a comparison of objectives and outcomes is made medical audit can be seen to address effectiveness. However, good practice criteria do not necessarily involve reference to patient health care outcomes. But as Bunker (1990, p. 532) points out, 'research on outcomes . . . will continue to be the central necessary ingredient in the effort to improve clinical practice.'

Any encouragement to health practitioners to review the quality of care they provide must be welcomed. However, the pursuit of medical audit predominantly re-emphasizes the efficiency and process dimensions. Medical audit is also a peer review procedure. It implicitly reinforces professional autonomy and the dominant position of the medical profession as definers and providers of care, and potentially works counter to the philosophy of general management, although the aggregate results of the practice of medical audit may be available to management. Further, it involves the implicit down-grading of care not provided by doctors, and suggests that medical care can be separated off from the care provided by other health care professionals.

An extension of medical audit to clinical audit schemes involving both doctors and other occupation groups is required, but this has been very slow to take root. Clinical audit would encompass the total health care provided to a patient. Ideally, this should extend not just to direct patient care as provided by doctors, nurses, and allied health professionals, but also to indirect patient care – the support services such as cleaning, food and so on – and would apply both to outpatient and inpatient care episodes, and also to general practice. Beyond this it could be broadened to involve the patient's own judgements of acceptability and satisfaction.

The proposed introduction of the internal market in the NHS may also be a spur to quality assurance concerns, though it may not leave them any less dominated by efficiency than at present. The purchasers of health care – the district health authorities and the general practitioners – will need information about the quality of care available in the providers' facilities (NHS, self-governing or private hospitals). At present, the only routinely available information relates to efficiency measures and accessibility (waiting-list times). The resource management initiative will add further information on the actual cost/price of care: another, though critical, efficiency measure. But if efficiency and price are the only criteria applied to guide purchasers' choice, a continuation of the current narrow approach to quality assurance will result. Questions need to be asked about the effectiveness and acceptability of the service, as well as about general clinical quality.

Insight into how the internal market might work in relation to quality assurance can be gleaned from recent Department of Health (DoH) guidance in a publication entitled *Contracts for Health Services: operating contracts* (1990). Considerable space is given to the issue of quality in the context of 'managing the contractual process' and specimen contract documentation is provided illustrating the quality issues, *inter alia*. The DoH points out that 'the move to a contract system and the funding of districts as purchasers from 1991 are above all aimed at improvement in the *quality* and *responsive-*

TABLE 3.1
Characterizations of criteria of evaluation in the NHS

Criteria	Currently	Possible future
Equity	Resource allocation	Market forces operating leading to greater inequity
Structure/process	Medical audit (to a limited extent) Performance indicators Waiting lists	Need to develop clinical audit across occupational groups for health programmes
Outcome	5 PIs QALYs (to a limited extent)	Reviewing services provided against criteria such as the 'Health for All by the Year 2000 Strategy' of WHO
Efficiency	Main criterion Value for money	Balanced perspective looking also at effectiveness: resource management initiative
Effectiveness	Low profile	High profile
Acceptability	Patient satisfaction surveys	Public health report, incorporating a survey of consumer need and perceptions of provision: encouragement of the active consumer (opening up the potential of litigation)

ness of patient care' (p. 6, italics added). Exactly how quality is to be defined and interpreted, and to whom patient care is to be responsive is however left unelaborated.

The emphasis remains mainly on value for money and efficiency: '[Health authorities] will be expected to use the contractual process to achieve value for money and to extract efficiency gains from the providers' (p. 17). But there are some signs of a broadening of concern. In particular, the purchaser is advised to draw up clear objectives 'as to the nature and quality of services that will best meet the needs of their residents' (p. 6). However, the objectives will have to be stated in specific terms if they are to be used to evaluate the service provided. In addition, the contract will contain a statement which describes the type of services required and the quality issues the provider is expected to address. 'Quality assurance regimes' are stressed, and the necessity for the provider to give evidence of whether it can meet the quality standards on offer. Such guidance must be welcomed, but it remains to be seen whether it results in the adoption of a broader approach to evaluation.

The White Paper also raises the issue of equity. From one perspective, it follows the principle of wider access (encouraging shorter waiting times). On the other hand, general practitioners as budget holders may be discouraged from taking onto their list prospective 'high-cost' patients. In such a scenario, inequity not equity would be a criterion for evaluation! But another aspect of equity, the provision of services according to relevance to health needs, may in the future be more dominant, through the annual review of public health at local level and because of the pressures of the internal market. If health authorities reassess the services that are required to meet the needs of their populations, this too may encourage market research of prospective consumers.

Turning to the criterion of effectiveness, the challenge relates to the elucidation of explicit and specific service objectives, stated in such a way that they can be used as a part of the evaluation process. In particular, for the pursuit of an outcome approach to evaluation, these need to be expressed in terms of potential changes in health status and the quality of life. Sound and relevant objectives can be found, for example, in the World Health Organization's *Health for All by the Year 2000* strategy. While measuring health is conceptually and technically a difficult process, many attempts have been made and await wider application (see, for example, G. T. Smith, 1985 and 1989; Roberts, 1990). Table 3.1 provides a summary of the current and a possible future situation regarding criteria and dimensions of quality.

Conclusion

The above discussion has highlighted four criteria as keys to evaluating health services: equity, efficiency, effectiveness and acceptability. None on their own is adequate. Further, these criteria do not in themselves amount to an interrelated, theoretically based approach to evaluating health services. Accordingly, the discussion has made extensive use of Donabedian's framework of structure–process–outcome.

Current pressures in the NHS are reinforcing an efficiency orientation. Movements towards medical audit are not in themselves sufficient. A broad perspective is required which looks at the process of care provided to the patient, across occupational groups. But it is even more critical to shift focus from the process dimension of quality to embrace outcome. A higher profile needs to be given to effectiveness considerations.

Any evaluation of health services is value-based. The criteria used in practice will vary in relation to the location of the evaluation (national versus local) and according to the power base of those doing the evaluation. The need to include the consumer's voice has been stressed. This can occur within clinical audit, within the development of good practice protocols, as well as through enquiries into patient satisfaction after episodes of care and wider market research on the adequacy of local services. Evaluating health services has become a cost and efficiency exercise; it is time to add a human and moral dimension. Evaluation is about making value judgements, which are themselves ethical comments. The future is to look beyond efficiency to equity, effectiveness and acceptability. The challenge is to develop and apply a procedure for evaluating health services from the varying perspectives of the constituent actors. In this way, the politicians, the managers, the health professionals and the consumers can meet together to come closer to a shared understanding of the value of their health services.

References

Aaron, H. J. and Schwartz, W. B. (1984) *The Painful Prescription: rationing hospital care*. Washington, DC: Brookings Institute.

Bainton, D. (1986) Quality assurance (personal communication).

Bunker, J. P. (1990) Variations in hospital admission and the appropriateness of care: American preoccupations, *British Medical Journal*, 15 September, 301, 531–2.

Carr-Hill, R., Dixon, P. and Thompson, A. (1989a) Too simple for words, *Health Service Journal*, 15 June, 728–9.

— (1989b) Putting patients before the machine, *Health Service Journal*, 14 September, 1132–3.

Charlton, J. R. H., Lakhani, A. and Aristidou, M. (1986) How have 'avoidable deaths' indices for England and Wales changed, 1974–78 compared with 1978–83, *Community Medicine*, 8, 304–14.

Charlton, J. R. H., Silver, R., Hartley, R. M. and Holland, W. W. (1983) Geographical variations in mortality from conditions amenable to medical interventions in England and Wales, *Lancet*, 25 March, 691–6.

Cm. 249 (1987) *Promoting Better Health – the Government's Programme for Improving Primary Health Care*. London: HMSO.

Cm. 555 (1989) *Working for Patients*. London: HMSO.

Department of Health and Social Security (1983) *Performance Indicators: national summary for 1981*. London: DHSS.

— (1990) *Contracts for Health Services: operating contracts*. London: DHSS.

Donabedian, A. (1980) *The Definition of Quality and Approaches to Assessment* (volume 1 of *Explorations in Quality Assessment and Monitoring*). Ann Arbor, Michigan: Health Administration Press.

Ellis, B. W., Rivett, R. C. and Dudley, H. A. F. (1990) Extending the use of clinical audit data: a resource planning model, *British Medical Journal*, 21 July 301, 159–62.

Gabbay, J., McNicol, M. C., Spiby, J., Davies, S. C. and Layton, A. J. (1990) What did audit achieve? Lessons from preliminary evaluation of a year's medical audit, *British Medical Journal*, 15 September, 301, 526–9.

Green, A. and Harrison, S. (1989) Efficiency and perversity in hospital services, *Health Services Management*, 85, 134–6.

Gudex, C. (1986) *QALYs and their Use by the Health Service*. York: Centre for Health Economics, Discussion Paper 20.

Hanson, T. and Mowbray, D. (1988) Clinical service review: a framework, *Health Services Management*, 84, 178–82.

Jenkins, L., Bardsley, M., Coles, J. and Wickings, I. (1988) *How did we do? The Use of Performance Indicators in the National Health Service*. London: CASPE Research.

Kerruish, A., Wickings, I. and Tarrant, P. (1988) Information from patients as a management tool – empowering managers to improve the quality of care, *Hospital and Health Services Review*, 84, 64–7.

Long, A. F. (1985) Effectiveness: definitions and approaches. In A. F. Long and S. Harrison (eds), *Health Services Performance*, London: Croom Helm, 10–56.

Moores, B. and Thompson, A. (1986) An all consuming view, *Health Service Journal*, 3 July, 892–3.

Mullen, P. M. (1983) Performance indicators – is anything new? *Hospital and Health Services Review*, 81, 165–7.

National Audit Office (1988) *Quality of Clinical Care in National Health Service Hospitals*. London: HMSO.

— (1989) *The Next Steps Initiative*. London: HMSO.

Roberts, H. (1990) *Outcome and Performance in Health Care*. London: Public Finance Foundation, Discussion Paper 33.

Royal College of Physicians (1989) *Medical Audit – a First Report: what, why and how?* London: Royal College of Physicians.

Smith, G. and Cantley, C. (1985) *Assessing Health Care*. London: Croom Helm.

Smith, G. Teeling (1985) *Measurement of Health*. London: Office of Health Economics, Current Health Problems no. 77.

— (1989) *Measurement and Management in the NHS*. London: Office of Health Economics, Current Health Problems no. 91.

Smith, P. (1990) The use of performance indicators in the public sector, *Journal of the Royal Statistical Society*, 153, 53–72.

Treasury (1989) *The Government's Expenditure Plans 1989–90 to 1991–92*. London: HMSO, chapter 14, Department of Health.

Wickings, I., Harvey, J. and Kerruish, A. (1989) Proof of the pudding, *Health Service Journal*, 31 August, 1070–1.

4

The Audit Commission

Mary Henkel

The Mandate and the Organizational Framework

The Audit Commission was created under the Local Authority Finance Act, 1982. By 1990, it had not only made a significant impact on local government but also extended its remit to the National Health Service. In assuming this task, the Commission made it clear that it would adopt essentially the same operating model as it had evolved for local authority audit. Local auditors would work across the health and local authority sectors and the key criteria would be the same.

The birth of the Audit Commission had been a milestone in the history of local government audit. Auditors were now legally required to concern themselves with far more than financial probity. They had to satisfy themselves that authorities had 'made proper arrangements for securing economy, efficiency and effectiveness'. The Commission's code of practice, published in 1984, made it clear that it was now mandated to examine and advise on the management of local authorities (Audit Commission, 1984; Day and Klein, 1990).

The earlier District Audit Service had laid the ground for the changes, through collaborative management projects with individual authorities and the development of some comparative statistics and performance measures against value for money criteria. But now the demands on the entire workforce were to alter. To meet their new responsibilities, auditors were to develop new working styles and have access to expertise and analytic tools well beyond those of accountancy. The Commission established a central structure to reflect a new image and provide the requisite leadership and resources. It was built round four directorates under the leadership of the Controller: finance and administration (to manage the Commission's own resources), operations, special studies and management practice.

The operations director was responsible for the work of the local auditors, 70 per cent of whom are employed by the Commission in the

District Audit Service; the rest are in the private accountancy firms that undertake nearly one third of local audits. But the onus for developing the Commission's extended audit function was laid on the special studies and the management practice directorates.

The special studies director was charged with the annual programme of national studies authorized under sections 26 and 27 of the 1982 Act, the purpose of which was to identify critical areas for the improvement of local authority performance. The programme determines the particular 'flavour' or focus of the annual audit in almost all authorities. When the Commission extended its work into the NHS it created two special studies directorates, one for health and one for local government.

While special studies were to be concerned with discrete areas of authorities' activities, the management practice directorate concentrated on improving general standards of local-authority management.

By 1987, the Commission claimed to have established, primarily through the work of these two directorates, an 'overall methodology' for 'integrated audit' of economy, efficiency and effectiveness. It included using profiles of local authorities and performance measurement statistics (these provided a quantitative framework for authorities to compare themselves within 'families' or clusters of authorities matched by socio-economic characteristics); special studies; local value for money projects identified collaboratively by auditors and their authorities; and reviews of authorities' overall management arrangements (Audit Commission, 1987a).

This chapter will outline the main evaluative criteria against which the Audit Commission assesses the work of local, and now health, authorities and the key influences on those criteria. It will then discuss the continuing value of the Commission's perspectives and methods in the context of the particular demands of public sector evaluation.

The Commission's Criteria

The Audit Commission has structured its work round the values of economy, efficiency and effectiveness. These values are linked with a more fundamental assumption that local authorities are accountable to a tax paying electorate for the proper use of the resources allocated to them. The fiduciary responsibilities of audit remain.

The three Es framework is used in the following analysis of the Commission's criteria, although in practice the distinction between economy, efficiency and effectiveness is difficult to sustain. Their meaning in use was shaped by the Commission's conception of the optimum management model for local authorities; by its own political purposes, in particular to gain the confidence of local authorities, whilst attempting radically to change their culture; and by the technical problems of defining and measuring effectiveness.

The Audit Commission was installed as part of government's drive to control public expenditure and to impose a disciplined, instrumental model of management in the public sector, based on economic concepts of rationality (Minogue, 1983; Bromley and Euske, 1986).

From 1984 the Commission, through the management practice directorate, advocated a more integrated, value-driven concept of corporate management. In this model, politicians and officers have distinct roles but all are subsumed within a conception of the 'well-managed' council. Since 1988, with the publication of *The Competitive Council*, the vision or mission of the local authority has been more sharply delineated by the Commission. It is to manage change in a policy environment where public authorities can no longer take their role for granted. The boundaries between the public and private sectors of the economy have been substantially broken down. The local authority's primary tasks are to enable the provision of quality services within a national policy and resource framework and to monitor that provision. In order to survive, the authority must determine where it will compete to provide directly and where it will leave that task to the commercial and voluntary sectors. Such decisions require a corporate management structure and a strategic planning capacity that combines relative simplicity with flexibility. A key to its success will be its capacity to 'keep close to customers' and so to respond to their demands and their verdicts on services. The Commission's management papers demonstrate its acceptance of the climate in which the twin imperatives are quality and expenditure control.

However, from the beginning, the Commission sought to demonstrate that its task was not a simple one of control. It was primarily to enable authorities to provide 'value for money'. This meant that it would identify, and seek to change, central as well as local government policies that stood in the way of this objective.

Value for money was to be clearly distinguished from cost cutting. Thus, while accepting economy as part of its remit, the Commission has, where possible, linked it with efficiency. And the definitions of economy and efficiency in the code of practice (Audit Commission, 1984) both incorporate the notion of quality. An authority exercises economy if it 'acquires resources in the appropriate quality and quantity at the lowest cost'. Efficiency entails securing 'minimum inputs for any given quality and quantity of service provided' or 'maximum output for any given set of resource inputs'.

The Commission's initial strategy was to direct auditors to look for 'value improvements' rather than 'cost reductions' (Audit Commission, 1986a). In practice this meant that they would first locate areas of local authority expenditure where costs could be reduced without affecting services.

Perhaps the clearest benchmark against which the Commission measures the performance of local authorities is that of the potential savings identified in the course of 'value for money' studies and subsequently achieved. These constitute part of the Commission's annual reports but they are listed as 'value improvements' or 'value opportunities': resources that authorities could use to better advantage in other ways. What is not recorded is whether the savings are so used or whether they represent reduced overall expenditure.

However the figures are used, costs are frequently the starting-point of inquiry. The special studies report on the probation service (Audit Commission, 1989a) interpreted 'value for money' largely in terms of service effectiveness. But it began from the premise that community-based intervention is substantially cheaper than prison sentences, using that as an argument why the probation service should concentrate its resources on people who have traditionally been given custodial sentences. The Commission's local authority profiles direct attention to their patterns of expenditure. They are expected to justify unit costs higher than the average for their cluster or 'family' of authorities.

At the same time, the Commission frequently criticizes authorities on the grounds that their expenditure on particular forms of resource, such as maintenance of property, or whole services, like community-based services for elderly people or people with learning difficulties, is too low (Day and Klein, 1990). In doing so reports often stress the transitional costs of moving to more economic or efficient use of resources. You have to spend to save.

Between 1983 and 1987, the Commission concentrated most heavily on promoting efficiency. Its work has focused attention on the importance of information systems and good predictive models, so that authorities know how they are spending their money and can prevent uncontrolled over-estimates of demand for service. However, again, efficiency was linked not simply to control but also to value for money. Above all, it was increasingly promoted as a means of enabling authorities to shift expenditure to their own priorities. The report on the management of secondary education (Audit Commission, 1986b) advocated an activity led staffing model and the closure of small and under-occupied schools on grounds of rational allocation of scarce resources. But the study itself and the follow up report (Audit Commission, 1988b) stressed the opportunity costs of failure to take such action. Within a climate of resource control, authorities were encouraged to see how they could use what they had more creatively to achieve their own purposes. The theme was sustained in the Commission's property management handbook (1988b). Authorities were enjoined to perceive their property as a 'dynamic resource', a key to the development and implementation of effective strategic planning.

In 1987 the Commission made a firm commitment to shift the emphasis of its work towards promoting effectiveness (Audit Commission, 1987b). It also significantly enlarged the assumptions on which that work was based. Originally, effectiveness was defined as 'how well a programme or activity is achieving its established goals or other intended effects' (Audit Commission, 1984). The emphasis was on services and authorities reaching their own objectives. And the Commission drew clear lines between its own expertise in management and that of the professionals whose task it was to define standards of service and develop professional practice that might achieve them.

As the Commission's own work began to expose the poverty of professional thinking about setting standards of effectiveness and quality (Henkel, 1991), and as some departments began to invite special study teams to help define such standards, they abandoned the reticence about professional boundaries that had inhibited them in, for example, the study of secondary education (Audit Commission, 1986b). They put forward explicitly normative models of service delivery in their studies on mental handicap (1987c; 1988c; 1989b). They promoted models of effective professional practice in their report on the probation service (1989a). And they tried to develop specific indicators of effectiveness in their work on performance measures (Audit Commission, 1988e). The Audit Commission thus set itself up as a source of national standards and norms against which local organizations could assess themselves and be assessed.

It also began to break down, and, in effect, redefine what is meant by effectiveness. It introduced the notion of 'service effectiveness' (Audit Commission, 1988e) and incorporated input and process issues into its analysis of what must go into performance measurement. The 1988 action guide identifies a key set of questions for local authorities as 'Is the service getting to the right customers, in the right way, with the right services, in keeping with its stated policies?' This makes it possible to use such measures of performance as amounts and levels of service delivered, opening hours and response times and numbers and categories of service users. Service effectiveness thus merges with efficiency measures. The Commission has not abandoned its interest in outcomes of service but itself has so far produced only a limited range of outcome measures.

Commission documents have, however, laid strong emphasis on targets and targeting. The language of targets has, at least in part, replaced the language of objectives and underlined the importance of setting and achieving intermediate outcomes, such as specific rates of employment for offenders on community-based court orders. At the same time the need to 'target' certain services to certain groups, the 'right customers', has been stressed. Targeting in this sense links with different purposes in different contexts, albeit within a single value framework: limiting expensive services to the most needy groups and marketing services that might bring revenue to attract new customers.

Three main themes emerge from this discussion. First, the criteria used by the Commission have to be understood within the context of its political role and purposes. Words such as efficiency, effectiveness, value for money and performance do not denote precise and fixed ideas, any more than other apparently less definitive expressions; their meanings shift with the priorities of those who use them and their function is as much emotive as descriptive. The Commission follows its own advice that performance criteria and measures must motivate those whose actions they are seeking to change. The connection it has made between economy and efficiency with local authorities' capacities to maximize control over their own destinies exemplifies the point.

Second, the Commission has made management the key to local authority success and sought to contrast it with a passive concept of administration (Audit Commission, 1986c) and an expansionist and pluralist concept of professionalism (Audit Commission, 1988a and 1989a). The planned management of resources is seen as more likely to provide quality services, commitment to professional leadership more prone to result in the triumph of quantity over quality. Good management is depicted as bringing coherence, direction and effective accountability, whereas the dominance of a professional culture tends to encourage 'loose network(s) of independent practitioners' and to result in services lacking shared and explicit standards or cogent evaluative systems.

A third, but integrally linked, point is that the Commission's special studies and its work on performance measurement have laid the foundations of a national evaluative framework for local government services.

So far, then, it could appear that the Commission has been committed both to greater local authority autonomy and to stronger central authority. The concept of management put forward assumes that local authorities will have significant degrees of freedom to shape the 'enabling authority' according to their own visions. And the Commission has tried hard, albeit with limited success, to persuade central government to lift restrictions on local authority rights to capitalize on efficiency savings and so give its incentives strategy more substance. At the same time, its development of evaluative criteria and structures within which to measure and promote their achievement has reinforced government aspirations to reassert a sense of central authority in the public sector. The next section will seek to establish more precisely the Commission's position by addressing the question of whose criteria it is seeking to install.

Whose Criteria?

The Audit Commission's work is strongly rooted in the perceptions and practice of the field. Its special studies directorate is structured round a core of analytic expertise, in statistics, operational research and economics. But individual studies draw on secondments of specialists, academic, managerial or professional, from the relevant field and consultancies with people at or near the top of the management and reputational system. Special studies teams have strong field-based networks and rely heavily on them to help them select special studies topics and to identify best practice within them from research and other literature and from current work. They test this through team debate and analysis and fieldwork in authorities selected with a bias towards those perceived in the field to be at the leading edge of developments. Does this mean that they can claim that their criteria are predominantly inductively determined? Is their function primarily that of interpreter, disseminator and marketer of field-based values, knowledge and methods?

Undoubtedly, this is one of their functions. They convey in lucid prose and arresting diagrams norms, issues, solutions to problems and promising projects derived from the field. But these are framed not only by the Commission's key criteria but also by certain a priori assumptions which can fairly be described as conforming to the views of the government of the day: that policies must be structured primarily by resource constraint; that management is the key to good public services; that the public sector should be subject to disciplines and principles derived from the market, such as competition and 'closeness to the customer'; and that accountability should be understood primarily as accountability to taxpayers.

Moreover, while the Commission repeatedly proclaims its neutrality on specific government policies, it not only takes them for granted in the criteria on which reports are based, but actively promotes them. Evaluations on such matters as secondary school management (Audit Commission, 1986b) and value for money in the probation service unequivocally proclaim the need for school closures and amalgamations and for changes in the objectives of the probation service (Audit Commission, 1989a). Policies on competitive tendering are actively endorsed (Audit Commission, 1989b). Thus while the Commission is eclectic and responsive to the field in the knowledge, methods and models of good practice it adopts, the value framework within which it operates has more in common with central than with local government.

The Audit Commission's Continuing Contribution to Evaluation

The last part of this chapter pursues the themes of centre and periphery within the Commission itself and in government. It can be argued that much of the Commission's authority derives from commitment to a strong top-down or centre-periphery model of evaluation and implementation and from its concentration on quantitative analysis developed within a managerial perspective. This section will first briefly demonstrate how these characteristics are reflected in the Commission's special studies and in its approach to embedding performance review in local authorities but also how they are also being modified. It then discusses the case for the Commission to accommodate a greater variety of perspectives and knowledge in its work and sets that in the context of the particular characteristics and demands of public-sector evaluation.

The Commission's special studies play a key role in its pursuit of its central objectives: to promote greater economy, efficiency and effectiveness in local management. They are targeted on aspects of local, and now health, authority management selected as important and susceptible to substantial improvement in performance. That is essential: they are expensive, highly labour-intensive and long-term exercises. The national component has a two-year time-scale and the local audit follows in the third year.

The methods the special studies teams currently use, particularly the combination of technical analysis, wide consultation in well-established networks and carefully selected fieldwork sites, ensure that the results are relatively robust, provided the policy framework remains reasonably stable. (An exception was the study *Towards Better Management of Secondary Education*, some of whose key arguments were undermined by the provisions for schools to opt out under the Education Reform Act, 1988). The Controller of the Commission has recently pronounced himself sufficiently satisfied with the special studies model to translate it into the newly assumed NHS audit task (Smith, 1990).

The system is highly structured from the centre. The national reports lay out evaluative criteria, the arguments for their adoption and the action that needs to be taken by local or health authorities and central government if they are to be met. They are converted into audit guides to enable local auditors to carry through the exercise in their own authorities. The guides contain detailed evaluative tools and, often, resource, planning and predictive models which can be used by local managers to improve or change their approach to the key issues. They also carry detailed advice to the auditors on the conduct of the audit, although auditors exercise discretion, in collaboration with local managers, as to the main focus of their study. Progress in the authorities following the audit is measured and recorded locally and nationally.

However, the studies must be assessed on two dimensions: their success in providing a technical product, that is, management and monitoring tools for long-term use; and their potential to initiate or sustain a process of reappraisal and change in local bodies. The studies perform well on the first count, for they continue to find authority services where the infrastructure for efficient management is not in place: for example, information systems which can show managers what resources they have, how they are deploying them and at what cost, and whom services are reaching. And their audit guides are widely praised in local authorities for the comprehensive technical guidance they contain.

A study carried out at Brunel University (Henkel, 1991) suggested that the second purpose could flounder unless the study was 'owned' by local managers or members with power to influence the political process. Without such support, local auditors could be dismissed by local personnel as having neither the professional nor the political understanding to make authoritative evaluations or provide the impetus for major change. They were sometimes seen as furnishing technical or accountants' solutions to complex political or specialist professional problems.

The Commission and some local auditors themselves have drawn the conclusion that auditors need additional management consultancy skills, particularly in the management of change, if they are to realize the extended concept of audit contained in the Commission's mandate. Auditors would then be better equipped to carry the role which they find is in practice required of them: to negotiate and collaborate with local authorities to devise local solutions to problems rather than attempting to impose a national formula.

Such a role is consistent with the Commission's professed overriding aim to help create local management strong enough to adapt to continuing change. But, as Day and Klein (1990) point out, it inevitably entails tension. Auditors cannot exchange the audit role for that of consultant, much as some authorities would like them to do so.

The Audit Commission has invested substantially in a second strategy to strengthen local management through systems of performance review. The handbooks they have produced (Audit Commission, 1986c, 1988e) provide two main kinds of help. First, they present models in which performance review is linked into strategic and operational planning and management.

Second, they suggest a framework for reviewing departments' performance, in which key issues are identified and guidance given on how performance that addresses those issues might be analysed and where to look for measures or indicators linked with that analysis. Special studies reports constitute a major source of such indicators.

There is now a substantial literature on the pitfalls awaiting those who develop performance indicators (see, e.g. Pollitt, 1986, 1988, 1990; Cave et al., 1988; Burningham, 1990). And the Commission is aware of many of them: the problems of overload, bias and ambiguity; the risk that performance indicators result in distortion of service priorities; the difficulties of constructing indicators of outcome as against input and process; the danger that quantitative measures will drive out qualitative forms of appraisal. A practical and simple analysis is provided of the different levels of management at which different indicators will be useful, along with a demonstration set of indicators that could be used as an annual monitoring device by a local government committee (Audit Commission, 1988e).

However, there are significant gaps in the advice offered on performance review. It is grounded primarily in quantitative analysis. And, as indicated earlier, it has little to say about outcome as opposed to output of services. The last four pages of the 1988 *Action Guide* contain some suggested approaches but primarily in the spirit of stimulating debate. Assessing the contribution of services to people's lives is acknowledged to be 'difficult and still at an early stage'. The Commission stresses the contribution to be made in this field by experimental projects and by research. Its thinking is reminiscent of Rivlin's advocacy of 'systematic experimentation' (Rivlin, 1971). In areas where qualitative evaluation of output and outcome is needed, the Commission suggests inspection as one resource, user or customer studies as another.

Here the Commission is arguing for performance review to draw on multiple sources of evaluation. But it raises the question whether the Commission should itself incorporate a wider repertoire. In the current climate, there is a particularly strong prima facie case for it to get to grips with the user or customer perspective on organizations. Many current formulations of public management are rooted in private sector markets in goods and services. These assume that the critical dynamic for managers, now that so many of the boundaries between the public and private sectors have been broken down, is that between managers and customers (*The Competitive Council* (Audit Commission, 1988a) referred to earlier reflects this same view).

Barnes and Miller (1988) argue that it is possible to develop performance indicators that are client- or user-centred instead of service-centred. Managers using indicators would then perceive the amounts and combinations of services received by different users and so get a comprehensive outline of the impact of service provision on individuals and how that may vary. Such an approach might raise different questions for managers, even if it is still primarily quantitative.

A qualitative approach is, however, adopted by Kellaher, Peace and Willcocks, if in a slightly different context. They are building on their already substantial research into evaluating consumer experience of residential care (e.g. Willcocks, 1984; Willcocks, Peace and Kellaher, 1987) and exploring the feasibility of structuring staff self-evaluation systems round user perceptions and wishes. Their work assumes that the interests of staff and users in residential settings are not wholly reconcilable, but that if service providers are serious about quality, they must face the challenge of insight into users' wants and experience without imposing their own frame of reference on them.

That presents a serious challenge to the Commission. It works within a top-down managerial perspective and a dominant ideology in which quality of service must ultimately be subordinated to tight resource control. The consumer viewpoint might be heavily distorted. At best, it might be clear and challenge vigorously. Its first document on performance review (1986c) declared a commitment, in that context, to ensuring that all stakeholders felt they were gaining from it.

Fully articulated customer perspectives may challenge not only resource allocation decisions but also distributions of power in designing and operating services. The complexities of their views and the intensity of their feelings in some circumstances could threaten the clarity and certainties which the Commission's work has injected into public debate. The Commission might use the customer view, as it has other sources of knowledge, as an incisive critical weapon. But it might also be compelled to distort it by the force of its need to incorporate it into its own frame of reference and to meet the objectives of reconciling multiple interests.

There are two issues here which those concerned with public sector evaluation must address. The first is whether the critical dynamic is indeed that between managers and customers. Policy theorists (e.g. Rhodes, 1987; Hambleton, 1988; Pollitt, 1988) have challenged this idea on a number of grounds, only some of which can be considered here.

They first argue that conceptualizing public service users as customers or consumers is an error or even a deception: most users lack even the power of consumers in the private sector; many do not, and cannot, pay; they are unable to find alternatives. Some are compelled against their will to receive services or accept intervention in their lives. Thus, for a number of reasons, the capacity to threaten profitability by removal of custom does not exist.

It is further pointed out that identifying the key relationship as being between managers and individual recipients of services is a mistake. It ignores the rationale for a public sector: not only can many people with most need for public services not pay for them, but the purpose of public services goes far beyond individual need. Failure to provide may mean a decrease in the quality of life of whole families, streets, housing estates, neighbourhoods and so affect the working of other social institutions and the economy. Individual transactions are not the only important relationships involved. The second issue concerns the range of interests which public sector evaluation might be expected to encompass and how. Pluralist evaluative theory assumes that there are always several sets of stakeholders in evaluations. But different theorists go on to draw different conclusions. Some advocate working from the managerial perspective, since managers hold the power to make changes (Wholey, 1983). Some suggest that the role of the evaluator should be to adopt the perspective of users, because they do not have power (Scriven, 1980). Others take the line that the evaluators' first and most significant tasks are to identify the range of stakeholders and assist them to negotiate their views and demands (Guba and Lincoln, 1989).

Within this perspective, the complexities of incorporating effectiveness into the Commission's mandate begin to be more fully displayed. If they were taken seriously, they could threaten its key merits: its clarity of values, focus and quantitative analytic expertise and its willingness to prescribe clear courses of action, within a managerial framework. Alternatively, their incorporation might ultimately be a fiction. Complexity and conflict would be submerged by the twin forces of the drive to clarity and dominant interests. These also constitute strong reasons why an evaluative body can never be wholly independent. It can be critical and institutionally separate but, if coherent, will inevitably reflect particular perspectives deriving not simply from a balance of power but also from the need to employ a persuasive language and a convincing base of knowledge.

The ideal solution might then seem to be to institutionalize pluralism and establish evaluative institutions that would give a strong voice to a multiplicity of interests: managers, professionals, trade unions, users and tax payers. But, as our political culture has been moving further away from pluralism, that is unlikely to happen, and if it did there is no guarantee that users would acquire power at all commensurate with that of other interests.

For these reasons, given that the Audit Commission has built up a position of power and that its mandate to evaluate effectiveness unarguably includes impacts upon service users, the argument that it should incorporate the user/customer voice then looks stronger. It is better for that voice to be there, even if it is distorted. Moreover, if it is used as a source of critique by the Commission against other powerful groups such as professions, they too may be encouraged to seek out the user voice and find ways of aligning themselves with it that will give it more real strength.

If we are serious about the quality of public sector evaluation and its potential as a force for change, ways need to be found of sustaining the long acknowledged tension between the drive to integrate differences in the interests of action and to disintegrate in the interests of democracy.

References

Audit Commission (1984) *Code of Local Government Audit Practice for England and Wales.* London: HMSO.
— (1986a) *Report and Accounts.* London: HMSO.
— (1986b) *Towards Better Management of Secondary Education.* London: HMSO.
— (1986c) *Performance Review in Local Government: a handbook for auditors and local authorities.* London: HMSO.
— (1987a) *Report and Accounts.* London: HMSO.
— (1987b) *The Way Ahead.* London: HMSO.
— (1987c) *Community Care: developing services for people with a mental handicap.* London: HMSO, Occasional Paper no. 2.
— (1988a) *The Competitive Council.* London: HMSO, Management Paper no. 1.
— (1988b) *Surplus Capacity in Secondary Schools: a progress report.* London: HMSO.
— (1988c) *Local Authority Property: a management handbook.* London: HMSO.
— (1988d) *Community Care: developing services for people with a mental handicap: audit guide.* London: HMSO.
— (1988e) *Performance Review in Local Government: a handbook for auditors and local authorities: action guide.* London: HMSO.
— (1989a) *The Probation Service: promoting value for money.* London: HMSO.
— (1989b) *Preparing for Compulsory Competition.* London: HMSO, Occasional Paper no. 7.
Barnes, M. and Miller, N. (eds) (1988) Performance measurement in personal social services, *Research, Policy and Planning,* 6.2, special issue.
Bromley, P. and Euske, K. (1986) The use of rational systems in bounded rationality organisations: a dilemma for financial managers, *Financial Accountability and Management,* 2, 311–20.
Burningham, D. (1990) Performance indicators and the management of professionals in local government. In M. Cave, M. Kogan and R. Smith (eds), *Output and Performance Measurement in Government: the state of the art, London: Jessica Kingsley,* 124–42.
Cave, M., Hanney, S., Kogan, M. and Trevett, G. (1988) *The Use of Performance Indicators in Higher Education.* London: Jessica Kingsley.
Day, P. and Klein, R. (1990) Inspecting the Inspectorates. York: Joseph Rowntree Memorial Trust.
Guba, E. G. and LIncoln, Y. S. (1989) *Fourth Generation Evaluation.* London: Sage.
Hambleton, R. (1988) Consumerism, Decentralisation and local democracy, *Public*

Administration, 66, 125–48.

Henkel, M. (1991) *Government, Evaluation and Change*. London: Jessica Kingsley.

Minogue, M. (1983) Theory and practice in public policy and administration, *Policy and Politics*, 11, 63–86.

Pollitt, C. (1986) Beyond the managerial model: the case for broadening performance assessment in the government and the public services, *Financial Accountability and Management*, 2, 155–70.

— (1988) Bringing consumers into performance management: concepts, consequences and constraints, *Policy and Politics*, 16, 77–88.

— (1990) Peformance indicators, root and branch. In M. Cave, M. Kogan and R. Smith (eds), *Output and Performance Measurement in Government: the state of the art*, London: Jessica Kingsley, 167–78.

Rhodes, R. A. W. (1987) Developing the public service orientation – or let's add a soupçon of political theory, *Local Government Studies*, 13, 63–73.

Rivlin, A. M. (1971) *Systematic Thinking for Social Action*. Washington, DC: Brookings Institute.

Scriven, M. (1980) *The Logic of Evaluation*. San Francisco: Edgepress.

Smith, R. (1990) Enter the men from the Audit Commission, *British Medical Journal*, 301, 1269–72.

Wholey, J. (1983) *Evaluation and Effective Public Management*. Boston: Little Brown.

Willcocks, D. (1984) Consumer research in old people's homes, *Research, Policy and Planning*, 2, 13–18.

Willcocks, D., Peace, S. and Kellaher, L. (1987) *Private Lives in Public Places*. London: Tavistock.

5

An Overview of the Use of Performance Indicators in Local Government

David Burningham

Introduction

What is the future of performance indicators (PIs) in local government? Are they just another fashionable management tool, born in a crisis which will eventually pass away? This is unlikely. Local government is in a process of radical transformation, which some observers predict will result by the end of the century in slimmed down organizations whose function is to tackle the problems left by the market rather than deliver services (Hepworth, 1988). In the immediate future, local authorities are likely to remain significant providers of services, but a number of interconnected trends are discernible, which have significant implications for management and the use of PIs:

(a) renewed emphasis on the role of the chief executive and the need for a new style of corporate management in the 'competitive council' (Audit Commission, 1988; 1989);

(b) increased competition – externally from competitive tendering and through the creation of 'internal markets' with service-level agreements (CIPFA, 1988);

(c) a shift away from centrally negotiated pay schemes towards more flexibility for individual authorities, allowing them to determine pay scales in the light of local conditions. This is associated with an extension of performance-related pay schemes (LACSAB, 1989);

(d) the rise of the 'enabling authority', which, as direct service provision contracts, exerts its influence on behalf of the community, through other agencies (Clarke and Stewart, 1988; Brooke, 1989).

This chapter reviews the progress with PIs in the light of these trends and suggests ways of avoiding some of the difficulties which are encountered. It concludes with a check list for users of performance measures.

Criteria for Assessing Performance Measurement

Before describing the application of PIs in local government, it will be helpful to raise two sets of questions against which progress in their use can be assessed.

What type of indicators are being used? (Taking residential care for the elderly as an example) are they:

(a) *Management Statistics?* – simple quantitative statements which do not directly measure performance; (e.g. the number of elderly people sponsored in private and voluntary homes)

(b) *Partial Indicators?* – Partial measures the meanings of which are ambiguous without other data, especially concerning quality; (e.g. cost per client week).

(c) *Performance Measures?* – more comprehensive measures of performance. These are likely to be a cluster of PIs and supporting qualitative data rather than a single statistic, reflecting all relevant dimensions of domiciliary care.

Each of these levels of indicator can be further classified according to whether they are being used to assess economy, efficiency or effectiveness (the 'three Es').

How are the PIs being used?
Although the applications are varied, they fall into three distinct but connected groups:

(a) *Accountability* – PIs as an expression of the key areas of performance for which the organization, unit or individual is being held accountable by those on whose behalf the work is being done. Ultimately, in local government, this is through the council to the local community and to funding departments of central government.

(b) *Control* – PIs used by managers to get early warning if performance starts to fall below the expected level or norm, so that corrective action can be taken; used for assigning and assessing work in the allocation of resources within a department. They are not to be confused with the more public PIs to monitor accountability.

(c) *Development* – PIs as part of a learning cycle in a process of intervention and change of management, intended to improve performance.

No single system of indicators can satisfy the whole range of objectives under these headings. For example, PIs used for control purposes need to be more selective and computed more quickly than those for public accountability.

TABLE 5.1
The choice and use of performance indicators

Type of indicator	% of total
Management statistics	42
Partial indicators	37
Performance measures	21
Use of indicators	% of total
Accountability	63
Control	27
Development	10
The three Es	% of total
Indicators measuring:	
economy	41
efficiency	44
effectiveness	15

Progress So Far

A distinction should be drawn between the formal criteria and systems for a performance review (often impressive on paper) – as reflected in committee structures and documentation – and how the systems actually work in practice. Some authorities, such as Bexley, have well-developed systems of performance monitoring, while others are still in the formative stages.

There is no single comprehensive survey of current practice, but various sources give some idea of trends. These sources include the Audit Commission, the Local Government Training Board, the Institute of Local Government Studies, the Local Authorities Management Services and Computer Committee, supplemented by case studies. At the formal level it is clear that considerable progress has been made with the introduction of PIs. Whereas a 1980 LAMSAC survey showed that at the time a third of authorities appeared to have no arrangements at all (LAMSAC 1982), now almost all authorities have some form of performance review committee or sub-committee.

Also encouraging is the fact that with many authorities, the move towards different styles of management, and the adoption of supporting performance-review systems, accords with the Audit Commission's check list (1986) for the 'well managed council'. For example, the London Borough of Kingston (McCloy, 1988) includes the following among its management objectives:

(a) the need for 'greater delegation' and 'more strategic thinking';
(b) emphasis on 'the centrality of work for the community' together with a 'customer-centred approach to the planning of Council services';
(c) 'to have greater correspondence between Committee and Department to facilitate accountability';
(d) 'personnel policies that would utilise talents to greater effect, and in so doing seek to reward properly performance';
(e) 'to be more decisive concerning the respective role of client and contractor'.

This list is fairly typical of many councils, but in practice the choice and use of PIs is often inadequate for the pursuit of these objectives. A survey among nine authorities – each using, across all departments, about 400 indicators – (Burningham, 1990) revealed the details in table 5.1.

While it cannot be claimed that these percentages apply to all authorities, they do reflect two widespread patterns in the use of PIs. Firstly, a very high proportion of measures are simply 'management statistics' or at best only 'partial indicators'. Consequently, many of the measures fail one of the basic tests of the usefulness of an indicator (see appendix 5.1), namely that of ambiguity. Can a change in a particular indicator be unambiguously identified with a change in performance? One of the reasons for this is that so many measures (in this particular survey 85 per cent) concentrate on economy and efficiency – simply because the data are available – leaving questions about changes in quality unanswered. Since this is central to the assessment of user satisfaction and hence effectiveness, the 'customer-centred approach' is neglected in many measurement systems.

Further ambiguity often arises because the PIs are poorly presented. Too frequently they appear as a rather impenetrable mixture of statements and statistics. If the objectives underlying performance review are to be reached, much more thought needs to be given to the format in which they are presented. The visual presentation, for example, could in many cases be substantially sharpened, perhaps by an improved layout to enable members and officers to identify indicators for what are regarded as key or priority areas. Otherwise, the use of PIs will fall far short of the attainment of the laudable but ambitious objectives of the kind quoted above.

The second characteristic of local authority performance review systems is that the data generated are being used mainly for accountability purposes, usually in the form of annual service profiles presented to the relevant service committee or performance review committee. Far less emphasis is given to the role of indicators in the internal management functions of control and development. For example, in education, as one Audit Commissioner has commented: 'LEAs are awash with information – yet this is mainly used for LEAs wider monitoring or simply for inclusion in statistical reports. Few LEAs use the information to produce useful monitoring reports about individual schools, – to help governors, head teachers, and LEA staff to monitor and compare their performance' (Henderson-Stewart, 1990).

Because events are being monitored, the misleading impression is sometimes created that they are therefore under control. The Urban Programme for example, has, since 1985, been subject to output and performance measurement based on 53 output measures, but many of the shortcomings identified by the National Audit Office – insufficient attention to priorities, lack of co-ordination – still remain (Campbell, 1990; Burningham and Knight, 1987; Audit Commission, 1989). These problems can arise because PIs in local government are not always fully linked with other planning and review systems – a point examined later in this paper. As a result some performance review committees become sidings into which performance indicators are shunted as 'background information' rather than junctions through which they pass in a process of real evaluation and decision making. Such review groups become 'isolated from the main decision making system and even at odds with it' (Audit Commission, 1986).

Clearly some of the misgivings voiced about performance review in local government, from those subject to review, arise from a natural defensive instinct. Professional providers and specialists in service and support departments may resist because they see review systems as an encroachment on their freedom and professional judgement. Nevertheless, not all objections are defensive and some express genuine doubts about the effectiveness of a performance review. As one chief officer has commented:

> We make a considerable effort in preparing information for Service Profiles but is it worth it? Members appear to make little or no use of them. Although the Chief Executive has the establishment of a system of indicators as a priority in his list of objectives, it is not clear to all participants how they are going to help in the departments. For many of us it seems just another piece of paperwork, an exercise in window dressing, which has little bearing on the way things are managed.

This view is not typical of all departments, but it does reflect concerns that are not uncommon.

So as not to end this review of progress on a misleadingly negative note, the point made at the beginning of this section must be emphasized.

Considerable progress has been made: all authorities now acknowledge the need for systematic performance review; most have in place some arrangements for achieving this. What is needed now is to build on these foundations and make PIs operationally effective at all levels within local government organization.

The Quality Problem

It is universally acknowledged that the measurement of quality, which underpins the assessment of effectiveness, is the most difficult aspect of local government performance review. 'Improvements' in quantifiable aspects – costs and quantity of inputs and outputs of a particular service – have little credibility unless considered alongside changes in quality. In the private sector, it is often claimed, the assessment of whether the right balance has been struck between quality and quantity presents no problem. In the market-place the supplier is guided by the consumer, who will decide on the desired quality/quantity trade-off and pay accordingly. Since, in local government, as in other parts of the public sector, goods and services are often provided free (or subsidized) at the point of use, there are usually no sales revenue figures to guide suppliers.

This is an over-simplification of what happens in the private sector. Firms cannot rely on their sales figures to tell them whether they have judged quality correctly. Unlike most local authorities, they conduct regular surveys of user opinion. Moreover, the simple, two dimensional 'quality/ quantity' view of products and services is unhelpful. Private sector marketing experts and market researchers refer instead to 'product characteristics' and 'product position' – the place a product or service occupies in the market by virtue of its characteristics, compared with its rivals (Douglas, 1980). For example, when establishing what type of new car will appeal to various segments of the market, analysts will not evaluate its attraction in terms of basic transport plus varying amounts of an omnibus category called 'quality'. They will examine how the different combinations of characteristics offered – economy, comfort, prestige, performance – are evaluated by customers and influence their choice.

The characteristics model can be applied to assessment of local-government services. Take for example a leisure centre. This could be viewed in the conventional manner as a provider of a number of quite distinct activities, each measured in quantitative terms (attendance/revenue) with some estimate of quality (range of equipment; level of supervision). Alternatively the characteristics approach would examine the combination of reasons for which people use leisure centres – fitness, development of

TABLE 5.2
Sports and social facilities at leisure centres

Leisure Centre	Average A (Sport)	Average B (Social)
W	25	30
X	67	40
Y	55	60
Z	40	70

new skills; opportunity to socialize; somewhere to take the family – and the extent to which facilities offered are seen to meet these needs. Leisure centres run by various authorities may offer different combinations of these characteristics.

To take a simplified hypothetical example: assume the characteristics can be placed in two groups – sports facilities and 'social' facilities, i.e. shops, café/bar, lounge area (the latter a contribution to 'atmosphere' and 'social life'). Possibly with limited resources, a leisure centre offering more in the first group would offer less in the second category and conversely.

Suppose a sample of users is then asked to rate, separately, out of a scale of 100 both sports facilities and social life for four leisure centres run by different authorities. We might get the data shown in table 5.2, which can also be displayed graphically (figure 5.1), showing the average ratings for each authority.

The leisure centre W, scoring less on both scales than the other centres, could, other things being equal, be regarded as under-performing. However, one cannot say which if any, of the remaining three centres is more efficient or effective until we add data on unit costs and user demand, indicating preferred combinations of sports and social facilities. Revenue will provide an appropriate measure of the latter if the centres are being run on purely commercial lines. If, as is likely, the centres have non-commercial objectives – catering for disadvantaged groups or a youth programme – then attendance figures for target groups should be included.

In practice, the non-commercial objectives will probably justify the inclusion of other characteristics for evaluation, but the prescriptive point here is that as many relevant characteristics as possible should be assessed by means of user surveys, when trying to build up a picture of 'quality'

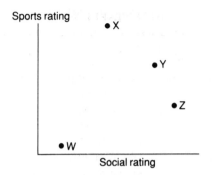

FIGURE 5.1
Sports and social facilities at leisure centres

and eventually effectiveness. Appendix 5.2, 'Yardsticks of Performance for Hounslow Leisure Services', although simplistic and fragmentary, with a mixture of inputs and outputs, is nevertheless on the right lines. This kind of assessment of user views on characteristics is also important in establishing relevant standards for quality assurance and drawing up service/contract specifications.

A high level of skill in the appropriate techniques is essential for effective valuation of user responses. This applies not only to the basic tasks of pilot surveys, questionnaire design and sample construction, but also to other survey methods such as user panels, group interviews and activity sampling. To this should be added 'encounter analysis' – the evaluation of front-line conversations with the public as a means of improving customer service (James, 1989).

At present, public opinion and customer research is in its infancy in local government, claiming only a minute amount of resources compared with private sector organizations of comparable size. Authorities will have to consider the most cost-effective way of achieving professional standards in their opinion survey work. Should independent in-house units be established or should the work be contracted out? If the latter, is it worthwhile for local authorities to club together to channel their demands to a professional service unit established for this purpose (Evans, 1989)? The impetus will come not only as a result of a 'more customer-centred approach' but also in the longer run a shift to councils as 'enablers' rather than 'providers'. This will require councils to be much more responsive than at present to the collective needs and aspirations of their communities (Jackson, 1988; Clarke and Stewart, 1988).

Making PIs Work

There are at least two sets of issues which are central to the establishment of effective measurement systems. First, there is the difficult role of the chief executive in a situation where corporate or general management is regarded with suspicion by professionals and specialists in various departments. Second, there is the perception that PIs are not really a significant part of the management process but a rather irritating exercise in paper-work. How can these difficulties be overcome? One response is to redouble efforts to increase the number of indicators. While there is some justification in this, especially with regard to improving effectiveness measures, the proliferation of indicators is not the solution.

Various case studies point to the importance, not simply of the choice of PIs, but of the way in which the indicators are introduced and applied to local government organizations (Burningham, 1990; Fletcher, 1985; LACSAB, 1989). Where PIs are bolted rather than grafted on, the results may be both frustrating and counterproductive. A number of practical steps, which are often overlooked, can be undertaken to secure the involvement and support of professionals in departments for measurement schemes. Firstly, a policy document can be compiled setting out a strategy for performance indicators. This would include:

(a)   a statement in operational terms of what it is intended to achieve;
(b)   an indicative timetable for the introduction of indicators (both this and (a) above will help to eliminate the competitive scramble, which sometimes occurs, to see who can introduce the most indicators);
(c)   guidance on the criteria for selection and use of indicators;
(d)   Criteria and mechanisms for the evaluation and improvement of performance measurement schemes.

Secondly, it is helpful to have a steering group to assist in the task of preparing the policy document and monitoring the subsequent developments. Its membership should comprise representatives of the departments and units using the scheme, together with relevant external agencies (including clients) and a member of the corporate management group, or whoever is responsible for co-ordination. This can provide a forum for evaluating experiences with PIs and establishing best practice. It also provides a point at which the dialogue and negotiation about indicators, and hence the sense of ownership so often lacking, can take place.

Thirdly, a realistic estimate is required of the resources needed to meet the aims specified in the policy document. Particular attention needs to be given to the question of resources for measuring effectiveness, especially the development of adequate survey methods for testing user opinion.

The steps outlined here provide a framework within which questions about performance review can be raised and answered. Without this security, prior to action, PIs will almost certainly have 'shallow roots' (Pollitt, 1990), extending only to the upper tiers of the organization. Four groups of questions (detailed in the check-list in appendix 5.1), should be raised.

- *Purpose* – To what aspects of the council's management activities are PIs expected to contribute? How will they be used?
- *Specification* – Do the selected PIs have the necessary characteristics for their task?
- *Integration* – Can the PIs be effectively integrated with the desired management practices and the way work is organized in the authority/ departments?
- *Evaluation* – Is the PI system itself being evaluated to assess costs/ benefits and incorporate new aims?

If these questions are to generate usable answers, they must be quite specific. They should therefore be asked with reference to the factors identified as essential to the good management of the particular organization. As strengths and weaknesses vary, it is difficult to generalize about what this list might comprise. However, the Audit Commission (1988) has specified eight key factors which characterize a well-managed council, together with the supporting tasks necessary to achieve them (see table 5.3). This provides a convenient starting-point for questions.

From this table it can be seen that performance review is a task which underlies almost all of the 'success factors' and should be a vital complement to undertaking the other key tasks. It is important to recognize that each success factor may require different types and ways of using PIs, applied at different points in the organization. Failure to acknowledge and act on this may result in PIs that are actually counter-productive to other key tasks. For example, PIs to assist in the objective of adapting to change need to be 'tin openers' rather than 'dials'. That is to say they should be indicators which help in an exploratory and interrogative process instead of providing exact answers. The aim should be to get certain issues onto the agenda of various committees for open-ended discussion about options for change. Indicators which are primarily dials may foreclose this kind of dialogue and inhibit the key task of thinking and planning ahead. However, elsewhere in the organization, and at other stages in the management process, indicators serving primarily as dials maybe entirely appropriate. This is certainly the case with the performance of ongoing operations and implementing decisions that have been taken on accountability and control.

TABLE 5.3
Key success factors in a well-managed council

Key tasks	Understand customers	Respond to electorate	Consistent achievable objectives	Clear responsibilities	Train and motivate people	Communicate effectively	Monitor results	Adapt to change
Manage internal relationships				X		X		X
Convert policy into action	X	X	X	X		X	X	X
Develop processes, people and skills			X	X	X		X	
Review performance	X	X	X	X	X		X	X
Think and plan ahead	X	X			X			X

Concluding Comments

The pursuit of good management in local government clearly requires the support of appropriate performance measurement schemes. On the other hand badly designed schemes may be more than just an irritating exercise in paper-work and may actually reduce the chances of attaining the three Es of economy, efficiency and effectiveness. To minimize these counter-productive aspects, PIs must be fully integrated with the best working practices and management structures of the local authority to which they are applied. This can only be achieved by a thorough analysis of the needs of the organization and the constructive involvement of all stakeholders during the introduction of the scheme.

Performance indicators used in local government should not be regarded simply as measures of well-defined costs and outputs in a static situation. The role of the local authority is changing. From being just a provider, it will in future take on a wider spectrum of tasks as lobbyist, promoter, co-ordinator and managing agent (D. Jackson, 1988). In this connection performance measurement can assist in the process of change by helping the authority to 'identify and articulate the collective needs and aspirations of its own community'. Much more attention must therefore be given to the assessment of user attitudes and experiences. It is only by focusing on outcomes in terms of quality and effectiveness that local government can decide what it is 'good at providing, as well as what it is not so good at accomplishing'.

Appendix 5.1: Performance Indicators Check-List*

I   PURPOSE
A)   For what purpose are PIs to be used? For example, to which of the eight 'success' factors (table 5.3) is it hoped that PIs will make a significant contribution?
B)   How are they to be used?
    i)   For use by officers, members, the public?
    ii)   For accountability, control or development purposes?
    iii)   As background information?
    iv)   For diagnostic purposes at the discretion of management?
    v)   As a regular cycle of audits?
    vi)   Will the use of PIs be confined to measures of departmental performance or will they be applied to different levels, to identify the performance of sections, groups or individuals?

vii) Will PIs be used to scrutinize all aspects of performance – economy, efficiency and effectiveness – or will attention be focused on one or two of these?

II SPECIFICATION

i) In the light of the previous analysis have all appropriate inputs/outputs and activities been identified?

ii) Do existing PIs match these requirements or are further refinements/PIs needed?

iii) Does each PI or group of PIs, meet the following operational criteria?**

Relevance – reflects the goals and objectives of the organization and is intelligible to users.

Congruence – complements other PIs in the scheme.

Ambiguity – a high or low indicator can be unambiguously identified with requisite performance. It can be adjusted for quality.

Cost – staff and data collection costs are reasonable.

Cheatproofness – indicator is not capable of being manipulated.

Aggregation – the indicator can be aggregated/disaggregated to meet the needs of policy formation and executive operations at different levels.

** Few PIs will score highly in each of these categories and therefore a relevant question is: What criteria do you use to determine the trade-off between any of the characteristics listed. Refer to priorities identified in section I – Purpose.

III INTEGRATION

Can PIs be effectively incorporated in the management processes/work of the council? Specifically:

i) How can the PIs be integrated with existing procedures for decision making?

ii) Does the scheme of PIs take account of:
a) the multi–task nature of departmental/individual work;
b) the pattern of working relationships, for example, co-operative tasks, liaison work?

iii) If PIs are to be incorporated in existing review mechanisms, then:
a) are they appropriate for the requisite managerial structure/style of management in each department;
b) do they distinguish between prescribed and discretionary work;
c) is the frequency of the use appropriate for sectional/individual levels of responsibility;
d) is the use of PIs linked with appropriate follow-up action, for example, changing tasks or resources?

* For a useful alternative list see Pollitt, 1987.

Appendix 5.2

Hounslow Leisure Services
Yardsticks of Performance

customer awareness of services is 12% up on market survey

area is first choice for families

less than 20% drop-out on Fitness course – and the next course is full. The course has 120% profit margin

15% increase in Passport to Fitness holders

33% increase in revenue from squash

shop turnover improves by 46%

23 from 25 scored on hygiene and cleaning inspection checklist

heating costs cut 3% in real terms

96% availability of supervision in weights room

staff attitudes showing clear improvement

75% of staff trained for required skills

revenue: cost ratio improved

comparisons survey with competitors shows HDSO offers better service

repeat bookings for Sports Hall extended from 6 months to 25 months ahead

staffing costs 2% below budget without deterioration in service

References

Audit Commission (1986) *Good Management in Local Government.* London: HMSO.
— (1988) *The Competitive Council.* London: HMSO.
— (1989) *More Equal than Others: the chief executive in local government.* London: HMSO.

Brooke, R. (1989a) *Managing the Enabling Authority.* London: Longman.
— (1989b) The enabling authority – practical consequences, *Local Government Studies*, 15, 55–64.
Burningham, D. (1990) Performance management and the management of professionals in local government. In M. Cave, M. Kogan and R. Smith (eds), *Output and Performance Measurement in Government: the state of the art*, London: Jessica Kingsley, 124–42.
Burningham, D. and Knight, K. (1987) *Co-operative Development and the Inner City.* London: North Kensington Task Force – Action for Cities Programme (mimeograph)
Campbell, M. (1990) *Local Economic Policy.* London: Cassell.
Chartered Institute of Public Finance and Accountancy (1988) *Accounting for Support Services: a practitioner's guide.* London: CIPFA.
Clarke, M. and Stewart, J. (1988) *The Enabling Council.* Luton: Local Government Training Board.
Douglas, E. (1980) *Managerial Economics.* Englewood Cliffs, NJ: Prentice-Hall.
Evans, W. (1989) Professional service units for public authorities, *Local Government Studies*, 15, 1–8.
Fletcher, C. (1985) *Performance Appraisal and Career Development.* London: Hutchinson.
Henderson-Stewart, D. (1990) Performance measurement and review in local government. In M. Cave, M. Kogan and R. Smith (eds), *Output and Performance Measurement in Government: the state of the art*, London: Jessica Kingsley, 106–23.
Hepworth, N. (1988) *What Future for Local Government?* London: IEA.
Jackson, D. (1988) Analysing the nature of local government today, *Public Finance and Accountancy*, 15–20.
Jackson, P. (1988) Local government as efficient government, *Economic Affairs*, 9, 17–18.
James, K. (1989) Encounter analysis: front-line conversations and their role in improving customer service, *Local Government Studies*, 15, 11–24.
Local Authorities Conditions of Services Advisory Board (1989) *Performance Related Pay – an Updata.* London: LACSAB.
Local Authorities Management Services and Computer Committee (1982) *Performance Review and the Elected Member.* London: LAMSAC.
McCloy, R. (1988) *The Chief Executive's Aims and Objectives.* Royal Borough of Kingston-upon-Thames (mimeograph).
Pollitt, C. (1987) The politics of performance assessment: lessons for higher education, *Studies in Higher Education*, 12, 87–98.
— (1990) Performance indicators, root and branch. In M. Cave, M. Kogan and R. Smith (eds), *Output and Performance Measurement in Government: the state of the art*, London: Jessica Kingsley, 167–78.

Evaluating Public Services: Reflections

Stephen Harrison and Christopher Pollitt

Each of the *Handbook's* four main sections will conclude with a brief set of editorial reflections, of which this is the first. The aim will be to identify any common themes which seem to have emerged from the foregoing contributions, and also to discuss any particularly striking points of difference or divergence.

The five chapters on evaluation do indeed yield several common insights. Three in particular stand out. The first is the difficulty of measuring effectiveness, and the continuing bias of many performance review systems towards measures of economy, efficiency and 'throughput'. The second is the need to recognize the multiplicity of potential 'stakeholders' involved in the evaluation of public services, and in particular to give more attention to the assessments which are or could be made by those who actually use the service. Third, there is the problem of 'rooting' evaluatory activities deep in day-to-day management and professional practice so that performance data are actively and regularly used by service delivery professionals and managers rather than being regarded by many of them as a tiresome, externally imposed exercise.

These three issues are, of course, interconnected. Effectiveness measurement is difficult partly because it necessarily involves going 'over the wall', beyond the organizational perimeter, to discover the extent to which service outputs eventually translate into impacts (outcomes) in the external world. This tends to be an expensive and time-consuming exercise, especially if an organization hasn't done it before. It is also conceptually difficult – problems of multiple causation and/or multiple attribution mean that it is frequently very hard to be sure to what extent the observed impacts can be safely attributed to the delivered output. And last but not least, the excursion beyond the organization brings the evaluator face to face with service users in their 'natural habitats'. This can be an upsetting experience if it turns out that the dimensions along which users assess services (and the weightings and judgements they make) differ significantly from those hitherto used by service managers and professionals. (Of course, the chances of encountering such unruly findings is minimized if users are consulted only 'on the premises' by means of management-designed 'tick-the-box' questionnaires which reflect management's own unmodified agenda.)

Divergence between what users seem to want and what service deliverers have previously decided these same users should have can be embarrassing. It may frighten professionals (and managers) who then respond by distancing themselves from such 'gimmicks' on the grounds that the service users are under-informed, biased, ignorant, confused, unrealistic or some mixture of these. Though understandable, such a reaction is arguably misguided. Looked at from another point of view the divergence is only to be expected, especially if users have seldom been consulted before. From this more optimistic perspective divergence represents an opportunity. It provides a basis on which to begin a dialogue between providers and users, a dialogue during which both sides can be expected to learn and to shift their own preconceptions somewhat. Users may indeed become more 'realistic' when supplied with more information – though that could as easily involve them in raising an lowering their expectations of the service. Equally, providers may come to understand that some particular procedure or activity which they carry out has a significance for users (welcome/unwelcome, trivial/ important) which had not previously occurred to them.

Such dialogues, when carefully articulated and supported, can help with the problem of 'rooting' performance measurement. When the managers and service deliverers can see that the system is measuring something which is actually meaningful to the individual users they deal with, the chances of their taking it seriously themselves is surely improved. To use again the private-sector term employed by David Burningham, there begins to be a shared vocabulary of 'product characteristics'.

It should be admitted, however, that most of the performance measurement systems of which the editors are aware are still some way off this level of integration. Where effectiveness *is* measured it tends to be effectiveness defined in some technical or professional way rather than along dimensions meaningful to service users. Users are beginning to be 'let in' here and there, but often only to the assessment of those aspects of a service which are at some distance from the sensitive professional core (such as hospital food or the choice of extra-curricular activities in schools). The optimist, however, could point to the distance covered in the development of performance measurement systems since 1980 and conclude that the integration of user judgements of effectiveness should be widespread before the end of the 1990s.

Ultimately, the question of selecting appropriate approaches to evaluation crosses the hazy border between the managerial and the political. As Mary

Henkel's chapter indicated, the attempt to incorporate user views into service evaluation may lead directly to demands from those same users for a greater institutionalized say in the design and operation of services. It is a long way in practice from the customer satisfaction questionnaire to the establishment of permanent structures for user participation, but not so far in logic. Such participation was successfully kept off the political agenda during the 11 years of the Thatcher administration (with the notable exception of the reform of school governing bodies) but now the rhetoric of 'quality' and 'customer responsiveness' has become so pervasive it may be hard to continue to hold the line against demands for new representative or participatory forms.

If there *were* to be significant developments on this front it would sharpen a tension already alluded to by several of our contributors, namely the balance to be struck between the interests of service users and those of the community at large (tax-paying or otherwise). Here, surely, we have crossed the border zone and are firmly back in political territory. Just as public-service managers are having to get used to setting clearer operational targets and answering for their achievement, so politicians may have to face up to the need to balance the interests of different sections of a diverse society more explicitly, more visibly and probably therefore more controversially than they have ever been obliged to do before. Those who still hold to the traditional tenets of liberal democracy may think that that would be no bad thing.

Part II

Controlling Public Service Professionals

6

Controlling Doctors

Brian Edwards

Introduction

All organizations that employ significant numbers of professional staff have to manage the sensitive interface between what the managers of the organizations want and what the professionals regard as an acceptable professional practice or standard. Nowhere is this boundary more sensitive than in health care. This chapter considers this boundary, describes the legal and other constraints within which doctors practice medicine and explores the notion of clinical freedom in the context of the internal market proposed for the National Health Service from 1991 onwards.

Clinical freedom was one of the founding principles of the NHS when it was created in 1948. What this has meant in practice is that provided overall hospital budgets were not exceeded, doctors practising in hospitals have had discretion to apportion the resources available to them (e.g. their time, beds, theatre sessions) between individual patients pretty much as they judged necessary and appropriate on clinical grounds. The criteria upon which they make these 'rationing' decisions (because that is what they are) is clinical priority, thus following through Nye Bevan's dream that 'medical treatment and care was to be made available to rich and to poor alike in accordance with medical needs and no other criteria'. The willingness of doctors to perform this rationing role in the context of infinite demand and limited resources has to be seen as the quid pro quo of clinical freedom. It has also had the effect of distancing politicians and managers from the rationing process at the point at which it impacts on the individual patient. Rationing by medical priority has always been easier to justify and live with than any other grounds. In general practice, where doctors are independent contractors rather than employees, clinical freedom has been even wider as a consequence of open-ended drug budgets. Provided the prescribing policies of general practitioners are judged by their peers to be professionally reasonable, there is no cash limit at all on the amount that they can prescribe in a given year.

These freedoms are, of course, never absolute. In the hospital and community health services, there are always limits to what can be done simply in terms of physical facilities and staffing resources. The ability of the managers to control the primary inputs to the system explains how cash limits are held intact year after year.

Professional freedom of the sort that has existed in the NHS since 1948 is a rare commodity. It is usually found at its greatest within public sector systems and at its lowest in the private health sector where economic criteria impose themselves most strongly on clinical practice, usually at the behest of the patient's insurers. When exercised responsibly, clinical freedom has enriched clinical practice in the NHS, and provided 'space' for clinical experimentation and development. There have been occasions when the freedom has been abused by individual consultants, usually in defending an empire or avoiding a legitimate challenge or complaint about treatment or care, but these are minor problems compared to the overall benefits to patients, the organization and the professions.

Legal Controls – Professional Boundaries

Doctors have to practise medicine within a legal framework that has over the years created boundaries and standards for clinical practice. The definitions of reasonable practice that are at the heart of the law of negligence are of necessity fluid, although there are examples of a more prescriptive position being taken on boundaries in fields such as termination of pregnancy. The law requires that a doctor should act reasonably and within his proper competencies. Thus, a physician who embarked on complex surgery would almost certainly be operating outside the definition of reasonableness, as might a general surgeon who embarked on neurosurgery. As medicine has become increasingly specialized, so have the boundaries of reasonable practice narrowed and managers need to take great care in seeking to encourage doctors to extend their range of work on economic grounds not to push too far. An interesting illustration of these pressures is the gradual move to day-case surgery which has been increasingly practised by some surgeons (and welcomed by managers because of the cost implications and productivity gains), but not by other surgeons who stubbornly decline to shift their traditional practice. Argument, persuasion and peer pressure are the ways forward; prescription is simply unacceptable even in the private sector.

Boundaries between doctors and other professions are often an area of conflict when professional skills begin to overlap each other. Clinical biochemists and psychologists are well established examples of professionals who have skills that are complementary to those of the doctor and which need to be made available to patients. As the boundaries move and shift so the area of tension and conflict will change. One of the areas of greatest conflict at present is the challenge by medical laboratory scientific officers to the legitimacy of doctors' rights to direct and manage the overall entity we call the hospital laboratory. The most appropriate solution is almost always to combine professional leadership and managerial authority in the doctor in charge, but the personalities and competencies of the individuals involved often make this stance of principle difficult to sustain in every case in the real world. The boundary between nurses and doctors has been shifting over the years and looks set to change again as an extended role is developed for nurses. Recent decisions to permit nurses to prescribe are but one example. The primacy of the doctors has never been seriously challenged by the nursing profession, but some midwives have strenuously fought for their right to independent professional practice. Everybody is watching with interest the recent move to permit a non-medically trained individual to undertake (albeit under medical supervision) some minor surgical procedures, such as the stripping of varicose veins. These shifting professional boundaries are an inevitable feature of a healthy and growing organization that is adjusting to new technologies and patterns of treatment. The tensions produced have to be managed with diplomacy and skill, rather than stifled.

Another powerful control mechanism is the General Medical Council, which has created a framework of standards within which doctors are trained and practise medicine. The Council was first established in 1858 to regulate medical education and offer some protection to qualified medical practitioners from competition from unqualified practitioners. All doctors who practice in the United Kingdom are required to be registered with the General Medical Council. This registration can be temporarily or permanently withdrawn if the Council judges an individual doctor to be unfit to practise, or if, after due inquiry, they decide he or she has been guilty of serious profession misconduct. Since 1980, the Council has also on occasion granted only conditional registration, thus limiting the doctor's professional freedom.

Setting professional standards is also very much part of the role of the postgraduate medical colleges. They exercise this mainly through their training programmes and examinations, success at which is almost invariably judged to be obligatory for progression to the status of hospital consultant. Appropriate postgraduate training under the auspices of the Royal College of General Practitioners is also now an essential prerequisite for general practice. The Colleges inspect local training facilities and arrangements and operate a system of formal accreditation for training. Loss of recognition can have a significant impact on the staffing structure of hospitals and its reputation, which is why college inspections are taken so seriously by the professional staff – a concern that should be matched by the manager. A more recent development has been the move by some of the Royal Colleges, and the Royal College of Pathologists in particular, to contemplate a more substantial move into the accreditation field, way beyond that required for training, thus offering an assurance of quality to anybody who decides to buy services from a particular laboratory. Through their influence over training, their inspections and the overall professional standards they seek to create, these colleges have a powerful influence over standards, but in so doing they also often constrain the boundaries of acceptable clinical practice.

A new and exciting recent development has been the change by the profession in its attitudes to medical audit. Medical audit is the systematic, critical analysis of the quality of medical care, including the procedures used for diagnosis and treatment, the use of resources, and the resulting outcome and quality of life for the patient. An effective programme of audit will help provide reassurance to doctors, patients and managers that the best possible quality of service is being achieved within the resources available.

By 1991, all hospital doctors and general practitioners working in the NHS will be required to participate in audit programmes. This represents an enormous step forward in the overall field of quality assurance and was one of the few aspects of the 1989 White Paper on the future of the National Health Service that the professions have broadly welcomed. To be really successful, medical audit needs to be undertaken in private (i.e. within the clinical community), at least at the level at which individual patients and clinicians are concerned, thus permitting doctors to be frank and self-critical in a way that adds to their knowledge of the outcomes and efficacy of clinical practice. There will, of course, be occasions when the judgements about individual cases will lead to recommendations for improvements to either the organization of the hospital or the deployment of resources, and, at that point, the audit process needs to inform a wider audience of health care planners and decision-makers if changes are to be brought about. An example might well be findings that would support a move to concentrate certain types of surgery in a more limited range of centres because they achieve better results. Each DHA will appoint one or more Local Audit Committee(s) who will produce an annual plan and a report which indicates the broad ground which they have covered and a summation of the results.

The system will also incorporate the right of a manager to ask for an audit review of a particular specialty if he considers there to be problems and this new (at least in its formalized sense) and potentially powerful ingredient in the doctor/management relationship should help ease those problems that lie in the difficult grey area of acceptable clinical competence. Whilst the audit processes must be seen as primarily educational, they ought to have the effect of exposing really poor professional practice – once exposed, these standards will usually rise as a consequence. Where they do not and the problems persist, the clinical community will first try to solve the problem itself, using peer review. Where this fails, the manager will be asked to help resolve the issue on a more formal basis. At that point disciplinary procedures come into play.

Medical Managerial Machinery

Most hospitals in the National Health Service have developed a means by which medical practice can be co-ordinated and judgements made about priorities both within specialty groups and across the whole of the clinical community. These 'cog-wheel' committees often include representatives of other disciplines and are usually formally linked into the managerial framework of the unit or district concerned. The executive powers of these committees are usually quite limited but their advice on priorities is very influential and they have provided a reasonably effective mechanism for the co-ordination of clinical activity.

In one or two places, these 'cog-wheel' structures have evolved into a more powerful managerial format involving the appointment of an individual doctor as a director of service, e.g. head of surgery. In this role they move beyond the light-touch co-ordination traditionally exercised by chairmen of divisions into a managerial mode with executive powers sanctioned by management, usually including the day-to-day control of the budget. This has been seen as a positive and creative development by many doctors änd managers, and it is likely to spread quickly through the NHS. Clinical directors will, however, have to tread very carefully in areas where they seek to impose their views and judgements on colleagues to protect clinical freedom from unreasonable intrusion by their colleagues, which may be just as strong as that from managers. Individual clinical freedom will survive even within a medical hierarchy.

General practitioners have also evolved a structure for co-ordination and representation in a mechanism based on local medical committees and many of the larger practices have a *de facto* leader in the form of a senior partner.

Nevertheless, sturdy individuality is, and is likely to continue to be, a dominant characteristic of general practice.

Mirrors, Bubbles and Incentives

One of the most effective means of persuading doctors to change their clinical practice is to enable them to see their performance contrasted with others – using mirrors. The first reactions are usually to challenge the accuracy of the mirror ('the data is wrong!'), but once that hurdle has been jumped, doctors operating at the extremes will often adjust their practice quite quickly. The development of performance indicators on a national scale is one example of this in practice. Making the indicators available to parliament and the public certainly produced a strong negative reaction initially, but now they seem to have become part of accepted practice, although the indicators still need interpreting with care. Conversations between doctors and managers are usually at their most productive when they are localized and focused in to a narrow and discrete area of clinical practice about which both parties are well informed. Thus, exhibiting within a region the wide range of average lengths of stay for cataract operations can have a significant influence on those at the wrong end of the scale. Accurate comparisons of bed and theatre utilization between hospitals and day-case rates between consultants in the same specialty are also powerful adjuncts to conversations with doctors about improved efficiency. Provided they are constructed soundly, mirrors are a powerful managerial tool – often all the manager has to do is to display the mirror for professionals themselves to recognize they are out of line and to take corrective action of their own accord.

The traditional way of creating financial boundaries for doctors is to control inputs to the system (beds, supporting staff, operating theatres, outpatient clinics, etc.). Whilst doctors are prepared to manage the choices within these 'bubbles' the system works well. The manager can retain his overall cash limit and strategic control over investments and the doctors have a substantial amount of freedom within the 'bubble' to practise medicine in a way they judge to be professionally acceptable. The best balance is achieved when the construction of the 'bubble' matches sensible clinical territories and when, within it, there is substantial freedom to divide resources between different heads of expenditure and retain some or all of the savings generated for reinvestment in that service.

Creating effective incentives to improve organizational performance is as valid in the National Health Service as it is in any other organization. Professional staff are not usually motivated to improve efficiency for the sake of it, but they will normally react very positively if they can have some say in the reinvestment of any savings they may help to generate. The programme of reshaping mental health services has been given a substantial push forward when health authorities have committed themselves to investing some or all of the income from the sale of land on the old mental hospital sites back into mental health services. The new move to develop resource management in hospitals and community units is at its most productive when management has developed a sensitive and effective network of incentives that reward effective performance. Every health care unit could gain substantial benefit from an 'incentives analysis' which identifies all the disincentives that are operating in their units and replaces them with positive ones that take the unit forward.

Personal Contracts of Employment

One of the most recurrent arguments in recent years has centred around the pressure to move hospital consultants' contracts from the Regional Health Authority to the District Health Authority level in non-teaching districts. The contracts have always been held at district level for consultants practising in teaching hospitals. At its simplest, the assertion is that, as consultants have a decisive impact on DHA resource utilization, they should be employed by them. The consultants have always resisted, on the grounds that they needed to have some distance between themselves and local managers, who might be concerned with short-term financial measures at the expense of proper professional practice.

In their recent White Paper (Cm. 555, 1989), the government sidestepped the issue and determined that some elements of the contract of employment (annual leave, study leave, locum cover, etc.) should be devolved to DHAs as managing agents, but the primary contract of employment will remain with RHAs. Perhaps more important though is the new arrangement whereby each consultant will be required to agree an annual job plan with local managers. These plans will specify a consultant's primary duties and set out clearly a series of fixed sessions that have to be met. These fixed points are usually those that involve other staff, e.g. theatre sessions, outpatient clinics, etc. In addition, the job plan is likely to specify emergency responsibilities and approved special interests that involve the use of significant resources. Job plans will be reviewed annually and that conversation will represent a vital and new component in the ongoing relationships between doctors and managers.

Since 1948, consultants in the hospital service have been eligible for merit awards which at the highest levels almost double their salary. The system was created following an inquiry by Lord Spens (Ministry of Health, 1948), whose committee concluded:

- That the wide diversity of ability and effort amongst hospital specialists made it impossible to recommend a single simple scale of pay that could be applied to all.
- That if the recruitment to, and status of, specialist practice was to be maintained, specialists must be able to feel that more than ordinary ability and effort received adequate reward.
- That a significant minority of specialists should have the opportunity of earning a salary comparable with the highest which can be earned in other professions.

The system provides for four levels of award:

212 – A+   Awards worth about 95 per cent of basic salary
742 – A   Awards worth about 70 per cent of basic salary
1729 – B   Awards worth about 40 per cent of basic salary
3952 – C   Awards worth about 18 per cent of basic salary

The number of awards available each year is strictly limited to about 35 per cent of those eligible, thus making the system very competitive. The cost of the award scheme in 1989/90 was over £70 million for a total of 6635 awards.

The process of deciding who receives the awards has been clouded in secrecy for many years, but with effect from 1989 the processes have changed and the Regional Health Authority Chairman and up to five NHS managers now join the selection process at the 'C' award level within each region. The chief executive of the NHS Management Board has joined the National Awards Committee which co-ordinates the whole process and determines the higher awards. The criteria for granting awards will remain predominantly centred around notions of professional excellence, but significant contributions to the management of the organization are likely to score more highly than has been the case in the past. University academic (clinical) staff are eligible for the awards if they have six or more honorary clinical sessions and the costs are met by the local health authority.

Inevitably, a system that dispenses such valuable awards has its critics – usually among those who do not have an award. However, in recent years many of the old disparities between clinical specialties have been largely corrected, although the balance against women is still substantial – about 22 per cent of women consultants held awards in 1989, compared to 35 per cent male consultants. With effect from 1993 all awards are to be reviewed at five-yearly intervals.

Clinical Freedom and the Internal Market

The introduction of an internal market is bound to affect established inter-
pretations of clinical freedom as well as the relationship between doctors
and managers. Many doctors have declined to share a sense of corporateness
or common good with manager colleagues, but instead have focused their
total allegiances on their specialty and their patients. This has often led
them into arguing their corner for more resources in highly emotive terms,
in public, sometimes using the tactic of rubbishing the organization they are
proclaiming to defend. This not only weakens the system of rationing based
upon a broad consensus of medical need, it also erodes the organization's
self-image and its standing with the community at large. Organizations that
are regularly exposed to public criticism from within their own ranks rarely
succeed and few survive. In the world after 1991, the most successful
hospitals will be those that create and sustain a broad consensus about
priorities and where doctors and managers share a common sense of corporate accountability and loyalty.

Every hospital will have to organize its affairs within the framework of a
series of contracts from District Health Authorities. The hospital manager
must be able to make a direct connection between what those contracts
require and the clinical practice of the doctors working in the hospital. If he
or she does not, the hospital will face financial ruin, particularly if doctors
want to provide services that no DHA is prepared or able to pay for. A lot
therefore hinges on the shape of the new contracts. For some specialties the
contract is likely to specify 'services within a budget' with perhaps a
descriptive analysis of the range of clinical work expected (probably using
DRGs or some similar way of classifying clinical activity). This is a development of current practice that still leaves the clinician with both a substantial
span of clinical discretion and the prime rationing role. In other specialties,
the contract is likely to be more specific and might, for example, begin
to specify expected numbers of particular surgical procedures (e.g. hip
replacements).

The first round of contracts will probably reflect existing clinical practice.
The problems will arise once the contracting authorities begin to seek to
change existing practice in a direction they judge to be in the community's
interests, and what is more, they have the financial levers to enforce their
view of priorities.

Health authorities will also have the ability to switch their focus from the
traditional control over inputs to the alternative of specifying preferred
outcomes, a move that some commentators would regard as a significant
challenge to established thinking about clinical freedom. Whilst it may

represent a challenge, it does not signify the end of clinical freedom – decisions about how to treat individual patients are never going to form part of the contract (although the day-case option may well be pursued with some vigour) and in all specialties the consultant will continue to be expected to use his clinical judgement in determining the priority of access between individual patients. What we can expect therefore is that clinical freedom will be exercised within a somewhat different framework.

It will be apparent from this analysis that the greatest tensions are likely to arise between practising clinicians operating in the provider hospitals and units and those managers operating at the District Health Authority level, who, with their authorities, will in time begin to play a much more explicit role in defining priorities based on outcomes than ever before. We should not jump to the conclusion that this relationship need always be antagonistic and hostile. The relationship could be developed into one that is positive and mutually reinforcing. DHAs will still want to pay regard to the advice and skills of local provider hospitals in shaping their contracts and they will have a substantial and long-term interest in the organizational health and status of the hospitals within their district, who will always be their main providers. The relationship can therefore be seen as symbiotic and in the best-managed parts of the NHS will be exactly that.

In the new competitive world, patients are for the most part likely to take professional quality and standards for granted and will judge the practices with which they are registered and the hospitals to which they are referred on other softer criteria, such as the ability to get speedy access, the way they are treated and respected and the way their overall experience is valued within the system. Doctors and managers cannot, however, avoid a common responsibility for sustaining technical and professional excellence, even if their customers take it for granted. Effective medical audit systems are one important way of securing this objective.

It is also likely that consultants will become more mobile during their careers, as the NHS becomes internally competitive and NHS trusts have the freedom to vary national pay agreements. We can anticipate more flexible or part-time contracts designed to attract back into clinical practice the growing number of women in the profession. Women represent an enormous untapped resource of highly skilled professional manpower that will have to be tapped by imaginative employment practices.

The internal market also represents a challenge to general practice, with its new performance-linked contracts and the option of managing a practice budget. General practitioners will remain independent contractors and a good deal of their clinical practice will remain outside any system of cash limits – particularly prescribing, although, in this field, there will be a whole series of measures to stimulate downward pressure on those GPs operating outside reasonable limits. Those practices that elect to operate a budget will find themselves in a new and very powerful relationship with the hospitals to whom they refer patients.

First impacts of the proposed budgetary systems are likely to be felt in services such as pathology and radiology, where GPs are bound to demand a quicker and more responsive service, a pressure that must be inherently good for the system. As GPs with budgets generate savings for reinvestment in their practices, we are also likely to see a shift in the balance between primary and hospital care, with some expansion of professional support to GPs from specialist nurses, physiotherapists, occupational therapists, chiropodists and psychologists.

In the new internal market, GPs will be able to seek just an opinion from a hospital consultant, a rare event in current practice, where reference to the out-patient clinic usually leads directly into treatment, if that is judged to be appropriate by the consultant. The consultant/GP relationship is bound to change as a consequence and in so doing affect their respective relationships with the managers of the service.

The relationship between GPs and the Family Practitioner Committees (which holds their contracts) is bound to change as these authorities are reconstituted in 1991, and the profession loses its powerful control over them. For the first time the GPs' contracts are going to be managed. Many GPs will welcome the sort of extended support this arrangement can provide for their practices; others will resist stoutly any attempt to 'interfere'. Tough but intelligent diplomacy will be the prime skill of the successful FPC general manager.

Whatever the new world looks like doctors will remain the prime asset of the National Health Service. Managers must therefore create an organizational climate which understands and respects the need for doctors to practice medicine according to acceptable professional standards, an organization which permits clinicians maximum personal discretion when they get to the level of treating an individual patient. Given a closer alignment of objectives and mutual respect, this ought to be possible.

References

Cm. 555 (1989) *Working for Patients*. London: HMSO.

Flynn, R. (1992) *Structures of Control in Health Management*. London: Routledge.

Harrison, S. (1988) *Managing the National Health Service: shifting the frontier?* London: Chapman and Hall.

Ministry of Health and Department of Health for Scotland (1948) *Report of the Inter-Departmental Committee on the Remuneration of Consultants and Specialists* (the Spens Report). London: HMSO.

7

The Case of Local Authority Social Workers

Alan Butler

How do social services managers try to control their staff? What particular problems are posed for the social-service manager, and what forms of incentive, if any, are available to them? Following a discussion of the traditional difficulties that social-service managers have in this area, I shall briefly examine some of the innovative techniques which are currently being imported into social work in order to enhance control and accountability.

The Context of Accountability: The Role of the Elected Representatives

The question of social work accountability is a complex one. In the classic model of a private company an employee is accountable to an immediate line manager or superviser and ultimately to his or her employer. Because of the nature of the social work task the position there is more diffuse. The major stakeholders would appear to be some or all of the following actors:

The social workers' employing agency, mediated through a line manager and supervisor.
The professional organization(s) to which the individual worker belongs.
The organization may have an ethical code of practice and a set of good-practice guidelines.
The service users – or consumers as we are now enjoined to call them.
Those others who may be connected or related to the service users and share some interest. Examples include relatives of the dependent elderly, foster parents of children admitted to care, etc.
The wider community. This may be a specific organization that has referred

an individual to the social work agency, or it may be that society in general has an interest in a piece of social work activity. For example, running a group for potential juvenile offenders may impact negatively or positively upon people living in a particular geographical area.

Fellow workers. Social workers often perceive themselves to be working in 'teams' and on certain cases may share some of the work with colleagues, to whom there is some degree of accountability.

Personal accountability. Regardless of occupation, we all carry some personal responsibility for the work that we do, so we are accountable to ourselves. I do not want to take an overly precious view of social work, but it has certain characteristics which promote the need for personal accountability. Because of the hidden nature of much of social work, and the fact that the 'work' itself is often so intangible, self-regulation and personal accountability are essential.

Finally, because social work is largely conducted in a local authority setting, there is accountability to elected political representatives. This usually involves local councillors but may on occasion also include members of parliament.

Contracting

Implicit in many of these proposals is the notion that what is being offered to the client should be much more open and available to public scrutiny. As long ago as 1970 Mayer and Timms were pointing out in *The Client Speaks* that many clients did not understand why the social worker was visiting them nor what the preferred outcomes should be. In other words the two parties to the enterprise did not share a common agenda (Rees, 1974).

An explicit contract, signed by both parties after adequate discussion, is one way forward. The clients would be encouraged to say what they wanted from the service. The worker would indicate what they or the wider service might provide, how regularly and to what level of quality. For example, an elderly person may contract for the delivery of so many meals per week, of a certain standard, to be delivered between certain clearly stipulated times. Any failure to meet the contractual requirements would give the client clear grounds for complaint. Standards and frequency of contact would thus be established and managerial control mode more possible. Similar forms of contract may be entered into with prospective foster parents. There the monetary conditions of the fostering arrangement would be explicit as well as the level and frequency of visits that they might expect from the designated social worker. Any failure to visit with the agreed regularity could once again be brought swiftly to the manager's attention.

Case Management

Case management also relies upon an overt contract between client and social worker. This concept emerged out of a series of action research projects conducted by the University of Kent Personal Social Services Research Unit and Kent Social Services Department (Challis and Davies, 1990). Essentially, they began by trying to devise a scheme whereby elderly people could be maintained in their own homes, independent of residential care. A controlled trial was conducted whereby half of the cohort who met the criteria for residential care were so admitted, whilst the other half remained at home. Those who remained at home had a sum of money earmarked for their use to the order of about two-thirds of the cost of residential care, and a case manager to administer it. The case manager's task, in close consultation with the elderly person concerned, was to weave together a mixture of formal and informal services, up to the cost of the allocated budget, which would enable them to maintain an independent life at home.

The assessment procedure concentrated upon the problems experienced by the clients and not just upon their eligibility for existing services. Moreover, carers and neighbours were drawn into the care planning. An attempt was made to mobilize and co-ordinate local resources so that a tailored package of care could be provided. An essential part of this was the delegation of the budget to the individual case manager. The results of the experiments were that older people were accommodated in their own homes for longer, that in general they expressed greater levels of satisfaction than those who had been admitted to residential care and that ultimately they tended to live longer.

One of the crucial aspects of this series of studies for social-work management was the role of the devolved budget. Social work managers began to realize that by giving social workers their own budgets to administer they could inject into social work some of the elements of the market-place. Efficient social workers could shop around for the best buys on behalf of their clients, and use any savings or surpluses for the good of the clients of their sector of the services. The extra discipline of budgeting and contracting meant that the social work practised had to be more overt and open to public scrutiny, with clearly stated objectives and targets.

Many social-work departments are now importing the idea of the case manager into their own practice and expanding the concept to cover other client groups. Discrete areas of social-work activity within a department, such as the fostering unit or the meals service, are also being given their own budget heads and encouraged to work within defined financial peri-meters. For the social-work manager this means that the control of practice is that much clearer and a little easier to exercise. The work undertaken by the social worker has to be more clearly described, the role of the client is more precise and the use of the budget opens up the possibility of adopting commercial standards of performance. However, there are doubts about how far this model can be extended into the heartlands of social work practice.

Quality Assurance

A further attempt at imposing management control upon social-work activity is the introduction into departments of quality assurance systems together with the adoption of various performance indicators. John Crook, Director of Social Services for Bradford, outlined five features which underpinned the necessity for adopting these approaches in his own department (Crook, 1990).

First, his organization was dissatisfied with the lack of clarity as to expected performance. Secondly, the organization could not clearly define its objectives and targets. Thirdly, he felt that as a consequence the ability to empower users and carers with respect to the services and procedures of the organization was severely impaired. Fourthly, the White Paper *Caring for People* demanded greater clarity and definition of purpose. Finally, there was the need to break away from the old bureaucratic mould which he believed impeded change. Crook suggested that, by concentrating upon the development of outcome measures, staff could be presented with realistic and achievable objectives and clear statements as to what they should be doing. Once the task of completing operational objectives was accom-plished, appropriate operational standards could be established.

Peter Brewer (1990), from Wiltshire Social Services Department, speak-ing at the same seminar, explored some of the practical problems incurred when establishing a quality assurance/inspection unit. The inspection pro-cess would focus upon the quality of service delivery to the department's clients.

> This will serve to illuminate the performance and co-ordination of policy, resources and staff within clearly defined areas of work. Areas of inspection will be agreed and the outcomes of inspection considered by the Director of Social Services. The results of any inspection will be fed back to those whose work has formed part of the area of inspections; the Director of Social Services will have executive control of the results of the inspection. The

results will enable good practice to be acknowledged and shared across the department.

The author steers clear of any discussion about sanctions for staff who do not measure up to the required standards of practice. However, it is implicit in points seven and eight of the code of practice for inspection, which are:

7   Upon completing an inspection, those undertaking the inspection will provide those staff who have been inspected, and their line managers, with a draft report of their findings and, when feasible, will meet with such staff to discuss the contents of this report. The purpose of this exercise will be to clarify facts and allow any agreed amendments to be included in the final inspection report. Following discussion of the draft report a final inspection report will be prepared for discussion by the Directorate.

8   Following receipt of a final report the Directorate shall agree what further action arising from the report should take place.

The whole system envisages greatly improved resources for both collecting and analysing information and measuring the cross-currents of activity within the department. A number of obvious performance indicators have been adopted. These include monitoring unallocated work and measuring response times to referrals. Greater efforts will be made to collect the consumers' views of the services being provided and to obtain feedback from other agencies.

Any element of managerial control is, in the documentation at least, always put in positive terms. So it is assumed that staff performance will improve when they get accurate information about their own performance. No mention is made of what might happen if it does not. Similarly, great emphasis is laid upon staff development and training, with the carrot rather than the stick seen as the way forward. It is asserted that 'A personal commitment by each individual to the standards must be the ultimate aim. Non-adherence or non-acceptance of the standards must be challenged and seen to be challenged. The standards must be owned by the organisation as a whole' (Brewer, 1990).

One of the criticisms frequently levelled at these techniques (Butler, 1991) is that by concentrating upon things that are tangible and measurable (waiting times, etc.) the real essence of the work is missed. Moreover, a strict adherence to performance indicators may result in a form of organizational distortion whereby people start to, say, shorten waiting lists (measurable) by curtailing interviews with clients (incommensurable). This would seem to be a particular dilemma for social work because of its invisibility, lack of homogeneity, and the subtlety of its procedures and processes.

References

Bell, L. (1990) Social service departments: preparing for the 1990s, *Public Money and Management*, 10, 23–5.

Brewer, C. and Lait, J. (1980) *Can Social Work Survive?* London: Temple Smith.

Brewer, P. (1990) Developing concepts of quality. In *Social Services and Quality Assurance*, Lancaster: Social Information Systems, 9–19.

Butler, A. (1991) *A Performance Indicator Guide to Sheltered Housing*. London: Institute of Housing.

Challis, D. and Davies, B. (1990) *Case Management in Community Care*. London: Gower.

Crook, J. (1990) Quality and outcome measures in social services directorates. In *Social Services and Quality Assurance*, Lancaster: Social Information Systems, 47–53.

Fischer, J. (1973) Is casework effective? *Social Work* (USA), 18, 5–20.

Freidson, E. (1970) *Professional Dominance*. New York: Atherton.

Howe, D. (1986) *Social Workers and their Practice in Welfare Bureaucracies*. Aldershot: Gower.

Larkin, G. (1983) *Occupational Monopoly and Modern Medicine*. London: Tavistock.

Mayer, J. and Timms, N. (1970) *The Client Speaks*. London: Routledge.

Mullen, E. J., Dumpson, J. R. et al. (1972) *Evaluation of Social Intervention*. San Francisco: Jossey-Bass.

Pearson, G. (1973) Social work as the privatised solution to public ills, *British Journal of Social Work*, 3, 209–27.

Pithouse, A. (1987) *Social Work: the social organisation of an invisible trade*. Aldershot: Avebury.

Rees, S. (1974) No more than contact: an outcome of social work, *British Journal of Social Work*, 4, 255–80.

Satyamurti, C. (1981) *Occupational Survival*. Oxford: Blackwell.

Shaw, I. and Walton, R. (1978) What use is social work training? *Community Care*, 18 January, 22–3.

Toren, N. (1972) *Social Work: the case of a semi-profession*. London: Sage.

Wilding, P. (1982) *Professional Power and Social Welfare*. London: Routledge.

8

The Management of Staff: the Case of the London Fire Brigade

Graeme Salaman

The management of staff, under whatever circumstances – public, private, commercial, non-profit, voluntary – historically displays a movement, an oscillation, around two opposing poles: the need to direct and control staff and the need to engage their commitment, intelligence and creativity. The first, as Alan Fox (1974) has put it, seeks to reduce the need for trust; the second attempts to build it. The first option, having destroyed trust by control, makes further control necessary; the second, by establishing management confidence in staff, confirms such confidence. The first option seeks to remove discretion from staff and locate it safely among expert, reliable managers and professionals; the second requires staff to make their own work decisions in the light of their experience, judgement, skills and commitment to the goals of the enterprise. The first cannot allow such discretion. Thus the first destroys skill, while the second depends on it. Skill is dangerous organizationally. The skilled worker, by virtue of the skill, has discretion. But how to be sure that this discretion is used 'correctly', or that the skilled do not 'abuse' their autonomy to resist management or achieve privilege?

Many organizations show an ambivalent attitude towards these tendencies, frequently displaying both at any time – a high trust approach to managerial or professional staff and a low trust to some or all shop-floor staff, as, for example, in hospitals. But this over-simplifies the picture. Historically, even with respect to the management of staff and the design of blue-collar jobs, it is possible to trace a long-term, if interrupted, movement between these two poles, a movement encouraged by developments in labour markets (excesses or shortages of skilled labour); technological developments which make possible (but do not determine) the deskilling or reskilling of labour, developments in management thinking, and in the nature of consumer and competitive pressure.

These tendencies in the design and control of jobs are paralleled by tendencies in the form of organizational control overall, that is to say, in the extent and way in which the centre exercises control over the constituent departments, operating companies, regional offices, etc. that constitute the organization as a whole. Again a variety of tendencies are apparent, which vary in the degree of concentration of decision-making and the extent to which decision-making is governed by rules (or by reasonably autonomous judgement). In some highly centralized organizations decisions (and information) are concentrated at the top. In others, characterized by high levels of bureaucracy, decision-making is distributed quite widely but is governed by formal regulation and procedure or by elaborate policy requirements. In others, managers are free to make decisions but are bound by tight control over expected standards of performance: the means may be open to choice, but the ends are tightly defined.

We are currently in a period of considerable discussion of both these issues: the control and design of jobs and the control and design of organizations. As a result of a number of factors – the performance of Japanese companies, which encourages interest in the nature of Japanese organizations and work design; growing competitive pressures, which force the need for improved efficiency and effectiveness; increased demand from consumers for better quality and more varied products and services, which forces the development of more committed and flexible workers – there is now enormous interest in ways of improving work performance of organizations and those who work in them.

This is seen to require efforts to enlarge the skills and deploy the intelligence and creativity of staff in their work and to gain their commitment to the goals their work serves, efforts to change attitudes and behaviour through enlarging skills and redistributing authority and responsibility, within the context of achieved levels of staff commitment. And this, in turn, is seen largely to be achieved through the manipulation of three interrelated elements: job content (flexibility), organizational controls (business units, work-group responsibility for quality, etc.), and culture change programmes. The first requires staff to work better and work more. The second requires them to take responsibility for what they do. The third ensures that they use this responsibility responsibly. Hence the current enthusiasm for such programmes. Thus, for example, in a much-quoted case at Nissan, supervisors and their teams have been given responsibility for communications within the team, quality, continuous improvement of quality and productivity, maintenance, high levels of attendance and timekeeping, training on the job, within the context of thorough-going attempts to achieve ideological and attitudinal control (Wickens, 1987, p. 184).

The upgrading of skill is usually sought in terms of 'flexibility'. The flexible firm is one which can readily adjust the labour it employs, the way that labour is utilised and the wages paid to current levels of output (Rubery et al., 1987, p. 131). Three means to achieving this flexibility have been identified: financial – the easy manipulation by management of reward scales and systems; functional – the variation of individuals' job content in response to production pressures; and numerical – the variation of payroll size and form through the use of part-time, short-term, temporary staff contracts.

The redistribution of authority and responsibility to accompany skill is sought through a number of initiatives, all of which have in common the attempt to generate feelings of personal responsibility for quantity and quality of work among staff. This is frequently expressed as achieving 'ownership' using, revealingly, the language of property to describe an attitude which, if achieved, is of course highly beneficial to senior managers. This 'ownership' is sought via such initiatives as performance-related pay systems; the restructuring of organizations into strategic business units; the allocation of responsibility for quality and quantity of output to shop-floor workers; the promulgation of specialist service departments as discrete 'profit centres' within organizations. There is evidence that many organizations are showing active interest in these developments – see, for example, the decentralization of British Rail and the Post Office – which are characterized by an increased emphasis on action at the individual as contrasted to the collective level. This tendency is facilitated and encouraged by the theory and practices of Thatcherism (see Salaman, 1989). This individualistic focus is displayed in the high levels of current interest in, and expenditure on, selection, performance review, reward systems (e.g. performance-related pay and performance review in the NHS) and training and development (often around the theory of competencies; see Boyatzis, 1982).

The London Fire Brigade

Our interest in this chapter is not, however, in the application of these tendencies within our chosen public sector organization, the London Fire Brigade, but in the manner in which a study of the impact of a programme of change within the LFB illuminates the key dynamic underpinning these fashionable and pervasive developments: the relationship between the three component elements – skill, control and commitment. The case discussed below suggests that under some circumstances skilled workers may not be entirely amenable to all aspects of managerial control. They may refuse to accept, precisely by virtue of their skill and how they are controlled, every aspect of ownership for organizational priorities. Skill and ownership and commitment/acceptance may pull in different directions. Indeed, because employees retain skill and some autonomy they may define managerial directives as legitimate and at the same time be able effectively to resist them. It will be argued that the case of the LFB suggests that current assertions that organizational effectiveness, quality and productivity can be increased through upgrading skill and delegating ownership depends critically on the achievement of a degree of ideological consensus, and furthermore, that within public-sector organizations, the inevitable divergence of attention between task-focused work-force and politically focused senior management can, when allied to other 'fracturing' features of organization and management, create a powerful conception of opposed interests.

One significant element in this is the nature and organization of the work tasks characteristic of some public-sector work, whereby staff may be able to claim sole and direct concern for life-saving, emergency, even dangerous work. Another is the spatial and temporal fracturing of this work from management within some public-sector organizations, whereby staff can define themselves as distant from management, and management as distant from the realities of the work – while being nearer to the influences of politicized decision-making.

Specifically, this case study explores how far certain aspects of the organization of work give rise to the development of lines of organizational fracturing, which in turn have significant implications for the legitimacy and effectiveness of managerial control. In the case of the LFB it will be argued that the informal development of solidarity, at the station or watch level, based on shared skill and shared tasks, served as a basis for distance from and resistance to managerial policies and control. Fracturing and differentiation was accompanied by a rhetoric which argued that corruption of senior management's priorities by political influences and the purity and value of firefighters' behaviour and motives were directly concerned with the realities of firefighting.

During the last years of the Greater London Council, the London Fire Brigade was required not only to implement equal opportunities law, but also the more far-reaching GLC equal opportunities policy. This was in response to the extremely small numbers of non-whites within the LFB. Prior to 1979, when the LFB's application to the Home Office for exemption from the provisions of the Sex Discrimination Act was rejected, women had been formally excluded from admission. After that date this was no longer possible. Thus, from the time of the installation of a Labour administration of the GLC in 1981, a vigorous and far-reaching programme of equal opportunities initiatives and training was introduced; monitoring systems to scrutinize applications and selections; the review of selection systems and procedures and standards; initiating a series of training seminars for all station officers and divisional officers, informing them of their responsibilities under the law and GLC policy. External initiatives included carefully targeted recruitment advertising, 'outreach' visits to schools and clubs, special advertising materials featuring blacks and women, plus pre-selection courses for those who failed the selection process and who were from deprived categories. The objectives of these positive actions was explicitly to encourage, inform and in some cases to prepare an appropriate quantity and quality of applications from previously disadvantaged groups. These initiatives were accompanied by annual recruitment target figures: in 1985, 30 per cent non-white and 3 per cent women.

Thus senior LFB management publicly committed themselves and their organization and staff to the implementation of equal opportunities law and GLC equal opportunities practice. But to a very considerable degree the station officers, and the organization as a whole, resisted these policies and obstructed their implementation. A measure of this is the low level of non-white and female recruitment when the programme was at its height: less than 10 per cent of male applicants were non-white in 1983, and women constituted only 0.8 per cent of applicants. The strongest indication of resistance, however, was obtained during research discussions with station officers.

Station officers were strongly resistant to the equal opportunities initiatives. They argued that, while in principle they supported the achievement of fairness within the brigade, they insisted that EO programme was itself unfair, a case of positive discrimination aimed at achieving quotas: set numbers of recruits from the key categories regardless of their suitability. Furthermore, they maintained that selection standards were being modified – lowered – in order to expedite the recruitment of sub-standard applicants. Thus the implementation of EO policy was regarded as an obstacle to working efficiency. They also frequently argued that women did not make good firefighters, and, in order to be consistent, they had to insist that those women who had joined the LFB were less than competent. Their explanation of this raised another major theme: the opportunism and lack of integrity of senior management, who were seen to have bent with the prevailing political wind, for careerist reasons, regardless of the consequences for firefighting efficiency. Their thinking displayed an artful immunity from critique. If a woman or non-white firefighter failed at their work this was taken as evidence of their innate unsuitability; if they were not seen to fail, this was taken as evidence of senior management's opportunistic manipulation of standards, for firemen *knew* that women couldn't do the work properly.

Station officers were highly resistant to senior Brigade managers' policy on equal opportunities. They saw it in negative terms as institutionalized unfairness foisted on them by a management cynically prepared to sacrifice efficiency for politics and career advantage. These attitudes need to be explained. They can be explained in terms of aspects of station officers' work and organizational location and the implications of these for their attitudes towards senior management. But these were not the terms in which senior GLC and LFB officials explained station officers' resistance. They explained it in terms of the racism and sexism of fireman or in terms of firemen's racist organizational culture. Both explanations are circular; both merely redescribe the behaviour. Neither explains why firemen held these views and resisted their managers' policies.

Such an explanation must assert the *collective* character of firemen's reactions to resistance. The views were not only widely held amongst firemen, they had a distinctly moral character. Firemen felt they should resist management and should support each other in this resistance. Where did this collective response come from? Essentially two sets of factors were responsible: those that set the station officers and firemen (the 'watch') apart from management ('us' and 'them'); and those that encouraged the development of solidarity among the firemen ('us').

Station officers and the firemen with whom they work are spatially, temporally and organizationally or socially isolated from higher levels of management. Within the LFB the watch is the working unit. It consists of about ten firefighters plus a station officer. This group works shifts together, sleeps, trains, eats, passes time together. It shares danger, excitement and boredom together. As a result of these shared experiences it also develops relationships of considerable intensity within the watch. The station officer is inherently part of the watch and cannot manage the group without some measure of support and approval from its members. At the same time then as strong bonds develop within the watch, it is systematically separated from higher management by times of work (shifts versus office hours), space (where they work – in local fire stations or at regional offices) and by organization of work, the sort of work they do.

Furthermore, station officers felt estranged from senior officers. One aspect of this followed from the fact that, within the LFB, recruitment occurs through a single point of entry. This means that socially, employees of LFB are remarkably homogeneous, more so than organizations with NCO and officer cadre entry points. Paradoxically, however, while this social homogeneity supported the solidarity of the watch, including the station officers, it also supported the separation of the watch from senior management. If all firefighters start from the same starting-point, those who fare less well organizationally have to explain to themselves and others why their superiors have pushed ahead of them. The way they achieved this was in terms of their opportunism and careerism. Thus, organizational success is defined as a result of moral failure. This in turn affects the station officers' reactions to the policies promulgated and implemented by these senior managers.

Station officers' estrangement is further assisted by difficult authority relations between them. Station officers find it difficult to exercise tight and total bureaucratic regulation over members of their watch. Because they work closely together, because station officers rely on their watch, they are often prepared to accept or ignore some 'technical' infringement of the rules in order to demonstrate a spirit of give and take or to seek legitimacy. Managing by the book is not admired, indeed it is seen as weakness. Senior management, however, may well demand that management is by the book, particularly if something goes wrong or if external, politically inspired attention is brought to bear. Under these circumstances senior managers' concern for full infringement, with its consequences for the disciplining or suspension of station management, is seen by station officers – and not only those directly involved – as a search for scapegoats to placate the politicians, and therefore as further evidence of senior officers' cynical careerism. Station officers complained that senior managers played their role not to support and manage them, but to police them and, when necessary, to throw them to the wolves.

Conclusion

Our analysis of a particular, historically specific event within the LFB identified a marked resistance among LFB station officers to the implementation of GLC/LFB equal opportunities policy. It has been argued that while no doubt there were officers whose resistance was inspired by an innate conservatism and personal attitudes and beliefs, the size and pervasiveness of the resistance suggests a marked social dimension. It was not merely that the new policy and procedures caused a reduction in station officers' traditional rights in recruitment and selection, though this was significant. It was the fact that the origin, nature and implementation of the new policies was seen in terms of an existing fracturing of the management of the LFB, a fracturing (senior, office-based, non-shift-working managers from operational, junior, shift-working station officers closely identified with their watch) which was seen, by the station officers at least, as coinciding with a split between the values and activities of the job itself: the necessary requirement and dangers of firefighting in contrast to the politicized requirements of managerial expediency of senior office-based managers. This is not a new phenomenon. It is evident in industry when shop-floor workers complain of the irrationality of management decision-making. It is particularly evident within the armed services, where front-line troops complain, often with total justification, about the difference between their priorities and those of headquarters staff.

But in the case of the LFB, the feeling of being political scapegoats, cannon-fodder for Brigade managers' politicking, took the familiar form of a deep conviction, on both sides, of the untrustworthiness of the other, and of the difference in interest and perspective that divided them. These differences, it has been argued, were systemic products of a form of organizational structure which ostensibly seems to follow many of the dictates of current management thinking: differentiation and sub-division of working units under centralized policy. But the result, at least as far as the policy under consideration here was concerned, was not staff ownership of senior management decisions but a vigorous rejection. At least in this case, the relationship between skill levels, organizational control and work-force commitment did not comply with the current view. The fact that fire-fighters are skilled, and that their organizational control structure is fractured as described resulted in a commitment to the watch and to colleagues and to tasks which was as strongly opposed to senior management as it was internally solidaristic.

References

Boyatzis, R. (1982) *The Competent Manager: a model for effective performance*. New York: Wiley.

Fox, A. (1974) *Man Mismanagement*. London: Hutchinson.

Rubery, J., Tarling, R. and Wilkinson, F. (1987) Flexibility, marketing and the organisation of production. University of Cambridge: Department of Applied Economics (mimeograph).

Salaman, G. (1989) Employment relationships in economic recession. In R. Scase (ed.), *Industrial Societies*, London: Unwin Hyman, 64–9.

Wickens, P. (1987) *The Road to Nissan: flexibility, quality, teamwork*. London: Macmillan.

Controlling Public Service Professionals: Reflections

Stephen Harrison and Christopher Pollitt

From the late 1970s until the mid-1980s far more energy and overt attention was given to improving the financial management of the public services than to developing what have subsequently come to be termed 'human resource strategies'. This emphasis on the control of resources was essentially a strategy for what Salaman terms 'reducing the need for trust' rather than 'attempting to build trust' (chapter 8). Such relative neglect of the staff who actually deliver public services was noted in several academic analyses (Exley, 1987; Metcalfe and Richards, 1990; Pollitt, 1990) and even more so by the staff themselves. Among the latter the various groups of professionals and semi-professionals stand out as being of particular importance, not least because they exercise substantial discretion and frequently dominate direct contacts with service users. Since the late 1980s, however, the management of 'human resources' has moved to centre stage. The current emphases on building staff commitment to a 'quality' service, on making professionals more directly responsible for resource decisions and more generally on achieving 'cultural change' all speak to a realization that improving public services is as much a hearts-and-minds matter as an exercise in target-setting and financial control.

The crucial question, however, is 'how?' Winning the support of professionals for new approaches is a tricky business, and the degree of optimism concerning current management strategies clearly varies considerably among our three contributors. On the whole Edwards seems cautiously optimistic, while Butler and Salaman perceive a deep lack of trust for current styles of management among the professionals and semi-professionals in social work and the London Fire Brigade.

Here Edwards's imagery of mirrors, bubbles and incentives appears to be very useful. A successful restructuring of manager/service professional relationships seems likely to require a careful deployment of all three devices. Mirrors show back to the service deliverers the results of their own current and recent past practices. Bubbles enable professional teams to continue to exercise considerable discretion and inventiveness on their local 'patch', but sets this within a clearer strategic framework than existed previously. Incentives continuously reinforce appropriate behaviours and achievements. (Incentives are not, of course, confined to merit pay bonuses for individuals. On the contrary, a variety of non-financial and/or team/department-based financial incentives may well prove more effective and less divisive.) It would appear that in the cases of the London Fire Brigade and some social-work organizations service deliverers were being expected to alter their practices in the absence of any clear mirrors, with no guarantee of protected 'bubbles' and without much in the way of incentives.

It would be too much, however, to claim that the 'mirror/bubble/incentive' formula will guarantee professional commitment and cultural change. Clearly there are other background or historical factors which make the manager's task more or less difficult. In some cases mistrust of 'management' may be deeply ingrained, so that almost any pronouncements coming 'down from the top' may be regarded with profound suspicion. It seems that the attempts to increase control and enforce economy in the early and mid-1980s sometimes engraved resentment in the minds of service providers. Winning trust, in these instances, is likely to be a matter of quiet and patient work over time. Headline-seeking management 'initiatives' or glossy presentations on cultural change are unlikely to succeed. More radically, wholesale redefinition of the contents of service professionals' jobs or, beyond that, actual replacement of current service delivery staff with alternative categories of staff or with new recruits will very seldom be available management options. In other words, managers have no practical alternative to convincing the professionals who are already there that change is both necessary and potentially beneficial. In this task credible allies *within* the professional group concerned are worth their weight in gold.

Increasingly, therefore, the crucial issue seems to be the development of a cadre of professionals who continue to practise their particular skills whilst being trained for and assuming managerial responsibilities. We suggest this is as true of health care as it is of social work as it is of education – and perhaps even of the fire service. This may be a 'slow fix', but it is the one most likely to bear long-term fruit.

References

Exley, M. (1987) Organisation and managerial capacity. In A. Harrison and J. Gretton (eds), *Reshaping Central Government*, Oxford: Policy Journals, 42–56.

Metcalfe, L. and Richards, S. (1990) *Improving Public Management*. Second edition. London: Sage.

Pollitt, C. (1990) *Managerialism and the Public Services: the Anglo-American Experience*. Oxford: Blackwell.

Part III

New Approaches to Resource Management

9

Local Management of Schools: a New System of Resource Allocation and Accountability

Rosalind Levacic

The Education Reform Act, 1988 (ERA) is bringing fundamental changes in the way schools and colleges are managed and expected to render accountability. Local education authorities (LEAs) must delegate budgets to schools and colleges. In the context of decentralized resource management the national curriculum provides the chief means for regulating schools and LEAs. Budget delegation is being phased in from 1990–1 to 1993–4 and the national curriculum from 1989 until 1997. There is considerable concern that the speed of implementation demanded by central government, when local authorities' ability to increase expenditure is severely restricted by the community charge and the level of revenue support grant, will adversely affect the quality of education provision. The general message from the Association of Metropolitan Authorities' member LEAs is that they are 'coping . . . and . . . doing their best to plan and administer under very difficult circumstances' (Association of Metropolitan Authorities, 1989).

Local Management of Schools: an Outline of the Main Provisions

Under local management of schools (LMS) all secondary and primary schools must receive a delegated budget 'for the governing body to spend as they think fit for the purposes of the school'. Each school's 'budget share' must be determined by a formula, tightly prescribed in circulars 7/88 (DES, 1988b) and 36/88 (Welsh Office, 1988). These set out the framework within which LEAs must devise their LMS schemes for approval by the Secretary of State. A key feature of the formula is that at least 75 per cent of the LEA's aggregated schools budget must be distributed according to the number and ages of pupils at each school, though LEAs have discretion to determine the age weighting. All other factors which affect the costs of schools – size, the number of teachers high on the salary scale, premises and pupils' social background – have to be taken account of in the remaining 25 per cent of the budget. The DES approved 87 out of 97 schemes submitted to it for implementation in 1990/1. Most LEA formulae were approved only provisionally and require further modification by 1993 to meet DES stipulations.

Pupil-driven funding, together with 'more open enrolment' whereby schools must admit pupils up to their standard number, are designed to increase competition between schools (a school's standard number is the number of entry year pupils it admitted in 1979/80 or 1989/90, whichever was the greater). Additional competition can come from grant-maintained (GM) schools which are directly funded by the DES or the Welsh Office. A school can apply to the Secretary of State for GM status after following a set procedure which includes obtaining a majority vote of parents in favour. A GM school's budget is determined by the relevant LEA's formula and its pro-rata share of the LEA's expenditure on central services. As the budgets of an LEA's GM schools are subtracted from its revenue support grant, the possibility of schools opting out of LEA control puts pressure on the LEAs to operate LMS schemes which schools find attractive. By September 1990, there were 49 GM schools. Most of these schools were motivated by the desire to avoid LEA reorganization. Threats to opt out have become an effective means by which opponents have scuppered or delayed reorganization plans and thus made it more difficult for LEAs to rationalize school places and so reduce costs.

Changes in Accountability Relationships

The 1988 Education Reform Act is intended to bring about a fundamental change in the ways in which schools and LEAs are held accountable. Whether or not the model of accountability intended by the legislators will actually come to pass, there will still be significant changes. I am using the term accountability in the narrow sense defined by Kogan (1986, p. 25) as 'a condition in which individual role holders are liable to review and the application of sanctions if their actions fail to satisfy those with whom they are in an accountability relationship'. Accountability requires that an evaluation is made and that those to whom role-holders are accountable can enforce sanctions on those who are held accountable.

In the pre-ERA system head teachers were managerially accountable to the director of education, who is accountable to the local authority members. Governing bodies were, prior to the 1986 Education Act, instruments of the authority's education committee. In practice, this hierarchical line of accountability was attenuated. As Kogan (1986, p. 63) notes of the pre-ERA system:

> The preferred mode has been that of professional accountability and of teacher self-evaluation . . . a hierarchical relationship is suffused by a great deal of discretion to formulate the work involved in the core tasks of teaching and learning. Directors and heads thus speak with two voices to each other . . . the director or his [sic] subordinate play a key role in teachers' promotions and the head is dependent on the director for resources.

In the decades following the 1944 Education Act, schools were managed by education professionals in schools and LEAs who had been recruited from the teaching profession and professional accountability predominated. In the last 15 years or so, the political accountability of the educational professionals has been more patently enforced by members in some authorities who have implemented specific curricular and social policies, sometimes with publicized clashes with their directors of education. There has also been a growing climate of public distrust with the education service and its accountability to its clients in particular, which culminated in the 1988 Education Reform Act.

Under ERA the LEA retains weakened political accountability from its schools, with its powers to implement education policies and to intervene in its schools substantially reduced. LEAs are to be held more strictly accountable to the DES for the implementation of the national curriculum and for operating LMS schemes, the detail of which are subject to approval by the Secretary of State. The DES prescribed funding formula is thus crucial. Had LEAs been allowed to determine schools' budgets according to their own devices, this would have left LEAs with a potentially powerful instrument by which to control schools.

The 1988 Act builds on the 1980 and 1986 Education Acts to extend consumer accountability. This has two prongs. The first is market accountability, achieved by extending parental choice of school and ensuring that consumer sanctions bite via a pupil-driven funding formula. The second is strengthening participatory democracy at the local level. The 1986 Education Act removed the dominance of LEA governors on governing bodies; two-thirds are now parent or teacher governors or co-opted members. The 1988 Act makes governing bodies responsible for managing the school and holding the head teacher accountable to it. The governing body is charged with managing the school's budget, although it is envisaged that this will be delegated largely to the head, with the governing body formulating broad policies and approving the consequent budget. Governors have new powers to determine the staffing establishment, to appoint, promote, discipline and dismiss staff. However, the LEA remains the employer and is responsible for severance pay, unless the governors have acted unreasonably. The LEA's remaining duties include staff development and training.

The governing body of a school with a delegated budget is accountable managerially to the LEA. In extreme cases of mismanagement, which expressly do not include disagreements over the curriculum, the LEA is required to withdraw delegation and manage the budget itself. However, the governors can appeal to the Secretary of State for reinstatement of budgetary delegation. The governing body is also, in a weak sense, politically accountable to the parents of the school. As well as elections for parent and teacher governors, the governing body has to produce an annual report and hold an annual meeting with parents.

Thus the new governing body is modelled on the board of directors of a company. There are clear expectations that they should operate managerially rational procedures: 'It will be for the governing body, together with the head teacher, to develop and carry out a management plan for their school . . . The head teacher will have a key role in helping the governing body to formulate a management plan for the school, securing its implementation with the collective support of the school's staff' (DES, 1988b, p. 6).

However, as the Audit Commission (1989) points out, as a consequence of delegating resource management: 'Governors and head teachers must therefore see themselves as carrying primary responsibility for quality. But to discharge their own educational responsibilities, LEAs need assurance, independent of institutional management that education of a satisfactory quality is being provided. That assurance can come only as a result of professional monitoring, including direct observation (inspection).' Thus LEAs are expected to develop a much more effective role as quality assurers by monitoring and evaluating the performance of their educational institutions.

In essence then, the new wave of education legislation attempts to replace de facto teachers' professional accountability, conducted within a potentially strong framework of hierarchical political accountability to the LEA, with a fundamentally different model of much weaker LEA control, stronger accountability of LEAs to the DES and new elements of consumer accountability using markets and local democratic participation. Schools lose their de facto freedom to determine the curriculum and gain considerable independence from the LEA in managing resources.

The Development and Use of Management Information

Financial Information

Decentralized budgeting requires computerized financial information systems, since its information requirements are greater than the old system. Under this, recording expenditures on individual items on a school-by-school basis was not needed and so there was little evidence on school cost structures. LEAs have found disaggregating their education budget a time-consuming task. However, they have needed to do this as a preliminary stage in devising an appropriate funding formula. LEAs retain responsibility for financial probity and so are concerned to ensure that financial control is exercised. Most LEAs will act as the schools' banker, paying invoices on their behalf, rather than putting the school's budget income into a school bank account. Schools need accurate, regular and timely information on actual and committed expenditures compared to those planned, in order to make informed decisions. To accord with the spirit of LMS, financial record-keeping needs to be transferred to schools. The task is more efficiently done using computer software which integrates financial management with other aspects of school administration, such as time-tabling and pupil records. Information is then transferred between school and LEA either on line or by disk. Since financial information for control purposes is essential for LMS, systems to provide this are the LEAs' first priority. The larger authorities are already using computerized financial information systems and so have in-house expertise to draw upon. Small metropolitan boroughs tend to be less advanced; some were still using manual systems which LMS has forced them to abandon.

From the point of view of the school managers, financial control should be a routine matter. They should be able to rely on the LEA to provide and run a much more sophisticated system than a school could provide on its own. However, in the early years of LMS there are teething problems with malfunctioning hardware or software and inaccurate or delayed information.

Management information for school decision-making

Senior teachers and governors need to assemble and make use of a wider range of management information than just the financial information needed for control purposes. They need to develop systematic and comprehensive management information of their own in order to make effective decisions concerning the allocation of resources if LMS is to realize its intended purposes. These are to 'enable governing bodies and head teachers to plan their use of resources – including their most valuable resource, their staff – to maximum effect in accordance with their own needs and priorities, and to make schools more responsive to their clients – parents, pupils, the local community and employers (DES, 1988b, p. 3).

A significant trend in school management is the increasing advocacy of rational processes and procedures derived from management techniques in the commercial sector. The training materials produced by the LMS Initiative, a consortium of organizations led by the Chartered Institute of Public Finance and Accountancy, the Local Government Training Board and the Society of Education Officers, are a good example of the rational approach:

> A clear understanding of what is needed for good management is required in order to secure the best results and value for money for the school . . . Management is a cyclic process which involves:
> * identifying objectives;
> * planning how to reach them;
> * preparing a matching financial plan and budget;
> * controlling execution of the plan;
> * monitoring and evaluating achievement and expenditure;
> * varying the plan;
> * reporting achievement.
> (LMS Initiative, 1988, p. 4.1)

Schools are being urged to prepare and implement a school development plan whereby they focus on a few key policies for implementing curricular change and link this systematically with staff development and budgeting. Guidance on school development plans has been circulated by the DES (Hargreaves et al., 1989). This rational managerial mode of running schools is at variance with existing practices and with current views of how schools operate as organizations, which stress informal collegiality, especially in primary schools, ambiguity and micro-politics (Bush, 1989).

Performance indicators

As part of the pressure to adopt managerially rational techniques, there has been much government-inspired discussion of the use of school performance indicators, suggestive lists of which have been drawn up by Coopers & Lybrand (1988) and CIPFA (1988) (see also Hulme, 1989). Performance indicators have been advocated for two quite distinct purposes. One is as part of the process for evaluating the performance of schools and their managers in order to render accountability to the LEA and to consumers by openly publishing PIs. The second purpose of PIs is as internal management information to assist school managers in judging how far their objectives have been achieved and in deciding what needs to be done. There is a potential conflict between the two uses of the same set of PIs, as any organization has an incentive to distort information being collected for external PIs, which then renders them useless for internal purposes. Considerable anxiety has been expressed by school personnel over the implications of PIs. On the basis of this and pilot studies in eight LEAs, the DES has now considerably softened its line on PIs. In December 1989 the Minister of State for Education recommended PIs for internal school use and published a list from which schools can construct their own (DES, 1989c). It seems, though, that schools will be required to publish aggregated unadjusted national curriculum test results for pupils aged 11, 14 and 16 (DES, 1989a).

LEAs are still free to use their own performance indicators as part of their procedures for monitoring and promoting quality and holding schools accountable. There are considerable differences of opinion. The current chairman of the Association of County Councils Education Committee considers that a battery of externally published PIs will not work and so will not be used (stated in a private interview), while some LEAs, such as Surrey (1989), are proposing to develop statistical profiles of schools as part of their monitoring and evaluation procedures.

Implementation costs

The main categories of cost are new information technology, training in new management techniques and – much more difficult to assess – the opportunity cost of the time of those involved. Some of these costs are limited to the implementation phase, others, particularly the opportunity cost of time, will be a continuing feature of LMS. It has never been anticipated that LMS would lead to an overall saving in costs. Jobs previously done by the LEA will now be done in schools and the extra clerical time may well exceed central job savings. Computer hardware and software costs for LMS are estimated to be about £10,000 per secondary school and £5,000 per primary school with over 200 pupils, plus training for administrative staff alone at £800 per school. Local authority forecast spending on LMS is given in table 9.1.

There are additional costs for training heads, other senior teachers and governors. The DES is supporting between 70 and 60 per cent of local authority expenditure on LMS preparation through Education Support Grant and Local Education Authority Training Grants. Details are given in table 9.2.

The opportunity cost of staff time is much more difficult to assess. More

TABLE 9.1
Local authority forecast spending on LMS (£ million)

	1989–90	1990–1	1991–2	1992–3	1993–4
Clerical staff	2.3	9.3	15.0	18.0	20.0
Equipment and materials	25.3	30.4	25.8	29.0	16.4
Training of clerical staff	2.4	2.4	2.6	2.6	0.0

Source: Service Working Group for Education (1989)

TABLE 9.2
LMS preparation costs supported by DES grants 1989–1990 and 1990–1991

	1989–90 (£ million)	1990–1 (£ million)
Education Support Grant		
IT systems	12.0	23.0
Central LMS support	10.0	11.0
Clerical staff training	3.0	2.0
Governor's training	4.9	5.1
LEA inspection	1.9	3.0
LEA Training Grants		
Training for heads and senior teachers	2.5	8.0

Source: DES (1988a) and (1989b) and *Education* (25 August 1989)

time in total will probably be spent in managing school resources, given the extra people involved and the incentives for schools to actively manage their budgets. Some head teachers, especially in the primary sector, are concerned that LMS will leave them less time for teaching, curriculum development and providing the traditional professional leadership of an educator. Local authorities are concerned that LMS will lead indirectly to further expenditure, due to formula funding, which the government has not allowed for. Under centralized budgeting unexpected additional expenditure in one school could be covered by unplanned savings elsewhere. To prevent individual schools experiencing severe difficulties under formula funding, extra lubrication in the form of additional money in the budget is needed. Local authorities' estimates of education expenditure in 1990–1 were £800 million in excess of the government's, compared to a £500 million difference in the previous year. Many LEAs were able to increase school budgets by a few percentage points in 1990/1 but threats of charge capping in 1991/2 has caused a considerable number of LEAs to cut back on education spending.

Will LMS Take Root Successfully?

Given the unaccustomed speed of implementation, the fundamental changes in attitudes and practices that LMS requires and grave concerns as to whether LEAs can adequately fund schools in the early 1990s, will LMS actually take root successfully? There are a number of favourable indications that it will. The basic principle of decentralized resource management is widely accepted by all the main political parties and LEAs. This is because the principle that decision making is best delegated to the lowest possible level in an organization is widely accepted and also because of the growing advocacy of local participatory democracy. Secondary head teachers by and large welcome LMS. The general secretary of the Secondary Heads Association considers that its members are confident of their ability to cope with LMS since they already run a pretty extensive enterprise. 'Getting budgetary responsibility will enhance their position very considerably. They ought to become more effective educational leaders when they are in a position to translate their educational objectives into budgetary terms' (stated in an interview). This opinion is backed up by a growing band of headteachers, including primary heads, who have now experienced financial delegation pilot schemes which pre-date ERA and who offer favourable testimony. Generally, schools have been able to cope well with budgeting. They have welcomed the new-found freedom to vire between budget heads and have made considerable efforts to save on some items such as energy. This has enabled such schools to develop and implement curricular changes which previously were only possible with LEA support or directive. Under LMS, schools are encouraged to articulate school aims and relate their resource allocation decisions to these. It is, however, difficult to specify clearly how school aims, which are by their nature qualitative, can be related to specific educational objectives for which resources are explicitly allocated and which can be satisfactorily measured by performance indicators. The currently advocated means to deal with the fundamental problem of relating resource use to objectives is school developmental planning (Hargreaves et al., 1989), whereby a school carries out an audit, decides on its key priorities, implements specific policies and evaluates the results. This approach is still very much in its infancy (Hopkins and Leask, 1989).

More anxiety about coping is expressed by primary heads, especially in small schools where they also teach. However, this could be considerably alleviated by extra clerical support, which such schools have lacked in the past. Some small primaries in Cambridgeshire have coped successfully with financial delegation. Many heads of small primaries prefer delegation to having their budget managed by the LEA – not only to obtain greater flexibility but to enhance their career prospects. However, considerable financial pressure is being placed on small schools for being uneconomic and the high unit costs of surplus primary places has been heavily criticized by the Audit Commission (1990).

The success of LMS in terms of government objectives also depends upon the ability of governing bodies to act as boards of management and to promote the responsiveness of the professionals to clients' preferences. Crucial to this is the calibre of people who are willing to serve as governors, their ability to work together and with the head teacher. It is as yet too early to judge whether the responsibilities of LMS have attracted or re-pelled potential governors. Certainly an increased number of parents stood for election as governors and governing bodies succeeded in co-opting members from business, though not all have been active. Considerably more training of governors is now taking place. The legislation gives governing bodies considerable scope for interpreting their remit in different ways. Some are likely to continue as passive legitimators of heads' and school-determined decisions, while others will seek to impose policies not supported by the head and to intervene in the more detailed running of the school. In some schools there will be unproductive tensions between governing body and head teacher. Heads will need to adjust to being held accountable to non-professionals and develop skills in managing with a governing body.

The formula funding aspects of LMS are far more contentious, partic-ularly with respect to some of the DES restrictions. If there were a change in government LEAs would probably be permitted far more flexibility. The DES has sought to ensure that schools bear the costs of the resources they use and so has insisted that, except for schools with less than 12 teachers, the budget received by each school depends on the LEA's average cost of teachers, while the school pays the actual salary costs of its teachers. The teacher salary costs of schools with roughly the same number of pupils and in the same LEA can vary quite considerably because some have lower pupil–teacher ratios, more teachers at the top of the salary scale and teachers on protected salaries due to earlier school reorganizations. The government's insistence that schools must be funded according to average teacher costs in the LEA but pay the actual cost of their staff is part of the pressure being exerted to increase local flexibility in teachers' pay. Thus formula funding creates losers and winners when formula budgets are compared to historic budgets. Though schools are given a four-year transition period, this issue has generated a lot of heat, with teacher unions making dire predictions of job losses. This has been somewhat calmed by the so-called 'Rumbold concession', by which individual schools could be given up to ten years to adjust to losses in budget due to having teachers with protected salaries or high on the salary scale. However, LEAs may well find this protection difficult to finance, nor does it resolve the budgetary problems of a school which acquires an old, stable, staff structure in the future.

The main problem in the implementation of LMS will be the political furore caused by teacher unions, governors and local politicians over the cost-cutting measures forced on schools which experience reduced funding in real terms. There is considerable speculation that this will occur, not only because of the redistributive impact of formula funding, but because of inadequate expenditure on local authority education budgets, due to the community charge and the revenue support grant set by central government. There is a danger that unpleasant decisions about cuts will now be delegated to governing bodies, who will be less able to cope because of inexperience, reluctance to make individuals they know personally redundant, weakness in the face of union threats and the small size of their budgets. There can be little doubt that one of the linked issues on the LMS agenda, as far as the government is concerned, is increasing the efficiency of the secondary sector where, as rolls declined through the 1980s, a good number of LEAs failed to remove sufficient surplus places. Whether governing bodies will be forced to tackle the problem by dismissing staff in order to balance their budgets and deliver the national curriculum, or whether they will cut maintenance and materials in order to avoid the unpleasantness of dismissing teachers, remains to be seen. So far, the DES has failed to secure extra funds from the Treasury in order to lubricate the transition to LMS and attract people to work in schools.

Accountability in Practice

The secondary head's role as chief executive will be further accentuated, with heads of department and some deputies fulfilling more of the traditional role of an educational leader. As the job of primary heads pre-LMS was still predominantly that of an educational leader in a collegial setting, they may find the adjustment more difficult. There will not be time to sustain as much teaching, and curriculum issues will require more input from staff. The national curriculum is reinforcing the trend for primary teachers to specialize in curriculum areas and to co-ordinate their teaching.

In practice it looks as if LMS will considerably enhance the power of head teachers and the senior management team, because the other links in the accountability chain are weak. Up till now governing bodies have had little power. Heads are not used to being the executors of governing body policy; rather they look to their governors to be supportive. Most lay governors will not have the time or even the expertise to acquire and interpret the information they need in order to formulate and evaluate school policies themselves. LMS and the national curriculum increase the amount of professional knowledge required by teachers and so are a barrier to lay understanding.

The ability of LEAs to hold schools accountable must also be in doubt. While LEAs had the role of quality assurers before ERA, many did not accord it a high priority. The Audit Commission (1989) criticized existing mechanisms of quality assurance, noting that 'the amount of observation of teaching by inspectors and advisers is uneven and, in some LEAs, disturbingly small' and recommended more systematic record-keeping (Audit Commission, 1989, p. 1). DES back-tracking on performance indicators and its failure to promote value-added indicators as opposed to measures of education attainment which are not adjusted for pupils' background, means that much is being left to the discretion of LEAs. As these feel over-stretched by lack of money and excessive work-loads, their capacity to develop effective quality assurance mechanisms is questionable. However, since the LEA's role as producer has been substantially reduced, they now have a greater incentive to develop their regulatory role.

Thus, the most effective means of accountability would appear to be the market. The burgeoning of interest in marketing indicates that secondary schools, in particular, are taking competition seriously. Competition will flourish more potently where schools have spare capacity and are located near alternative schools. Squeezing out surplus places would reduce schools' incentives to compete. Competition also requires that customers have access to relevant and low-cost information. Since choosing a school is an infrequent event, school customers cannot build up information through consuming and comparing products. Publication of schools' national curriculum results, as well as other information about the school which puts the results into context, are vital for informing parental choice.

Conclusion

It would be a pity if the potential benefits of LMS to schools and their clients was put at risk by financial stringency, so that schools, instead of enjoying a new-found freedom to allocate resources, get bogged down in problems of retrenchment which are externally imposed, rather than resulting from their own failure to attract pupils or contain above average costs. In the face of the resulting political outcry, the DES is more likely to sweeten the pill by abandoning some of the measures required to secure schools' accountability. As well as adequate funding, a more systematic and comprehensive framework for the management education of teachers, as recommended by the DES School Management Task Force (1990), is needed to ensure the professional development of the heads and deputies upon whom the success of LMS so clearly depends.

References

Association of Metropolitan Authorities (1989) The workload of LEAs. In the Minutes of the Policy Committee, 21 September, item 10, P 89 93.

Audit Commission (1989) *Assuring Quality in Education.* London: HMSO.

— (1990) *Rationalizing Primary School Provision.* London: HMSO.

Bush, T. (1989) *Managing Education: theory and practice.* Milton Keynes: Open University Press.

Chartered Institute of Public Finance and Accountancy (1988) *PIs in Schools: a contribution to the debate.* London: CIPFA.

Coopers & Lybrand (1988) *Local Management of Schools.* London: HMSO.

Department of Education and Science (1988a) *Local Education Authority Training Grants Scheme: financial year 1989–90.* London: HMSO, Circular 5/88.

— (1988b) *Education Reform Act: local management of schools.* London: HMSO, Circular 7/88.

— (1989a) *National Curriculum: from policy to practice.* London: HMSO.

— (1989b) *Education Support Grant.* London: HMSO.

— (1989c) *Performance Indicators: an aide-mémoire.* London: HMSO.

Hargreaves, D. H., Hopkins, D., Leask, M., Connolly J. and Robinson, D. (1989) *Planning for School Development: advice to governors, headteachers and teachers.* London: HMSO.

Hopkins, D. and Leask, M. (1989) Performance indicators and school development, *School Organization,* 9, 3–20.

Hulme, G. (1989) Performance evaluation and performance indicators in schools. In R. Levacic (ed.), *Financial Management in Education,* Milton Keynes: Open University Press, 189–98.

Kogan, M. (1986) *Education Accountability,* London, Hutchinson.

LMS Initiative (1988) *Local Management in Schools: a practical guide.* London: CIPFA.

School Management Task Force (1990) *Developing School Management: the way forward.* London: HMSO.

Service Working Group for Education (1989) *Local Authority Need to Spend in 1990–91.* London: Service Working Group.

Surrey County Council (1989) *The Surrey Scheme of Local Management*. Kingtson-upion-Thames: Surrey County Council.

Welsh Office (1988) *Education Reform Act: local management of schools*. Cardiff: Welsh Office, Circular 36/88.

10

Resource Management in Universities

John Sizer

Introduction

Since the election in May 1979, economy and effectiveness, value for money, performance indicators, executive styles of management, devolved budgeting and accountability within institutions, and departmental and individual performance assessment have risen high on the agendas of the Treasury, the Department of Education and Science, the funding bodies (the University Grants Committee and the National Advisory Board for Higher Education and their successors, the Universities Funding Council and the Polytechnics and Colleges Funding Council), vice-chancellors and polytechnic directors, and university academics and administrators.

The Conservative government has been committed, not only to reducing public expenditure and encouraging a market economy, and, therefore, requiring institutions to seek additional non-governmental funding, but also to justifying their activities and accounting for their use of resources and their performance in terms of:

- *economy* in the *acquisition* and *use* of resources,
- *efficiency* in the *use* of resources, and
- *effectiveness* in the *achievement* of institutional, departmental and individual objectives, through the successful implementations of strategies and action plans.

The relationship between these elusive concepts in higher education is illustrated in figure 10.1. This requires, as elaborated in the *Report of the Steering Committee for Efficiency Studies in Universities* (the Jarratt Report) (CVCP, 1985), the development of strategic plans to underpin academic decisions and structures, which bring planning, resource allocation and accountability together into a corporate process linking academic, financial and physical aspects. Important aspects of *effectiveness* are responsiveness to, and relevance to, the needs of a post-industrial, advanced information

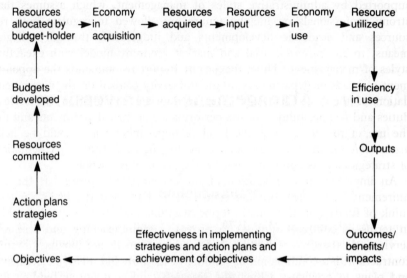

FIGURE 10.1
Value for money – the three Es

and manufacturing, technological society, including widening access to higher education as the 18-year-old population declines; contributing to the improved performance of the economy; matching competition in producing more qualified scientists, engineers, technologists and technicians; and developing the ability to adapt to change. Selectivity in the allocation of resources available for research; critical evaluation and rationalization of small, weak departments; and continuous striving for improved quality and excellence in teaching are other important dimensions of effectiveness. Thus, the government expects institutions to be accountable to the UFC and the PCFC, and through the funding bodies to the DES, the Treasury and Parliament, for providing *value for money* in terms of the three Es.

The government also wishes to reduce its commitments to funding higher education and expects institutions, through increased entrepreneurship and a market-orientated focus, to build up alternative funds. Reduced dependence on government funding and increased diversity of sources for funding, it is argued, will restore institutional autonomy, which implies the need for strengthened accountability mechanisms. Over-emphasis on government funding and excessive direction from funding bodies is seen to inhibit responsiveness, creativity, innovation and diversity of provision. There are, therefore, pressures on institutions, particularly universities, to change their 'culture' from the free oligarchic and consensus model, supported by administrative styles of management, which assumes that strong professionals on lifelong tenure are allowed to regulate both resources and academic developments and judgements through collegial means, to an entrepreneurial and market economy model with executive styles of management. Thus, the Jarratt Report recommends the appointment of heads of departments by the university council on the recommendation of the Vice-Chancellor after appropriate consultation, with clear duties and responsibilities for the performance of their departments and for the use of resources. It is the head of department who should be held *accountable* for the use of resources and for the successful implementation of strategies and action plans, not the department as a whole.

An important new dimension of the accountability process is the requirement on the new funding councils (the UFC and the PCFC) not to think of funding institutions in terms of grants and student numbers, but in terms of contracts (grants) to provide certain teaching and research services. At the time of writing, the funding councils are moving towards contracts with a combination of funding of institutional mission statements and plans to provide teaching and research, and competitive bidding for an increasing proportion of funding over the planning period; a high proportion in the case of the UFC and a marginal are for the PCFC. Governing bodies and managements will be held *accountable* for the implementation of institutional plans and contracts (grants) awarded. Competition between institutions for students has also been stimulated by a substantial increase in tuition fees for full-time home undergraduates, with a commensurate reduction in contract funding of institutions.

Furthermore, the philosophy is not simply to be one of employing dominant buying power to purchase teaching and research at the lowest cost, but of securing value for money in terms of the three Es, including responsiveness, relevance, innovation and creativity, selectively hard choices, quality and excellence. Whatever the methodology, it is clear that a key determinant of effectiveness is *quality*, both of teaching provision and research. All of this implies that institutional, departmental and individual performance assessment has not only become an important dimension of institutional and departmental management, but is likely to become more so.

The Role of Performance Indicators and Devolved Responsibility and Accountability

Publicly available performance indicators (PIs) are key inputs into the process of accountability, both internally within the institution and externally to funding bodies, governments and society. In a market economy model they should be an important source of market intelligence for consumers. The university sector has taken the lead in the development of a comprehensive, publicly available, set of PIs and management statistics to assist both institutional decision-making and internal and external accountability.

Planning and resource allocation, the central concern of the Jarratt Report, particularly during times of financial constraints and changing demands, involves making choices between mutually exclusive alternatives, each with its own combination of inputs, outputs, outcomes, impacts and benefits. Therefore, it is not surprising that current initiatives in the development and use of performance indicators in the United Kingdom flow from the conclusion in the Jarratt Report that: 'There is a recognized need for reliable and consistent performance indicators. These need to be developed urgently for universities as a whole and for individual universities as an integral part of their planning and resource allocation process' (CVCP, 1985, p. 22). This conclusion led to the joint recommendation to the UGC and the Committee of Vice-Chancellors and Principals: 'A range of performance indicators should be developed, covering inputs and outputs and designed for use both within individual universities and for making comparisons between institutions' (CVCP, 1985, p. 36), and the recommendation that all universities develop 'reliable and consistent performance indicators'.

The first set of *University Management Statistics and Performance Indicators* was published in 1987 (CVCP/UGC 1987), and further sets, with additional indicators, have been published annually (CVCP/UFC, 1990). In the initial list of 39 PIs, expanded to 54 in 1988, the joint CVCP/UFC Steering Committee has concentrated on input, process, and only two sets of output/outcome measures (destinations of graduates after six months and number of successful leavers), because considerable, and difficult, work is still being undertaken on effectiveness measures, particularly in the area of research and the longitudinal impacts of teaching outputs. The PIs are more useful, therefore, in assessing efficiency than effectiveness, but an institution can only be efficient if it is effective. Ongoing work on research output has focused on bibliometric methods of assessment at the level of the cost centre on subjects within universities, in particular, developing a methodology for collecting publication counts. In order to develop meaningful costs of teaching outputs (graduates) and research outputs and outcomes, the complex problems of joint product costing will have to be resolved. Cost per full-time equivalent indicators in the current publication are distorted because they relate teaching student FTEs to research and teaching costs. Work has also been undertaken to develop a set of indicators of institutional financial health that can be derived from the institutions' published accounts.

PIs and management statistics should inform decisions. They provide a starting-point from which academic and managerial judgements should be made, but the fewer the indicators the wider the gap that has to be bridged by such judgements. Having made decisions, a comparison of the expected and actual performance indicators should form one part of the assessment of whether past decisions have been successfully put into effect. Experienced and effective executive managements would not, and weak, ineffective managements cannot, rely on over-simplistic use of performance indicators. Decisions which PIs and management statistics should inform may be of a long-term or strategic nature or of a short-term tactical nature. They may be at an institutional, faculty or departmental level. Future analysis and institutional strategies and operational plans, as the Jarratt Report argues, should lead to departmental mission statements and plans, which identify the role and mission of departments, set out their objectives, strategies and action plans, and the progress measures, including PIs, against which performance will be assessed and monitored. For a further discussion and illustration of the use of PIs in formulating corporate strategies and plans in higher education institutions, and subsequently evaluating progress in implementation, see the recent report by a CUA/APA Study Group entitled, *Strategic Choice: Corporate Strategies for Change in Higher Education* (CUA, 1990). Longer term departmental strategies and plans have to be translated into annual action plans and budgets. Thus the Jarratt Report's constitutional recommendations included:

5.5(f) Budget delegation to appropriate centres which are held responsible to the planning and resources committees for what they have achieved against their budgets.

5.5(g) Developing reliable and consistent performance indicators, greater awareness of costs and full cost charging.

The key word in recommendation 5.5(f) is *achieved*.

Accountability is concerned with whether the head of the responsibility centre, be it an academic or service department, has successfully implemented the plan for which resources were provided, i.e. with what has been achieved not what has been spent. PIs can be used both in defining what it is planned to achieve and in measuring achievement. It has been observed elsewhere that the managements of some institutions appeared to confuse resource allocation with budget delegation, and view accountability in the narrow financial control sense of comparing actual with budget expenditure, i.e. living within one's budget (UGC, 1987). The CVCP also appears to take this narrow view of accountability in its guidance to universities on the structure and practice of financial management in universities (CVCP, 1988). It distinguishes between two complementary processes of *resource planning and allocation* and *accountability and control*, and recommends that the latter should be the responsibility of the finance officer and the finance committee. Financial accountability and control is only one aspect of accountability for achievement.

In many institutions PIs have been used in historical performance evaluation as part of long-term academic planning, but have still to be fully developed into a system of progress measures of performance as part of a devolved system of budgeting and accountability at the responsibility centre level, with performance against progress measures influencing decisions about future budgets, i.e. financial quantifications of action plans to implement strategies to achieve a set of objectives. Universities are slowly recognizing, and grasping the implications, that accountability is concerned with what has been achieved not what has been spent, and that performance indicators can be used by institutional and responsibility centre managers, both in defining what it is planned to achieve and in measuring achievement. As table 10.1 illustrates, many universities have yet to fully implement the recommendations of the Jarratt Report, particularly in respect of the development and use of PIs. Accountability also implies incentives at both the institutional and department level and rewards for good performance, as well as sanctions when it is unsatisfactory.

The UFC intends to take account of performance in its funding decision. All of this gives rise to questions as to whether sufficient consideration has been given to the changing roles of heads of departments and to their incentive, reward and career structure, as well as to management development programmes. This question is considered later in the paper.

Budget delegation and accountability also necessitate the development of new information and costing systems. The UGC/UFC *Initiative on Management and Administrative Computing* is addressing this need. Many universities' accounting systems were primarily concerned with stewardship and 'score-keeping' rather than with identifying and satisfying the needs of responsible managers for financial and other quantitative information for purposes of planning, decision-making and control (Sizer, 1989).

The concerns of heads of departments about PIs also have to be addressed further. As in the case of clinicians and their responses to attempts to introduce clinical management budgeting in the National Health Service, there is a great danger that heads of departments will *not* see that department performance indicators are primarily intended to help them manage their departments, to inform their decisions and assess their achievements. They may not feel 'ownership' of the performance indicators system, and they may regard performance indicators as constraints rather than aids.

Universities   157

TABLE 10.1
Extract from UGC follow-up to the Jarratt Report, March 1989

SUMMARY OF UNIVERSITY RESPONSES IN KEY AREAS	% positive response
I REDUCTIONS IN SIZE, NUMBER AND FREQUENCY OF COMMITTEE MEETINGS	
Review of committees since Jarratt Report	80
Annual or other ongoing review of committees	30
II INTRODUCTION OF BUDGET DELEGATION	
Progress made since Jarratt Report	47
Further delegation planned/ongoing development	35
Virement and accountability at delegated level	34
III MORE FULL COST CHARGING AND USE OF PERFORMANCE INDICATORS	
Performance indicators developed and in use	14
Performance indicators under development	11
More full cost charging since Jarratt Report	62
IV CHANGES IN EXECUTIVE RESPONSIBILITY	
Heads of Department with defined role and responsibilities	42
Heads of Department in a managing role	27
Heads of Department accountable for activity	23
Heads of Department responsible for resource management	23
V ESTABLISHMENT OF A PLANNING AND RESOURCES COMMITTEE	
Planning and Resources Committee established	64
Planning and Resources co-ordinates academic and financial planning	45
Planning and Resources responsible for corporate and strategic planning	50
Planning and Resources deals with resource allocations	26
Planning and Resources undertakes special reviews eg space planning	11
VI STAFF APPRAISAL AND DEVELOPMENT	
Staff appraisal scheme introduced	24
Pilot or planned introduction of staff appraisal	72
More emphasis on staff training	39
New training and development staff appointed	16

Source: UFC Circular Letter 16/89; *Strategic Choice: Corporate Strategies for Change in Higher Education* (report by a CUA/APA Study Group) 1988/90, p. 78.

This is because there is a conflict between the use of performance indicators by institutional managements when evaluating the accountability of departmental managers for teaching, research and services, and their use by departmental managers in internal management of their teaching and research activities. At the present time the emphasis is being placed on accountability rather than on their use as a tool for the departmental manager. *Performance indicators are best interpreted and employed by the managers who can influence their outcomes.* Their use as part of the accountability process should not dominate. The primary purpose of a budgetary planning and control system, and the supporting management information and performance indicators, is to help the budget holder to manage his own performance. Hence, he must have ownership of the system.

Heads of departments are also concerned that excessive emphasis will be placed on short-term cost efficiency at the expense of long-term effectiveness. They fear sight might be lost of the fact that you can only be efficient if you are effective, i.e. you can be inefficiently effective, but not efficiently ineffective. In particular, they are concerned that high costs per FTE imply both inefficiency and ineffectiveness. A high-cost department may be both effective and efficient because of the quality of its teaching and research outputs, outcomes, benefits and impacts. Hence the concern of heads of departments that these difficult measures of teaching and research performance are not only addressed, but also properly related to input and process measures of efficiency.

Research Planning, Selective Allocation of Resources and Accountability

The CVCP/UFC Steering Committee has recognized that one of the reasons why it is difficult to develop meaningful publishable measures of an institution's research performance is because research performance assessment, as with teaching quality assurance, has to start at the level of individuals and groups in departments (or organizational units), and build up through departmental and faculty assessment. For purposes of internal research planning, selective resource allocation, monitoring and accountability, it is necessary to develop individual or research group and departmental profiles of the nature of the research activity that is taking place within a department or other organizational unit, and to identify the research PIs that are relevant to the evaluation of that department's research activity. Guidance can be given to departments on the possible evaluation criteria and relevant PIs at each stage of research activity, i.e. input, process, output, outcome, benefit and impact (Sizer and Frost, 1985). The UGC's research selectivity exercises, which made limited use of research PIs, and the pressure on universities to be as selective internally as the funding bodies have been externally, have led to the recognition of the need to develop department research profiles and research PIs. These have been reinforced by an intimation from the UFC that its research policy could involve regular assessment of research performance.

The UGC informed the Secretary of State in 1986 that universities individually needed to draw up and carry out plans for the selective distribution of the resources they devote to research, and that the UGC would monitor their arrangements for this and report to ministers annually on their implementation. The second annual report to the Secretary of State (UGC, 1988) indicated that, despite financial constraints, overall since 1985 universities had made considerable progress in research planning and selective use of resources for research, and that there was considerable momentum within the system for further development. However, in many institutions, selectivity within departments and subject areas did not appear to have been fully integrated into mechanisms which brought planning, resource allocation and accountability into one corporate process linking academic, financial and physical aspects with the objectives of ensuring the economical, efficient and effective use of resources devoted to research. Very few institutions appeared to have developed mechanisms whereby the planning and resources committee, assisted by the research committee, was in a position to monitor the use of scarce research resources, and to hold heads of departments *accountable for* the implementation of departmental research plans which had been agreed with the planning and resources committee. The third annual report (UFC, 1989) concludes that the considerable momentum towards further developments in research planning and the selective use of resources is resulting in a very much heightened perception within institutions of the machinery, practices and procedures necessary to ensure that the institution effectively provides selectivity at all levels.

In order to develop departmental research plans and obtain an overview of the scale and use of resources for research, and also for teaching, as well as developing research profiles, it will also be necessary to develop output-orientated accounting systems. As in the case of output costing in the National Health Service, the accounting methodology problems are considerable, including all the problems surrounding absorption costing and joint product accounting in process industries. It has to be recognized from the outset that there is no one way of apportioning joint costs to cost centres or absorbing joint costs into cost units. However, unless they are addressed meaningfully, teaching and research process and output indicators are difficult to produce. The time is right to review methodologies to see whether an acceptable one can be developed and implemented, and more meaningful cost indicators developed for teaching and research processes and outputs. It is appropriate that the CVCP has established a working party under the chairmanship of Sir John Kingman, Vice-Chancellor of the University of Bristol, to enquire into the costs of teaching and, therefore, research also. Developments in information technology suggest that the feasibility of establishing data bases economically should not present a constraint, and the UGC/UFC Initiative on Management and Administrative Computing should allow this hypothesis to be tested.

Teaching Quality

One of the dangers of selectivity supporting research, and strengthening the mechanisms for research management and accountability, is that greater emphasis is placed on research at the expense of teaching. Successive DES ministers have considered that universities need to assign to teaching the same prestige as they have traditionally assigned to research, and have been pressing the universities over a long period to give greater attention to teaching quality. The CVCP (1986) offered advice and guidance to universities on the maintenance and monitoring of academic quality and standards. It undertook to monitor the extent to which universities followed this advice, to publish reports in 1987 and 1988 on the changes that had been made, and to give further guidance if necessary. It also agreed to introduce more effective systems of staff development and appraisal, and to promote the development of PIs of teaching quality. In 1988 a standing group was established, under the chairmanship of Professor Stuart Sutherland, to create an academic standards unit to monitor universities' implementation of procedures for teaching quality assurance; this action was perceived by some as a defensive measure to discourage the DES from sending HM Inspectorate into the universities. The CVCP (1989) accepted the recommendations of the Sutherland Committee and an Academic Audit Unit has been established. The remit of the Unit is as follows:

1   To consider and review the universities' mechanisms for monitoring and promoting the academic standards which are necessary for achieving their stated aims and objectives.
2   To comment on the extent to which procedures in place in individual universities reflect best practice for maintaining quality and are applied in practice.
3   To identify and commend to universities good practice in regard to the maintenance of academic standards at national level.

TABLE 10.2
CVCP Academic Audit Unit – an outline check-list for academic audits

It is proposed that the academic audit unit should monitor universities' quality
assurance mechanisms by examining and commenting on the adequacy of:
1 Universities' mechanisms for quality assurance in provision and design of courses
and degree programmes:
   • having centrally planned monitoring of courses and teaching
   • scrutinizing new courses or degree programmes (or revision of them)
   • monitoring course design in relation to student intake and non-traditional
   entrance
   • monitoring validation by the university of courses in associated institutions
2 Universities' mechanisms for quality assurance in teaching and communication
methods:
   • monitoring existing courses and degree programmes including data collection,
   such as student numbers, drop-out rates, classified results, etc.
   • monitoring postgraduate training and research, including appeals procedures at
   postgraduate research degree level
   • seeking external examiners' views
   • monitoring and informing students of their progress and exam performance,
   including appeals procedures
   • promoting innovative practice in universities, such as use of interactive video
   and expert systems
3 Universities' mechanisms for quality assurance in relation to academic staff:
   • assessing and monitoring academic staff
   • provision for staff development
4 Universities' mechanisms for quality assurance in taking account of:
   • external examiners' report
   • students' views on courses
   • views of external bodies – professional accrediting bodies and employers, etc.

Source: The Reynolds document and subsequent reports and various other CVCP codes of
practice, e.g., those on the external examiner system and university validation.

4 To keep under review nationally the role of the external examiner
system.
5 To report to the CVCP.

The scope of the required audits will be defined in terms of a standard
checklist (see outline draft in table 10.2) against which universities' internal
quality assurance mechanisms (as shown in internal guide-lines and mechanisms) will be assessed across the whole system. The aim is to develop

the check-list as the audit system evolves. The UFC expects institutions to put in place arrangements for assessing and improving teaching as soon as possible.

When Secretary of State for Education John MacGregor intimated that he expected teaching quality as well as price will be taken into consideration by the UFC when deciding where student numbers are placed, the UGC did not find a way of nationally assessing teaching quality. If the UFC is to take account of teaching quality when awarding contracts, and in monitoring their satisfactory fulfilment, it will have to develop an appropriate methodology. Can it rely, as in the Netherlands, on the university sector to create systems which it can draw upon and which merit public confidence, without the back stop, which exists in the Netherlands, of a university inspectorate? This is a key question in respect of accountability for teaching quality. The CVCP academic audit unit can monitor procedures employed in universities for self-evaluation and programme review, but it cannot be expected to assess the comparative quality of teaching by subject areas in all universities. There is an important distinction between *minimum quality assurance and comparative quality judgements*.

The UFC has acknowledged that appropriate machinery will have to be set up to consider and advise on these matters. Furthermore, it will also have to consider how to assess whether the quality it has contracted for has been delivered. The UFC may find it impossible to develop the capacity to make comprehensive judgements without substantial additional resources, but, more critically, without straining its wish that there should be minimum bureaucratic involvement on the part of the Council in institutions' affairs.

Teaching quality has to be addressed by departmental heads as 'responsible' managers as part of staff development and training, appraisal and accountability. The vice-chancellor/director has the key responsibility of establishing throughout the institution a 'teaching quality culture', which includes regular reviews of course structure and content, quality and quantity of teaching resources, quality of course delivery, staff development and appraisal procedures, extent of student and employer satisfaction, as well as external accreditation and assessment. Therefore, there has to be a process of *accountability* to students, employers, funding bodies, government departments and public, which starts at the level of the individual lecturer, through heads of departments, to the vice-chancellor/director, to provide assurance not only that a 'teaching quality culture' exists but is also delivered. Universities are being encouraged to make reports from the Academic Standards Unit publicly available, as are CNAA and HMI reports. The key question in a market economy is whether the reports are effectively communicated to prospective customers (students).

Various PIs, not necessarily publishable, need to be developed relating to each of those components of a 'teaching quality culture', in terms of adequacy of provision, quality of provision, economy of acquisition and use, efficiency, etc. (Sizer, 1990). A key question is, *How can you ensure that a proper balance is struck between the qualitative and quantitative aspects of performance assessment?* The quality of lecturers' performances in classrooms may be more relevant than staff-student ratios, but excessive SSRs will inevitably impact upon the quality of teaching.

Publishable PIs of institutional teaching quality are very difficult to develop. Bourke (1986), in his report on quality measures in universities for the Australian Commonwealth Territory Education Commission, spells out the difficulties in assessing teaching quality and some of the possible ways forward. The Joint CVCP/UFC Steering Committee has considered possible indicators, but concluded that some which are used within institutions, such as classifications of honours degrees, are inappropriate for making comparisons between institutions. It considers that there is a need for universities to undertake formal self-evaluation and appraisal of teaching as a matter of good practice, including the development of systems of individual teacher appraisal and student questionnaires. It will return to the issue of indicators of teaching quality, not only because of the CVCP's commitment to promote such indicators, but also because of its importance in a market-orientated system as part of the process of *accountability* and in ensuring that customers in the market-place are fully informed. The DES accepts that teaching quality is easy to recognize but difficult to measure; nevertheless it looks to joint initiatives by the CVCP and UFC to develop management information and performance indicators relating to teaching quality.

PIs, publishable and internal, are only one input into the process of quality judgement, quality assurance, accountability and performance assessment; peer review has a very important part to play. It occurs at every stage of a research project's life. The UFC's 1989 research selectivity exercise was essentially a process of 'informed peer review'. For teaching, it takes place when courses are accredited by the CNAA and professional bodies, externally examined, and inspected by HM Inspectorate. Many universities have introduced periodic internal departmental reviews, every three to five years, and most, if not all, use external assessors. Whilst it is difficult to identify output measures of teaching quality, the evaluation of institutions' procedures to be undertaken by the new CVCP academic audit unit should raise the level of awareness of the importance of teaching quality assurance at the departmental and institutional level.

If there is to be detailed external peer review of the quality of departments or subject areas, PIs should inform the peer review and help to narrow the gap that has to be bridged by peer judgements. PIs provide one starting-point for more detailed enquiry and questioning by reviewers. They indicate where performance differs, but not necessarily why it differs, or how to improve it. In the absence of performance indicators, the element of judgement may be too great; reliance on PIs in the absence of peer judgements is extremely dangerous. Peer review and performance indicators should, and must, complement each other.

Implications for the Roles of Heads of Academic Departments

Normally, professors are appointed on the basis of the excellence of their scholarship and research, and their capacity to provide academic leadership; limited consideration is given to their managerial abilities. Many would say they did not become academics in order to become managers of responsibility centres with delegated budget responsibility and accountability. The author directed a research project which examined the responses of nine universities both to events leading up to the UGC's grant letters of 1 July 1981 and to the letters themselves; their impact upon the organizational structures, management style, planning and resource allocation processes, etc., and upon the teaching, research, academic and administrative services, and related activities of institutions. In a comparative analysis, which was summarized in a final report to the DES (Sizer, 1987), the responses of, and different impacts on, institutions which faced substantially different percentage cuts in recurrent grants and/or student numbers were considered and summarised, together with the implications for the effective and efficient management of universities. In a subsequent paper (Sizer, 1988) managerial guidelines drawn from the comparative analysis were contrasted with the Jarratt Report on efficiency studies in universities and with a UGC analysis of universities' responses to the Jarratt Report. One of the guidelines related to the roles of heads of departments:

> Recognise the changing, more demanding, and at times conflicting managerial and representative roles of Heads of Departments, and the need for periodic replacement. Plan for succession and provide appropriate managerial and leadership training and development for current and future Heads of Departments. Ensure Heads of Departments do not neglect staff appraisal and development by implementing formalised departmental and university systems. Ensure as far as possible that heads have appropriate administrative support.

The case studies showed that the roles of chairmen and heads of departments changed substantially as a result of the financial reductions. They were under constant, and at times conflicting, pressures from the administration and their own staff. They became more involved in planning and resource allocation issues and in protecting their departments' interests. Their staff management role became more demanding and critical. Their own teaching, scholarship and research inevitably suffered. Some were unable to cope with the extra demands and the additional stress. They had insufficient time to respond to staff development needs and required more administrative support. There was a widespread belief that headships should rotate about every four or five years, if the leadership commitment was to be maintained and the pressures coped with. Subsequent developments have increased the pressures on, and have highlighted the changing roles of, heads of departments, as they are being pressurized to move to an executive style of management. They are expected to allocate research resources selectively, improve research performance within their departments, develop a 'teaching quality culture', bid for students in competition with other institutions, and act entrepreneurially, generating non-government funding. Furthermore, heads of departments have a central role in the new procedures for staff appraisal, which inevitably will change their relationships with departmental colleagues.

Should outstanding academic leaders should be forced into an executive style of management? That is, will executive styles of management stimulate or inhibit excellence in teaching, research and scholarship within academic departments? For many departments the question vice-chancellors face is not 'who should be head of department?' but, 'who amongst the suitable candidates is willing to be head of department?' The Jarratt Report recognizes that there is a danger that the managerial role may crowd out the teaching, research and scholarship leadership role of the eminent and the able professorial head. It takes the view that it is preferable to retain the managerial and academic leadership functions in one person, but where this is not practical the head of department must possess the requisite managerial skills and be encouraged to delegate some part of the responsibility for academic leadership to others. However, will all eminent and able professors be willing to play second fiddle to a less able academic who has executive management skills? Given the crucial roles of heads of departments and the increasing pressures they face, urgent consideration needs to be given to the provision of incentives, rewards and career structures, as well as to management development programmes.

The Way Forward

At the time of writing the Conservative government appears to be firmly committed to an entrepreneurial and market economy in higher education, as well as further strengthening of accountability for use of public funds. Thus it is to be expected that it will continue to press the CVCP and the

UFC to make further progress on the difficult and complex work to be undertaken in respect of longitudinal outcomes of teaching; indicators of research outputs, outcomes, benefits and impacts; separation of teaching and research costs; and, in particular, measures for teaching quality assurance and comparative teaching quality judgements. Performance indicators are becoming firmly implanted in the culture of institutions, but sight must not be lost of the dangers of abuse and misuse.

The government also wishes to see further progress in the implementation of the Jarratt Report by universities, and expects the UFC to continue to monitor its implementation. This will necessitate not only improving universities' accounting and information systems to support heads of responsibility centres, but also further consideration of the organization structures and of the roles and responsibilities of heads of departments and reward and incentive structures. In particular, it needs to be demonstrated that executive styles of management, and devolved responsibility and accountability, improve the quality of teaching, research and scholarship, i.e., that they improve the effectiveness of departments and institutions.

A more fundamental issue is the future role of the UFC. It has been argued elsewhere that the UFC has not the capacity to undertake comparative judgements of teaching quality, and that it may not prove possible to develop the capacity without substantial additional resources, but also without straining the UFC's stance on bureaucracy. In the end, it may be that if the government is committed to an entrepreneurial and market economy in higher education, it should rely on market forces and the actions of individual consumers to force institutions to take seriously the need to assess and deliver teaching quality, and to demonstrate to the market not only that they are striving to deliver it, but that they have in fact delivered, rather than contract funding by a monopolistic buyer (UFC) of FTEs from a cartel of institutions (CVCP) with limited countervailing power, other than an unwillingness to make low-price bids, as a surrogate for a competitive market. There is a danger that the UFC will fall between stools, neither a dirigiste national planning body nor an effective surrogate for a competitive market. If the institutions do not have a clear understanding of the role of the UFC, and its resource allocation processes, this will create a climate of uncertainty as to future funding prospects, and it will be extremely difficult to achieve effectively and efficiently resource management in universities.

References

Bourke, P. (1986) *Quality Measures in Universities*. Canberra: Commonwealth Tertiary Education Committee.

Committee of Vice-Chancellors and Principals (1985) *Report of the Steering Committee for Efficiency Studies in Universities* (the Jarratt Report). London: CVCP.

— (1986) *Academic Standards in Universities*. London: CVCP.

— (1988) *Guidance in Structure and Practice of Financial Management in Universities*. London: CVCP.

— (1989) *The Teaching Function: quality assurance*. London: CVCP.

Committee of Vice-Chancellors and Principals and Universities Funding Council (1990) *University Management Statistics and Performance Indicators in the UK*. London: CVCP.

Committee of Vice-Chancellors and Principals and University Grants Committee (1987) *University Management Statistics and Performance Indicators*. London: CVCP.

Conference of University Administrators and Association of Polytechnic Administrators Study Group (1990) *Strategic Choice: corporate strategies for change in higher education*. London: CUA.

Sizer, John (1987) *Institutional Responses to Financial Reductions within the University Sector*. London: Department of Education and Science.

— (1988) The management of institutional adaptation and change under conditions of financial stringency. In H. Eggins (ed.), *Restructuring Higher Education*, Milton Keynes: SRHE and Open University Press, 80–92.

— (1989) *An Insight into Management Accounting*. Third edition. Harmondsworth: Penguin.

— (1990) Funding councils and performance indicators in quality assessment in the United Kingdom. In L. C. J. Goedegbuure, P. A. M. Maassen and D. F. Westerheijden (eds), *Peer Review and Performance Indicators*, Utrecht: Uitgeverij Lemma, 155–81.

Sizer, J. and Frost, R. (1985) *Criteria for Self Evaluation of Department Research Profiles*. Loughborough University of Technology: Responsible and Responsive Universities Working Project, Working Paper.

Universities Funding Council (1989) *Third Report on Monitoring Research Selectivity*. London: UFC.

University Grants Committee (1987) *Report to the Secretary of State on Universities' Responses to the Jarratt Report*. London: UGC.

— (1988) *Second Annual Report on Monitoring Research Selectivity*. London: UGC.

11

The Civil Service and the Financial Management Initiative*

Andrew Gray and Bill Jenkins

> *'A little bit of freedom and a lot of grief.'*
>
> Civil servant's comment on the FMI

Many officials who have lived through the financial management initiative (FMI) share a sense of disillusion with its achievements. Of course, some express more positive reactions and some, fewer perhaps than might be expected, wish the whole irrelevancy would go away. But it will not. Indeed, part of the success of the FMI has been its sustained development into a central element in civil service management.

In the 1990s the civil service faces a world significantly different from the past: geographical dispersion, executive agencies and privatization; differentiated labour markets, conditions of service and pay systems. Above all, there is the dominance of systems for managing resources and meeting targets. This contrasts sharply with the early 1970s which, in the spirit of the Fulton *Committee on the Civil Service* (1968) and the White Paper *The Reorganisation of Central Government* (1970), emphasized policy strategy and personnel management. But most of this was lost in the economic crises of the mid-1970s, which resulted in new disciplines of cash limits. The arrival of Mrs Thatcher's government in 1979 marked a clear attempt to break with the past and to create a climate in which a new public sector management could be developed.

* This chapter is based on research supported by the Economic and Social Research Council and carried out between 1986 and 1989 by Andrew Gray, Bill Jenkins, Andrew Flynn and Brian Rutherford.

An Emphasis on Efficiency Management

'Policy is indigestible; management is not.'

Senior civil servant

The election of the new Conservative government in 1979 coincided with increasing civil service recognition of the need to create a coherent regime of resource management to remedy the financial indiscipline and operational weaknesses of the past. Influenced by new right thinking that the public sector was too large, inefficient and inherently wasteful, the new administration set out to reduce the scope and size of government and to promote a managerial culture in public sector organizations. In pursuit of these objectives the Government removed icons of the *ancien régime* (e.g. Programme Analysis and Review (PAR) and later the Central Policy Review Staff (CPRS)) and instituted a programme for cutting civil service manpower and eliminating waste. At the forefront of this was the efficiency strategy designed and co-ordinated by Derek (later Lord) Rayner, a businessman with unusually extensive experience and knowledge of civil service operations.

At face value the efficiency strategy has been a small-scale operation. The Efficiency Unit, directed on a part-time basis first by Rayner, then by industrialist Sir Robin Ibbs, and latterly by former Customs and Excise Chairman Sir Angus Fraser, comprises only half a dozen full-time officials. It has had the task of guiding and co-ordinating a series of departmental and interdepartmental studies to identify and eliminate inefficiencies in resource use and procedures. The emphasis has been on promoting greater value for money, removing obstacles to good management, and encouraging quick and effective implementation of feasible changes. Prime-ministerial interest has ensured that the programme has been given high priority. The identification of administrative savings was, however, only one of Rayner's objectives. His wider aim was to promote a managerial culture in central government administration. Under his direction and that of his successors the Unit has therefore been both catalyst and agent of change in a reform programme designed to enhance resource management.

Alongside the efficiency strategy went efforts to improve management information systems and administrative running-cost control in central government. Influenced by business practices in accounting and management science, the Treasury and the Efficiency Unit began to encourage the development of systems to support expenditure control. In the new, tighter, financial regime, some departments, especially those with large executive operations such as tax gathering, saw the value of a systematic approach to resource management, while a few ministers, in particular Michael Heseltine, argued for the development of information systems to aid both administrative and political management. Heseltine's management information system for ministers (MINIS), attracted interest even outside Whitehall, but it did not lead to a rush of innovations in other departments. For the Treasury and other advocates of change these developments confirmed that a more comprehensive reform of financial management was needed. The publication of the House of Commons Treasury and Civil Service Committee Report on *Efficiency and Effectiveness in the Civil Service* (Cmnd. 8616, 1982) provided them with the opportunity to launch such a programme. Thus the Financial Management Initiative was unveiled.

The Development of the Financial Management Initiative

The overall objectives of the financial management initiative (FMI) have been to improve the allocation and control of financial resources in central government, specifically by providing managers at all levels with (a) a clear view of objectives and the means to measure performance in relation to them; (b) a well-defined responsibility for making the best use of resources, including critical scrutiny of output and value for money; and (c) the information particularly about costs, and the ability to exercise this responsibility effectively.

The intention was to improve systems of resource management by building on existing departmental efforts and forcing others to follow suit. Departments were initially 'invited' to submit plans for improved systems to a newly established Financial Management Unit (FMU) (later succeeded by the Joint Management Unit (JMU) and then by the Financial Management Group in the Treasury), staffed by a small group of senior officials and management consultants. As with the Efficiency Unit, the FMU sought to shape and guide developments (there was no blueprint to implement) and to identify and publicize good practice. Early results were reported by two White Papers (Cmnd. 9058, 1983; Cmnd. 9297, 1984) and by a review from the National Audit Office (1987).

In essence the FMI was designed to promote accountable management, i.e. a system of delegated responsibility and accountability. Specifically, it has come to comprise three elements: top management systems (TMS), delegated budgetary control (DBC) and performance indicators (PIs). Departments have also been pressed to ensure that they have clear management plans and the structures for integrating and controlling these developments.

Top management systems represent the flowering of MINIS. Here the aim has been to provide senior officials and ministers with an overview of departmental objectives, activities and resources to inform objective setting, prioritization, and resource allocation, i.e. a specific link with the public expenditure survey (PES). Departments have been encouraged to design new systems in-house or to employ outside consultants and, in practice, many have used both. This use of consultants and in-house teams has also characterized the development of systems of delegated budgetary control. Here the aim has been to improve resource management by delegating financial management throughout the department and its agencies, holding managers responsible for their budgets and performance. Initially, delegation was limited to running costs although the intention was to broaden the scope as systems and managers progressed. However, for top management systems and delegated budgetary control to be effective it was essential for departments to be able to assess their performance. Thus the third element of the FMI has been the development of performance indicators. Work has been encouraged both to facilitate the operation of delegated financial management (e.g. by establishing cost control indicators) and, at divisional levels, to assess the effectiveness of programme expenditure.

From the outset departments were obliged to move forward on all these fronts and regularly to report progress to the centre of government. For some departments (such as Customs and Excise) these demands coincided with in-house responses to more general resource and operational pressures. In these cases the FMI innovations have been fairly easily accommodated. For others, however, the initiative has proved more problematic, especially where there were initially few qualified financial staff, only limited information systems and a tradition of centralized departmental control. Problems were aggravated where senior managers (and ministers) regarded the FMI simply as an instrument of the Treasury's scheme to reduce public sector resource consumption and where the government's quite separate policy for cutting civil service manpower placed limitations on the responsibilities which could be delegated to line managers.

For the co-ordinating and directing agencies at the centre of Whitehall the FMI has been less about institutionalizing new management systems than about changing the culture of civil service management. The fundamental concern has been with a holistic approach to departmental management in which systems and approaches are integrated. This emphasis has been critical in sustaining progress.

The Progress of the Financial Management Initiative

In 1987 the National Audit Office (NAO) reported on the progress of the *Financial Management Initiative*. Its assessment was generally encouraging.

In spite of minor reservations on the development of performance indicators and the differing speed of departmental change, it found much evidence of real achievement and little of serious shortcomings. A year later, however, the Efficiency Unit was less positive. In its report on *Improving Management in Government: the Next Steps* (1988), it expressed a concern with how far systems and practices had still to change. Although it praised some achievements in cost control, it argued that there was still a serious lack of accountable management, that outputs, clients and even value for money had been neglected and that there was insufficient managerial information or technical support. Its solution was to identify coherent activities which could be hived off into departmental executive agencies and managed essentially as separate businesses.

Does this imply that the FMI's progress has been severely limited? Our own research leads us to be less pessimistic than the Efficiency Unit but rather less encouraging than the NAO. Two factors in particular bear on this assessment: first, the highly differentiated tasks and environments of the civil service and, second, the inevitable tension in Whitehall between politics and management. How these factors impinge on a department and its operations will influence the pace and effectiveness of management reforms.

Nevertheless it is possible to give a broad assessment of the FMI. There can be little doubt, for example, that systems of delegated budgets are now in place in almost every department. However, the scope of the change varies. Decentralized budgetary control is most effective for the control of administrative running costs, which are discrete, measurable, and lie within departmental discretion. The principle progress has therefore not unexpectedly been made in relation to these costs rather than to those of programme expenditures which can be more difficult to measure and control (especially if they are led by demand).

The progress on performance indicators has followed a similar pattern. Development has been most rapid in relation to executive activities (e.g. tax gathering and transfer payments). On the other hand, progress has been less marked in policy work, i.e. policy formulation and regulation, or where running costs constitute a very small proportion of total departmental costs. The NAO observed that there were inherent difficulties in assessing the effectiveness of programme expenditures. This remains so, not least because these are the areas in which the FMI touches on the politically sensitive.

Similar constraints have influenced the establishment of top management systems. Again, in some form or other, these are now in place in every department. However, comprehensiveness and effectiveness vary and their lack of integration with other management systems reflects the complexity and nature of departmental activities and organization. In practice these information systems have also illustrated some of the operational issues raised by the FMI. The systems often depend for their data bases, for example, on large amounts of material generated and collated by lower level managers. However, the relevance of all this can be easily lost, especially when, as is often the case, programme information has to be somewhat arbitrarily extrapolated from establishment profiles. Thus, data provision has come to be regarded as an imposition impeding rather than facilitating efficiency and effectiveness and generally undermining the credibility and validity of the system. Top management systems have therefore progressed more effectively where their operational relevance has been clear to those using them.

For many observers the pace of these changes has, by Whitehall standards, been rapid. Many of the developments reported by the NAO, for example, were in place in some form or another within three years. One factor governing the effectiveness of this was the availability of the necessary expertise. If a department lacked not only systematic financial data but also personnel with the necessary skills (accounting, computing, etc.) to develop the systems, then it took time to establish itself. In some cases expertise was brought in through management consultancies and software acquisitions.

The cost of change is difficult to assess. The NAO indicated that the costs of introducing systems were only measurable in the broadest terms and that departments found it difficult to make any calculation of the cost effectiveness of the FMI other than in terms of changing management attitudes and practice. It concluded that it was unrealistic to expect a quantified assessment of the costs and benefits of the FMI.

Accountability and the Financial Management Initiative

The thrust of delegated budgetary systems is to push financial responsibility down the line and to hold individuals accountable for the management of resources. But what is meant by 'accountable' in this context? In essence it arises from stewardship, i.e. a relationship in which one party entrusts resources and responsibilities to another on the basis of given or assumed codes or understandings. Accountable management is the systematic extension of this relationship down and throughout an organization. Until the 1980s this concept was little spoken of in British government (notwithstanding its endorsement by the Fulton Committee in 1968). But the introduction of the FMI has altered that. The mechanisms of delegated budgetary control hold managers to account for the (especially financial) resources allocated and consumed. Also, through the development of performance indicators and other methods of evaluation, responsibilities and accountability become more visible, an argument used by the Treasury in White Papers on public expenditure (1986–9) which have included increasing numbers of departmental performance indicators.

Aspects of the FMI can also be argued to have strengthened ministerial accountability and facilitated external scrutiny. Top management systems, for example, are said to increase ministerial ability to control and account for departmental activities. Admittedly, few ministers have followed the example of Michael Heseltine, who published the details of MINIS. Nevertheless, a case can be made that the FMI reforms not only improve the efficiency and effectiveness of civil service operations but also assist in increasing the internal and external accountability of ministers as managers. However, this can hide paradoxes and problems in the new world of delegated budgets and tensions between politicians and managers.

Our recent research supports the contention that the practice of the FMI has yet to fulfil the accountable management ideal. In the exercise of responsibilities effective autonomy has tended to be limited and judgements dominated by input and financial criteria rather than by efficiency and effectiveness. Discretion is restricted and control is retained at the centre, in departments by ministers and senior officials and at the heart of government by the Treasury. In part this reflects the centralizing tendencies of the systems introduced and in part the inevitable tensions between political management and resource management. Ministers in particular view the world in political (and ideological) rather than in resource and policy management terms. They tend therefore to prefer to distance themselves from techniques such as the FMI or to use its results for political purposes.

Accountable management may therefore be restricted in both form and practice. Within central government and its departments discretions are limited and essential control is still centralized through the new systems. In terms of external accountability and control, ministers and civil servants still remain answerable in much the same way as before. Real changes may yet come, however, with the further development of executive agencies in which chief executives are made directly responsible for specified activities. But if one emphasis in this development is improved service to the client we might ask who the client is. One official reply is that the client is the minister, another that is the general public whose interest is guarded by the department or the government itself. Hence, ideas that departmental activities should be accountable to the public, other than in a general sense, find little favour at the centre of Whitehall, Hence, as with many recent changes, the rhetoric of the debate continues to mask the political reality.

The FMI's Contribution to Civil Service Management

The sheer persistence of the FMI suggests that it might stand as one of the most successful attempts at management reform in the civil service. Perhaps the lessons of 30 years of continuous upheaval are being learnt. However, if we wish to understand the implications for the future reform of resource management (i.e. consolidate the strengths and accommodate the weaknesses), we need to consider the implementation of the FMI more systematically. One way to make such an assessment is to consider the nature of the general contribution which the FMI has made to management in government. In a recent book *The Strategy Process* (1988) Mintzberg, Quinn and James identified three modes of management found in various combinations in modern organizations. The entrepreneurial mode is characterized by a pro-active approach to decision opportunities, by long-term decision horizons and by flexibility of response to changing circumstances. The adaptive mode is essentially reactive, short-term, and concerned with marginal adjustments. The planning mode is analytical, long-term and integrated. None is inherently preferable to any other; it is a matter of the organization adopting modes consistent with the management demands made upon it by different environments.

Our researches suggest that the FMI has indeed contributed to a more effective way of dealing with an environment of resource constraint. It has contributed to a more considered adaptive mode in central government. Its focus in practice on finance (input) rather than policy (output), on the readily measurable and controllable and on the enhancement of economic rationality has led to a more systematic consideration of the use of resources in the management of government. But this has tended to emphasize resource management for its own sake rather than for what these resources can produce. This has led to a frustration amongst both senior and middle managers, who see unrealized planning and even entrepreneurial opportunities in the new systems.

One reason for this imbalance in the contribution which the FMI makes to management stems from the limited use of top management systems and policy evaluation. Another cause is the way financial management has been developed independently of other management processes, notably those of human resources and policy. These problems arise, in turn, from an ambiguity of objectives in much of public management. The government's policy of restraining public expenditure led it to seek control of both departmental expenditures and manpower. This has resulted in some absurdities in management decisions which would not be tolerated in the type of private sector organization the government often uses as a role model. Thus, proposals for manpower which would contribute positively to effectiveness and even to revenue raising have been turned down because they would increase civil service numbers. In the course of our research we were informed of several occasions when this had occurred or when the ability to retain resource surpluses had been severely limited. Given this it is of interest to note that one aspect of the *Next Steps* initiative has been the attempt, for some executive agencies at least, to create a more flexible financial regime in which management can operate (Cm. 914, 1989).

Hence, the FMI needs to be extended in scope to allow more effective managerial discretion over resource allocation and consumption (e.g. in staff appointments, retention of savings, reductions in annuality rules, etc.) The view of the Efficiency Unit is that the establishment of executive agencies could provide the appropriate structural conditions for the FMI to make a more comprehensive contribution to management. This may well be the case. More attention, however, will need to be paid in this (as with management change in general) to the problems of implementation.

Implementing Management Reform: The Way Forward

The experience of the FMI adds considerable evidence to support our view that successful implementation requires strategies which systematically identify and plan for meeting the different sets of preconditions in the engineering of the management of change. These sets of preconditions are the technical, the organizational and the political ones. Each has to be provided independently and in concert, for each works with others to influence the character of the implementation process and therefore the success of the change.

In technical terms the FMI's initial development faced difficulties in both the availability of financial and related skills and also the design of the information systems. Both problems were recognized. Departments set out to recruit appropriately qualified staff and to invest in training programmes for those already in post, but these efforts were limited by manpower and financial constraints. However, resources were found to employ external consultants to diagnose, prescribe and in many cases to provide departmental management accounting systems.

Attention was also paid to organizational issues, particularly to the overall direction and co-ordination of the initiative and to its management within departments. The logic of accountable management, however, is one of differentiation. There is a need therefore for integrating mechanisms to prevent consequent fragmentation. The failure to provide these, for example, by linking human resources management processes such as manpower planning with financial management, has reduced the FMI's contribution to the planning and entrepreneurial modes described above.

The consistent provision of political authority has been perhaps the most distinctive feature of the FMI compared to previous reforms. Overcoming the resistance requires political drive. This emanated from Mrs Thatcher, even if she was not always supported by many of her cabinet and junior ministerial colleagues. It is this authority, however, which provided legitimacy for the efforts of the Treasury and others at the centre who directed the FMI.

Conclusions

With the publication of the Efficiency Unit's report on *The Next Steps* and the subsequent establishment of executive agencies, questions were raised about the future of the FMI. Has it failed or run into the sand? Will agencies take the FMI's developments further and provide real managerial freedom and efficiency? The agency programme has its merits, but it should not be seen as a replacement for the FMI. Indeed, agencies could damage some of its achievements, not least because of the way the idea is predicated on organizational disaggregation rather than integration. In spite of the criticisms made above, the strength of the conception of public management embodied in the FMI lies with its respect for external and internal departmental differences and its recognition of the need to provide an integrated management framework within which the manager can be granted increasing freedoms. To date the willingness actually to provide this framework has been lacking. But this is a political problem often based on a calculation of how far any system for managerial improvement can increase strategic political advantage, political support and, on occasions, aid survival. In brief, like many other past initiatives, recent management changes are seen as useful insofar as they serve (or fail to serve) political ends. These are not issues that the agency programme or other developments can immediately solve. When they are solved, however, the acronym will have to be changed, for then there will be no longer an 'initiative' concerned principally with 'finance', but simply and effectively 'management'.

References

Cm. 914 (1989) *The Financing and Accountability of Next Steps Agencies*. London: HMSO.

Cmnd. 8616 (1982) *Efficiency and Effectiveness in the Civil Service*. London: HMSO.

(The White Paper that announced the FMI.)

Cmnd. 9058 (1983) *Financial Management in Government Departments*. London: HMSO. (The first of two government progress reports.)

Cmnd. 9297 (1984) *Progress in Financial Management in Government*. London: HMSO. (The second government progress report.)

Committee of Public Accounts (1987) *The Financial Management Initiative* (HC 61, 1987–88). London: HMSO. (The Public Accounts Committee's assessment of the FMI.)

Efficiency Unit (1988) *Improving Management in Government: the next steps*. London: HMSO. (The report that argued for the creation of executive agencies.)

Gray, A.G. and Jenkins, W. I. (1985) *Administrative Politics in British Government*. Brighton: Wheatsheaf

Mintzberg, H., Quinn, J. B. and James, R. M. (1988) *The Strategy Process*. Englewood Cliffs, NJ: Prentice-Hall.

National Audit Office (1987) *The Financial Management Initiative* (HC 588, 1986–87). London: HMSO. (The NAO's evaluation of progress.)

— (1989) *The Next Steps Initiative* (HC 410, 1988–89). London: HMSO.

Treasury and Civil Service Committee (1988) *Civil Service Management Reform: the next steps* (HC 494, 1987–88). London: HMSO.

— (1989) *Developments in the Next Steps Programme* (HC 348, 1988–89). London: HMSO.

12

Changes in Resource Management in the Social Services

Norman Warner

Major changes took place during the 1980s in the way social services departments operate. There have been changing public and political expectations, together with new legislation and approaches to service delivery. Funding mechanisms have grown ever more complex. The sources of finance for a social services department have increased, even if the total amount available never seems quite enough. Local authorities generally have undergone considerable changes and their social services departments have not been immune from these. The cumulative effect of these changes has been a significant shift in the way resources are managed. Before exploring some of the major changes and their implications for resource management, it is worth outlining the context in which a social services department operates in the 1990s.

A Mixed Economy of Welfare

There will no doubt continue to be a few people who argue for the state to take over responsibility for the financing and provision of all welfare services; just as, at the other extreme, there will be people asserting that the state has no business in the provision of social services. The current position is an established public and political commitment – confirmed in well over 30 Acts of Parliament – to ensuring that there are publicly funded social services available to try to prevent vulnerable people slipping into such difficulty that they become serious social casualties. However, there is little prescription about how these services are provided and local authorities do not have to rely on direct provision.

The placing of statutory responsibilities on local authority social services departments reflects a concern that has been around for more than two decades about having a single focal point for social services in particular localities. Social services departments were established in 1971 with the purpose of integrating into a single department the services for children, for the disabled and elderly and for the mentally ill. This reorganization followed the Seebohm Report which wanted 'a single door on which to knock' for those in need of personal social services. Despite occasional outbursts to the contrary, this philosophy of integration of services for a range of client groups still holds the public and political middle ground. The government's decision at the end of the 1980s to make social services the lead agency for community care has confirmed the co-ordinating and integrating role of social services departments.

Social services departments have never been the only providers of social care and support. For example, they have always relied heavily on foster parents to look after many of their children in care. However, in recent years there has been a significant shift in the balance between local authority and independent provision of social care.

During the 1980s the government, somewhat inadvertently, allowed the social security system to stimulate a dramatic expansion of private and voluntary sector residential and nursing-home care. In ten years social security expenditure in this sector went from well under £100 million a year to about £1.3 billion. Voluntary sector provision of day care and hostels has expanded considerably, but often with public money. Many health authorities have funded hostels, group homes and residential care as part of the rundown of long-stay hospitals. New domiciliary care agencies have appeared. Housing associations have expanded into the field of social housing with care programmes, and housing authorities have built many sheltered housing schemes with integral support services. Although social services departments still run a lot of direct services themselves, they have become minority suppliers of some services in some parts of the country (e.g. residential and day care for the elderly).

What has happened in the past decade is the development of a true mixed economy of welfare with a larger – and growing – range of direct service providers. The social services departments still have extensive powers to ensure that particular services are provided but it is increasingly recognized that they need not provide the services themselves. They are becoming enablers, enforcers, planners and co-ordinators. The process is far from complete and developments have proceeded at a different pace in different parts of the country. Nevertheless a trend has been established and it has considerable implications for the way resources are managed.

Other Changes in the 1980s

There have been other changes at work in local government in the 1980s that have also had a considerable impact on the way social services are managed. These are described briefly below:

1 *Decentralization/devolution.* There has been a major shift in many local authorities towards decentralization of decision-making about service delivery. This has meant devolving more authority for making decisions to managers and staff who are closer to the people receiving services. This has often been done as an act of political or managerial faith without full understanding of all the consequences.

2 *Customers first.* A genuine change of attitude has taken place in many local authorities towards those who receive services. There is a real and growing wish on the part of many managers and staff to treat service users as customers. This involves consulting and negotiating more with the service users themselves, and changing the patterns of service delivery. This thread is closely associated with decentralization or devolution.

3 *New responsibilities.* In the early 1980s the rhetoric was that government would be removed from the backs of the people and that local authorities were not to be entrusted with new duties. The reality was a flow of legislation placing new responsibilities on local authority social services departments. There was the Mental Health Act, 1983; the Registered Homes Act, 1984; the Disabled Persons' Act, 1986; the Access to Personal Files Act, 1987; the Children Act, 1989; and the NHS and Community Care Act, 1990. Key features of much of this legislation were that it both increased the right of individual citizens to seek services from local authorities and at the same time extended local authority regulatory and 'social policing' functions.

4 *Contracting.* The 1980s has seen the emergence of some form of contract culture in local government alongside the greater emphasis on consumer choice. It began with compulsory competitive tendering for many local authority services. It has been reinforced by internal local government moves to decentralization, with many service departments like social services demanding to have proper service level agreements or contracts with central departments like finance, legal services, information systems and property management. It is now reaching further into social services departments through the changes emanating from the NHS and Community Care Act 1990. These lead towards an organizational split within departments between service purchasers and service providers, with contracts linking the two. This purchaser/provider split has profound implications for resource management, as will be described later.

5 *Managerialism.* Social services departments have been swept along with the surge of public sector managerialism in the 1980s. More directors of social services have no professional social work qualification and a few have no background in social services. As with the NHS, more general managers are being appointed at different levels within social services departments. The nomenclature of jobs has changed: e.g. team leaders

are increasingly team managers. Increasing numbers of social services staff are obtaining formal management qualifications. With public demand for services exceeding the ability to finance them, the emphasis in social services has shifted in favour of people who can manage resources carefully and creatively. Local authorities at risk of rate-capping or charge-capping do not want their social services run by people who regard these services as totally demand-led and who are unable to manage budgets.

6 *Performance review.* There has been greater public demand for more accountable local authorities; growth in the number of service providers; a growing concern with value for money in the public sector; and pressure to target limited resources on key targets. This has led in social services to a growing concern with performance review. There is an emphasis on assessing effectiveness and quality that was almost totally absent ten years ago. There is much more monitoring of performance with data being collected on outputs and even, occasionally, on outcomes. Individual performance is appraised more regularly and systematically and in some cases an individual's pay is influenced by performance assessment.

7 *Forward planning.* The thrust of managerialism, the pressure on resources and the growing understanding that it takes time to introduce new services has given a boost to planning. But the increasing emphasis on trying to plan ahead has often been frustrated by the public sector's obsessive preoccupation with annuality in the way it controls resources and by the attendant financial crises. However, some social services departments are developing three-year plans, usually as part of their local authority's medium-term planning process. This approach has been given some support by the government's decisions on community care. There has been considerable emphasis in the Department of Health guidance, not only on the need for joint planning with the NHS, but also on the need to plan ahead in developing community care strategies and plans. All this is a long way from the anti-corporatist rhetoric of the early 1980s that made forward planning difficult.

The Impact of Community Care on Resource Management

Most of the factors described above come together in the changes in community care set out in the White Paper, *Caring for People* and incorporated in the NHS and Community Care Act 1990. Those changes require a 'customer first' approach; devolution of management decision-making and budgets; contracting with a multiplicity of service providers – some in-house and some external; greater managerialism; performance review; and forward planning. It is worth describing in some detail the impact of the community care changes because they encapsulate how social services are having to change their approach to resource management. Under the community care changes, social services departments are required to put in place several key features:

- A system for assessing individual needs and ensuring appropriate responses in the light of those assessments. This is described as case management or care management; increasingly the latter term is used.
- Arrangements for contracting with various service providers to meet the collective needs expressed in the individual assessments. This is described variously as commissioning, contracting or service development.
- The treatment of external and internal providers of services on a more even-handed basis when contracts are awarded. This has the effect of turning in-house providers of services into business units trading separately within the social services department – the so-called purchaser/provider split.
- The establishment of independent 'arm's length' registration and inspection units. These will require in-house residential care providers to meet the same requirements of the Registered Homes Act as private and voluntary sector residential care providers.
- The preparation of community care plans in consultation with other agencies, especially health authorities.

The organizational implications of these changes are profound. Different social services departments are responding in different ways. Some are finding it difficult to face up to the full implications. The government announcement in July 1990 that full implementation of the community care changes would be delayed from April 1991 to April 1993 allows those who would prefer to change slowly to do so. Nevertheless, in the medium term it will be difficult to resist reshaping Social Services organizations and resource management systems in line with the government's changes.

The logic of these changes has encouraged some social services departments to separate their activities into different streams:

- care management for individuals;
- in-house service providers;
- contracting and service development;
- inspection or quality control;
- planning.

It is possible to group planning with contracting and service development, but the other activities usually stay as separate streams. The question then arises as to how resources are to be managed through this new organizational pattern. Here there are sometimes differences of view. The role of care management is crucial in determining how resources are to be managed.

Care Management

There is widespread agreement on five main roles for care managers:

- co-ordinating the assessment of individual need;
- developing an individual care plan with the customer and carer;
- securing the actual provision of services by in-house or external providers;
- monitoring the delivery of services from the customer's perspective;
- reviewing the assessment with the individual customers and their carers.

The dispute is often over the sixth role, as budget holder for buying the services in individual care plans.

Some people have argued that it is impossible for a care manager to reconcile the role of assessing individual need with the task of operating within an approved budget. Others have argued that resource constraints and therefore a rationing system are an inevitable part of health and social care; and that it is better for the reconciliation of individual needs and wishes with the budgetary reality to take place 'close to the customer'. Making these reconciliations at the local level through negotiation between care manager and member of the public seems likely to achieve faster service delivery than arbitration through reference to a remote bureaucratic hierarchy. However, there are strong centralizing tendencies in public sector management and only time will tell which approach prevails. What is clear is that influence over resource commitment is shifting towards care managers. Even where they do not actually commission the services directly, they are effectively writing a prescription for somebody else to dispense.

Care managers are unlikely to have total freedom to purchase whatever they want, even where they control the cheque book. They are always likely to be offering people services from a 'menu' of items, some of which they have obtained but many of which will have been commissioned by a contracting unit. Such units should, ideally, build up their picture of what services to buy in bulk from the care managers themselves because the latter should be 'logging up' shortfalls in service availability from their individual assessments. The contracting units are trying to balance several factors: service needs; quality control; price; and continuity of supply. In the early years the information available to them is likely to be deficient and this will make it difficult to form judgements over which service suppliers represent value for money.

Contracting

Those contracting for services face a dilemma. Do they opt for maximum competition with a long list of approved suppliers available to care managers and service users? This is likely to give little security to service suppliers and make for discontinuity of supply. This is a high-risk strategy, given the vulnerable nature of many of the service users – the elderly, the disabled and the mentally ill. Alternatively, do those commissioning services move more cautiously towards a contract culture involving more settled relationships with a more limited number of suppliers? This latter course seems the more likely medium-term outcome because it has several major advantages:

- it secures continuity of supply for individual users;
- supply is less likely to be disrupted by the unexpected withdrawal of suppliers or the buying-up of services by other authorities;
- a settled relationship is more likely to secure high quality services;
- the monitoring task is more manageable and cheaper without a huge number of suppliers.

It also helps with the transition to separate in-house service suppliers to have them operating on a more contractual basis within the local authority. These services have major problems of transition to a contract culture in many local authorities.

Some local authorities want to test whether – or to show that – their own in-house services represent value for money. The only way to do this is to separate out these activities (e.g. residential care, day care) into independent business units and operate them on a trading account and contracting basis. These separate units then contract with care managers or through contracting units for the provision of a given level of service at an agreed price for a specified period of time. The service agreement or contract needs to have reasonable periods of notice for major changes. The units themselves in turn have to develop agreements with other in-house providers of support services (e.g. finance, personnel) aimed at keeping their overheads as low as possible. The effect of this activity is to bring out the true cost of the local authority service so that it is comparable with external suppliers of a similar service. The unit costs of these in-house business units start to become crucial to whether care managers or contracting units want to buy their services in the longer term.

Local authorities differ in their comfort levels with this more business-like approach to running in-house care services. Budgetary pressures will push many along this path, particularly where there are alternative suppliers with whom they could enter into contracts. For the more adventurous authorities there is the prospect of more efficient and successful in-house business units selling their spare capacity to other authorities and reducing their charges to their own authority.

There are separate monitoring arrangements for these three different streams of resource management:

- Care managers have case-loads and keep individual care plans under review to ensure that the resources used continue to be appropriate for assessed needs.
- Contracting units carry out contract enforcement functions in respect of service suppliers, internal or external.
- All suppliers of residential care have to conform to the standards provided for under the Registered Homes Act, 1984. From April 1991 local authorities have had to enforce those standards through 'arm's length' inspection and registration units whose line management is independent of any management arrangements for local authority residential care.

Thus, as the management of resources has been divided into three separate streams, so the monitoring and quality assurance requirements have become more elaborate and demanding.

Planning

Further complexity is added by the obligation on social services departments to produce community care plans on a basis of consultation and agreement with other agencies, especially health authorities. This represents an attempt to knit health and social care more closely together into a 'seamless service' as far as the service user is concerned. There is also a wish on the government's part to secure better use of public sector resources through more integrated plans. However, there are still significant barriers to shifting resources across organizational boundaries, the most significant of which is the absence of any clear definition of what constitutes health care or social care. This can provide major scope for inter-agency friction in spheres such as mental health, services for the profoundly and multiply handicapped, dementia among the elderly and nursing home provision.

Nevertheless, a model for community care planning is starting to emerge in some authorities. This embraces some attempt at public acceptance amongst the agencies of shared principles underpinning service provision and some jointly agreed policy statements relating to the delivery of particular services. Increasingly, a wide range of agencies and some consumers are involved in the construction of plans. These approaches provide a basis for a social services department to produce plans after a process along the following lines:

- assessing future need, using information on historical trends in demand, social epidemiology data from health authorities and other sources and aggregating service demands from care managers;
- collecting information on sources of service supply and identifying shortfalls;
- adjusting policies and priorities and broadly allocating resources between major services;
- developing strategies for improving matching of supply to demand;
- devising critical success factors for plans (i.e. performance indicators and targets);
- monitoring actual performance against plan.

The Community Care Model of Resource Management

What is beginning to develop is a much more complex model of resource management for social services departments. Figure 12.1 attempts to capture the main elements of this model and the interaction of the different parts. There is no reason for thinking that this model is not transferable to the children and families services which form most of the remainder of a social services department's activities. It is likely that some departments will start to use it in whole or in part as they move to implement the Children Act, 1989, from October 1991 onwards.

Wider Issues of Planning, Management and Accountability

Changes in resource management in social services are starting to go beyond community care. A few social services departments have tried to improve the way they plan, manage and account for resources through more coherent management systems that encompass strategic forward planning and individual accountability. These changes point the way for the future. The evolving systems may embrace elements such as:

1 *Strategic management*, which is a process for balancing an organization's performance requirement (the sum of the internal and external demands on it) with its capability (the sum of the factors contributing to its ability to perform) at a pace appropriate to its situation.

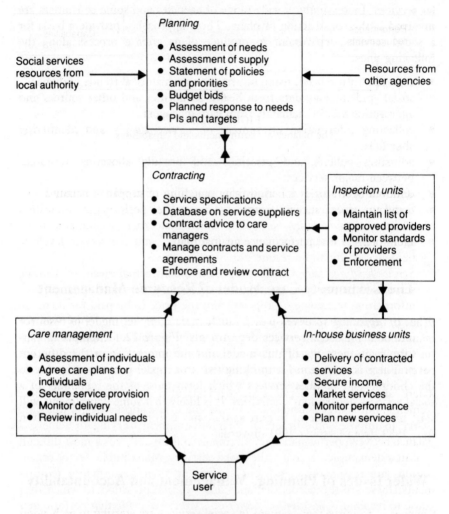

Social services
resources from
local authority

Resources from
other agencies

Planning

- Assessment of needs
- Assessment of supply
- Statement of policies
  and priorities
- Budget bids
- Planned response to needs
- PIs and targets

Contracting

- Service specifications
- Database on service suppliers
- Contract advice to care
  managers
- Manage contracts and service
  agreements
- Enforce and review contract

Inspection units

- Maintain list of
  approved providers
- Monitor standards
  of providers
- Enforcement

Care management

- Assessment of individuals
- Agree care plans for
  individuals
- Secure service provision
- Monitor delivery
- Review individual needs

In-house business units

- Delivery of contracted
  services
- Secure income
- Market services
- Monitor performance
- Plan new services

Service
user

FIGURE 12.1
The community care model of resource management

2 *Medium-term planning*, which is a process of producing plans for the
   development of services over a three-year period. They involve statements of policy and targeting of resources, and effectively place in the
   public arena the choices made by politicians and managers.
3 *Business plans*, which are statements of business objectives to be

FIGURE 12.2
The balance of requirements and capabilities

achieved over a shorter period than a medium-term plan – usually a year
– and the associated resources.
4 *Resource accountability statements*, which state each accountable manager's annual budget (money and manpower) and the service levels to
   be delivered for those resources.
5 *Service level agreements*, which represent a contractual means of defining
   services to be provided by support services (e.g. personnel, finance, law,
   information technology, property) and the price to be paid for them.
6 *Staff appraisal schemes*, which are a means of setting objectives for
   individual managers to achieve in a given period and appraising performance: these usually have a staff development element in the appraisal process and pay may be linked to adequate performance.

There are few social services departments that have adopted all these
elements, but a larger number are attempting to use approaches of this kind
to try to impose some order on their environment. Trying to achieve a
balance between performance requirements and capability is a most difficult
task in a demand-led activity like social services. Many public sector organizations are reasonably competent at defining their performance requirements: these are the needs, demands and external pressures to which they
chose to respond. Considerably fewer effectively reconcile that performance
requirement with their capability. In a well-managed organization with
realistic plans, these two factors should be in balance, as shown in figure
12.2.

Some social services departments are trying to assess their capability more
carefully to see if the cash, manpower and other resources available to them
match the performance requirements. Capability includes the clarity and
effectiveness of management, the structure of the organization and the
values and habits of staff. Where the capability has deficiencies, these either
have to be made good or politicians have to be persuaded that their expectations have to be reduced in terms of performance requirements. This is not

always an easy task but the existence of proper planning, review and budgetary processes make it easier.

Medium-term planning is being given greater momentum by the community care changes. Some social services departments have been trying to produce medium-term plans for their main client groups (the elderly, the mentally ill, children with a learning disability, those with a physical disability) that articulate:

- policies
- service needs
- priorities
- resources
- service targets
- previous performance.

These plans are often produced after consultation with health authorities and other agencies and sometimes with the involvement of service users.

In some authorities there are regular review mechanisms in which particular services are reviewed each year. This can lead to proposals to expand services or to cut them back or to reshape them. These reviews may be integrated into the planning process and their results incorporated into the medium-term plans. To be effective these reviews and plans should be integrated into a local authority's budgetary process, so that proposals for growth or savings from reviews or plans are taken into account when each year's budget is set. This is not easy to do unless an authority's programme for reviews, planning and budgetary processes dovetail into each other. This means having the results of reviews and medium-term plans ready by each autumn, when information on the next financial year's resources becomes available. When resources are going to be scarce – as has often been the case for some local authorities with rates and charges capped – then timely service reviews and medium-term plans have made it easier to reach judgements on priorities for resource allocation. It is the absence of proper service review arrangements and medium-term planning that has revealed an air of crisis management in some authorities when there have been resource cut-backs in social services.

Until recently strategic management, medium-term plans and annual budget exercises have not been linked effectively to individual management performance. The idea of business plans for parts of a social services department is starting to fill this gap in a few authorities. In simple terms, business plans connect strategy with service delivery. The business plan shows the targeted resources (cash, manpower, buildings, etc.) for delivering specific service changes and the order in which they are to be made. Collectively these changes in service delivery amount to a strategic change of direction for particular client groups, set out in medium-term plans. The business plans themselves can fulfil the role of action plans for individual managers and provide a basis for appraising individual performance.

Conclusion

Social services departments are starting to change their patterns of service delivery and resource management in the direction described above. However, they are not behaving in a uniform way; any generalization is likely to be inaccurate and many authorities have only taken a few hesitant steps along the paths described. The direction is often set by a few authorities, with others following with varying degrees of reluctance and enthusiasm. The costs of transition are considerable but it is almost impossible to give reliable figures. Many, if not most, local authorities have not devolved support services (e.g. finance, personnel) budgets or staff to their social services departments. This makes both the costing and delivery of change more difficult. In some authorities the management capability is insufficient to introduce the full range of changes described.

It is likely to be well into the 1990s before nearly all social services departments have managerial control over the full range of resources they are attempting to manage. It will be even longer before all have the kind of planning, management, budgeting and accountability systems described above – systems that would enable them to say they are managing their resources strategically with some kind of balance between performance requirements and capability. Nevertheless a directional change is taking place along the lines described.

Most social services departments will deliver the main ingredients of the community care changes described above by April 1993. This will force them to adapt their planning and management systems and devolve more responsibility for resource management lower in their organizations. In turn they will have to divide their budgets up more accurately between different internal managers and this will expose many inadequacies in budgetary provision and control.

Probably the most serious problem facing social services in these changes is the inadequacy of their information systems. Most social services departments rely for much of their financial and management information on mainframe systems run by and for the local authority's central departments. These systems are not geared up to organizations with a large number of decentralized units making their own resource management decisions. There is great difficulty linking financial, manpower and service information for most social services managers.

The result is a need for major investment in new social services information systems which build from the bottom up. The care managers need systems that support their case-load management work. The direct service providers require up-to-date data on costs, usage and income. The planners and service developers need systems which aggregate information from the care managers and service providers. For the most part these systems exist in only the most rudimentary form in a few authorities. There is a minimum investment requirement of about £100–£200 million over three years or so to bring social services information systems up to some minimum standard of what is required to effectively manage devolved care systems, and the separation of service providers from service purchasers. Many politicians are unwilling to make the investment required and some central departments are reluctant to see their authority crumble, with resources being shifted from them to a service department like social services.

Some politicians are also uncomfortable with some of the changes taking place. They see resource commitments being made at lower levels in social services departments and wonder if both political and financial control is being lost. In some respects they *are* losing political control over detailed decisions about service delivery, but financial control tends to be greater with more precise budgets issued to more accountable managers closer to the service delivery point. However, these managers start to expose service shortfalls more precisely and publicly and this increases political nervousness. Some politicians consider they are being asked to be accountable publicly for a myriad of resource decisions over which they have little control.

Politicians are also being asked to commit themselves more to medium-term plans which in turn commit resources for several years ahead without any great certainty that those resources will be available. There is a growing mismatch between the forward-planning approach of the new managerialism and community care implementation and the year-on-year uncertainty about local authority funding. This requires social services managers to handle ambiguity and conflict with increasing political sophistication and public exposure. Not all these managers are up to the demands made by the changing patterns of resource management in the social services departments of the 1990s.

To secure the service delivery benefits of the management changes described, many politicians will have to change their roles. They will have to concentrate more on shaping strategic policies, agreeing medium-term plans, settling the broad allocation of resources between major service areas and monitoring policy outcomes. They will have to stop interfering in detailed budgetary and operational acceptance of the need for more investment in information systems and adequate personnel and financial support for managers delivering services: what one government minister has called 'administrative slum clearance'. These support changes will mean politicians transferring power, responsibility and funding from central departments to service departments in many local authorities.

13

Resource Management in the National Health Service

David Symes

The History and Scope of the Initiative

The resource management initiative in the NHS started in 1986 as an experiment at six large acute hospitals. The intention was that the different approaches adopted in these sites would be evaluated before any extension. Earlier attempts to improve the accuracy of cost information related to individual medical specialties had led to tensions between doctors and accountants at many of the 'management budgeting' pilot sites. In response the 1986 initiative was announced by the then NHS Management Board, with the agreement of the Joint Consultants Committee, a national committee representative of the Royal Colleges of individual medical specialities.

The initial progress at the experimental sites encouraged the government to extend and accelerate the initiative to complement the introduction of explicit contracts between purchasers and providers of health care – one of the main features of the reforms which they proposed following their review of the NHS. As a result 50 more sites were added to the programme in March 1989, and a further 50 in January 1990. In May 1990, 30 more were announced, bringing the total to 136, which represented about half of the large acute hospitals in England and Wales. The objective was to extend it to all 260 such hospitals by 1993. Formal evaluation of the six experimental sites was carried out, but the results were not available until the spring of 1991 (Buxton et al., 1991). Many doctors, therefore, perceived the extension of the initiative as a leap in the dark, while recognizing, albeit reluctantly, that the allocation of resources within hospitals, following the government's review, would require improvements in costing data. This was allied to a growing realization that their clinical practice could be threatened if unrealistic contract prices were to result in short-term closures of services.

The initial phase of resource management at most of the experimental sites involved a review of management structures and processes. An increasingly popular organizational 'solution' was to establish clinical directorates along the lines of the structure adopted at the Johns Hopkins Hospital in Baltimore and subsequently Guy's in London. This concentration on structure was supported strongly by then director of financial systems on the NHS Management Board because it was a visible statement of the primary objective of the initiative which was to 'put doctors and nurses into the driving seat in managing the resources they use'. Changing the decision making structure was not in itself sufficient to achieve this objective and early attention had also to be given to improving information systems and providing management support to the clinical directors.

The provision of support to clinical directors tended to take the form of a business manager and a nursing officer, although sometimes the nurse would be the business manager as well. Indeed, sometimes the nurse was the clinical director with a business manager in support. Differences in the salaries of those nurses and administrators drafted in to support clinical directors threatened at one time to thwart the initiative and required the introduction of new national pay scales to ensure equity.

These cultural changes were not limited to the experimental sites, however, and some large acute hospitals were practising resource management without being recognized or disseminating their success. One such hospital introduced 'clinical leaders' who were supported by a nursing officer and an accountant. Each quarter they would meet to review activity, staffing and financial information on a specialty basis, using simple graphs based on a few numbers drawn out of existing reporting systems. What made this hospital's approach work was that when the graphs showed that changes in behaviour or additional money might be needed, the discussion was not a face-off between accountants and doctors, but was used to examine a range of possible clinical responses. This was because the nurses, along with their knowledge of the clinical options, had also been trained to assert themselves and therefore challenged the doctors' initial assessment of what could be achieved.

At another hospital a rapport developed between its manager and medical staff as, together with the accountant, they tried to establish realistic prices for the provision of a range of specialized treatments paid for by the Regional Health Authority. On this occasion the persistence of the manager in involving doctors in the identification of the data needed to plan and monitor service levels resulted in the development of a joint database. Throughout this process the manager instilled among medical colleagues the belief that data should only be collected if the resulting information had the potential to lead to changes in behaviour.

At these two hospitals resource management was taking place, with doctors being actively involved in the management process, prior to their later inclusion in the 'roll out' programme. Both hospitals illustrate the importance of seeing resource management as a continuing process rather than as an 'initiative'. They also make it clear that organizational issues other than structure and systems are involved in putting doctors and nurses into the driving seat.

A useful framework for considering some of these wider organizational issues is the 'happy atom' of McKinsey's quoted by Peters and Waterman in their study *In Search of Excellence* (1982). This '7S framework' recognizes that successful organization change requires the parallel development of strategy, systems, skills, structure, symbolic behaviour (or style), staff and shared values. Like the game of cat's cradle played with a loop of string, it is possible for someone with skill to change the shape of the 'cradle' by pulling at threads in a particular order. If they succeed, all elements remain connected and the shape remains stable, although different from before. If someone without skill tries to repeat the process, more often than not the threads are not pulled in unison and the cradle becomes unstable and falls apart. The same can happen to organizations if attempts are made to alter their shape (or culture) by concentrating on one or two of the 7S qualities without recognizing the need to address the others.

Those experimental sites who saw the 'initiative' as being about structure and information systems began to find it difficult to move beyond improving their data collection and analysis to purposeful dialogue among clinicians about using resources to provide both better and more cost-effective patient care. One result of this was the growing recognition that the introduction of resource management by professionals would require a programme of organizational development over about three years, in addition to reviewing information systems and decision-making structures.

Figure 13.1 illustrates the scope of activities which have to be addressed if resource management by professionals in hospitals is to be achieved. The activities represent a hierarchy, with changes in behaviour resulting from dialogue based on intelligent analysis of meaningful data.

The remainder of this chapter focuses on each of these aspects before prescribing a sequence of activities which need to be addressed by any public service contemplating introducing resource management by professionals.

Data Collection, Coding and Processing

The day-to-day provision of caring and healing services to patients requires the availability of data about who the patient is, what their health needs might be, where they live, who their GP is, etc. To speed up the processing

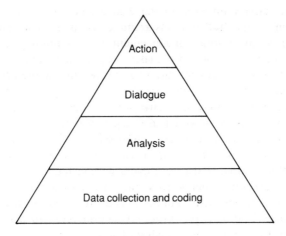

FIGURE 13.1
The scope of activities affected by resource management

of these individuals, hospitals have increasingly become dependent upon computer systems linked to a master index of present and past patients. Some of the experimental sites did not possess such a computerized patient administration system and a first priority for them was to make decisions about which system to purchase and how it would link to other data sources with which it would need to be integrated if accurate costs were to be provided to clinicians.

In considering these alternatives a number of sites decided that they needed to purchase completely integrated systems incorporating patient administration, nurse management, theatre management, pathology, radiology and pharmaceutical management systems, using ward-based terminals for 'ordering' services for individual patients. Systems developed in the USA for individual patient billing provided many of these facilities, but they were not in use in all American 'for profit' hospitals, because their running costs added to the overheads which needed to be recovered before profits were earned. Such a leap forward in data processing made major demands on the ability of staff to learn how to operate the new systems. Training became more important, though often as an afterthought, in an attempt to force the square pegs of existing staff into the round holes of the information system purchased for them.

At the same time evidence from the USA had indicated that the categorization of patients into groups of related diagnoses had helped in the reduction of the costs of acute hospitals. Research carried out at Yale

University had been used by the federal government to price related treatments in such a way that hospitals knew in advance what resources they would attract when treating certain conditions. In the past the hospitals committed resources and passed the cost along to the federal government or the insurer. The researchers at Yale had reduced the thousands of possible diagnoses and treatments to 467 diagnostic related groups (DRGs). The adoption of DRGs in the USA, when it changed from a 'pass along' payment system to a 'prospective payment' system, assisted in reducing overall costs as surplus capacity was squeezed out. This led the director of financial systems on the NHS Management Board to investigate the extent to which the DRGs used in the USA could be transferred to the UK (which had been in effect a prospective payment system since the introduction of cash limits). The use of DRGs appealed to doctors because it could release money for other clinical purposes and might provide them with data which could be used for auditing their quality of service.

One result of this was to involve doctors at some of the experimental sites in testing out existing DRGs. The initial work indicated that it would be possible to adopt DRGs to reduce the work-load data to a more manageable range, to which individual costs might be attributed. Later work with DRGs has indicated the need for modifications because some of the groupings are not homogeneous and in fact hide two, three or sometimes four different clinical treatments, each of which has different levels of resource use. This finding, and the knowledge that the length of stay of elderly patients was related more to their home circumstances than the condition from which they were suffering, led many doctors at the experimental and roll-out sites to look for a more flexible way of grouping their work-load.

These doctors sought a classification of diagnostic codes which would be hierarchical, with mutually exhaustive and exclusive categories. The basis of the DRGs, however, was an international classification, based on 18 major causes of death, which had none of these characteristics. This was a problem which had been faced by a GP in Loughborough when trying to analyse his own clinical work-load. He had developed, over a number of years, a classification which appealed to his fellow doctors in hospitals adopting resource management and which had the benefit for accountants of being able to fit onto the international classification and the 467 DRGs based upon it. This clinical classification was used increasingly in the resource management hospitals because it allowed individual doctors greater flexibility to create for themselves meaningful groupings of diagnoses and treatments. It therefore had value to them for medical audit purposes. The classification required further development and its later development costs were eventually met by the Department of Health, in recognition of the extent to which this UK clinical classification met with support from doctors.

The ability to group diagnoses and procedures in a meaningful way has encouraged many doctors to become more involved in improving the accuracy of coding. This was previously carried out by clerical staff whom the doctors rarely saw or talked to. The importance of accurate coding to the doctors at resource management hospitals resulted in these forgotten people being brought out of their basement offices and in some cases placed alongside the doctor's medical secretary. The coding of diagnoses and procedures then became a matter for discussion between clerical officer and doctor. This change in the status and importance of the coding clerks was accelerated by the government's review of the NHS, with the realization that accuracy in coding where a patient lives helped in the early recovery of costs from the appropriate health authority.

At one of the experimental sites the initial concentration was not upon structure or information systems, but upon the skills of doctors to process data about the profile of care which they would wish patients with particular conditions to experience. Elements of these profiles were then associated with standard costs and actual performance compared on a retrospective basis with what was expected and budgeted for. The resulting comparisons allowed clinicians to review their own use of resources and to use this as a basis for discussion with their colleagues. This is an example of fitting the information systems around the perceived and stated needs of those staff who possess the skills to undertake the processes required to achieve the organization's objectives (or mission/strategy). Although slower to show results, this approach of working with staff and designing systems from the bottom up achieved more in the medium term than those approaches which started from structure and imposed information systems upon staff.

Intelligent Analysis

The clinical information system, which was developed at this experimental site, illustrated the benefits of clarifying what pictures intelligent people would wish to see and would act upon. Early on, a further experimental site was added to the original six, in recognition of the advances made when it was a management budgeting site. The calculation of standard costs had progressed, following much detailed leg-work by accountants working with the heads of clinical support departments. The wealth of data which had by then been harvested was augmented by further information system development which built on existing systems, rather than replacing them with new systems. The breadth and depth of data available to this unit was most impressive and called out for a friendly way of interrogating the resulting database. An executive information system was purchased and was soon able to allow managers and clinicians to view related, previously collected data items in an informative and investigative manner. Sufficient data existed to gain an overview and to ask progressively more detailed questions. While this unit progressed from data collection to data analysis the generation of a climate for dialogue between clinicians remains to be addressed.

Preparing for Dialogue

The NHS system of performance indicators drew attention to extremes of performance and people became defensive about being at one extreme or the other in any national distribution. This was despite the fact that being at one of the extremes might be an objective which was being striven for. Experience with the use and abuse of performance indicators in the NHS suggests that when professionals and managers are presented with pictures which differ from their intuitive feel for what is happening their responses fall into one of the following categories:

1 *Data inaccuracies*: The picture is not true because of inaccuracies in the data.
2 *Data classification*: The picture is untrue, not because of data problems but because of the misleading way in which local data has been classified.
3 *Action already taken*: The picture is true and there is no problem with the way it is classified, but the necessary action has already been taken.
4 *Action about to be taken*: The picture is true, action has not yet been taken, but the necessary action is known and is about to be taken.
5 *The action required is outside my/our short-term control*: The picture is true, action has not yet been taken, nor is it about to be taken, but the necessary action is known; however, it requires capital investment or manpower approval which can only be taken with someone else's agreement.
6 *That's interesting (or oops!)*: This is where the picture has illuminated something about the process of health care locally which was not known and is worth investigating further.

Experience in the NHS suggests that about 20 per cent of pictures based on clusters of indicators of performance survive to the sixth category. The fifth and sixth represent the value of data collection and intelligent analysis, however, the cost which has to be set against this lies in the first four categories. This trade-off can appear to be a waste of time for some professionals and will continue to require auditors of professional performance to develop a sympathetic and trusting relationship. This sort of relationship is not arrived at without effort and needs to be prepared for.

To overcome potential antipathy to performance review and medical audit it is important that the professionals whose performance is being audited identify their own safe zones, being asked to account for variations outside this only when a significant change in quantum is required to move from outside to inside this zone. If a small change moves them from outside to inside the safe zone the picture is of little value.

The Lessons

A number of lessons emerge from the experience of the NHS in attempts to put professional staff in the driving seat and to take greater responsibility for the resources which they commit in treating individual patients:

1 It makes sense to involve existing staff in identifying what questions they need to have answers for, in order to carry out their role, before they are asked to specify what they want from an information system or they are presented with a solution that works somewhere else.

2 Clarifying roles in this way may alter the relative power and status of groups of staff and needs to be handled carefully.

3 Resource management represents an attempt to alter the culture of a hospital and, while structure and systems have a role to play, changes in these aspects have to be congruent with other factors such as skills, style, shared values and strategy (or purpose).

4 Organizational development of this degree is likely to take about three years. In the early days much preparation will be required with little achievement to show.

5 The tendency to go for a quick IT fix at the expense of adequate preparation will in the medium term prove to be mistaken and in the long term expensive. In developing information systems, failing to prepare is tantamount to preparing to fail.

6 The ability to measure the quality of care provided to individual patients and to compare this with an expected profile for groups of treatments should be seen as a major objective of resource management. A spin-off from this would be that such data can then be associated with standard costs to allow the quantifiable three Es of economy, efficiency and effectiveness to be integrated with qualitative measures of performance so that an informed dialogue can take place.

7 Professional staff need to be involved at the start if they are to ensure that the pace of change is one with which they are comfortable and to avoid solutions being foisted onto them.

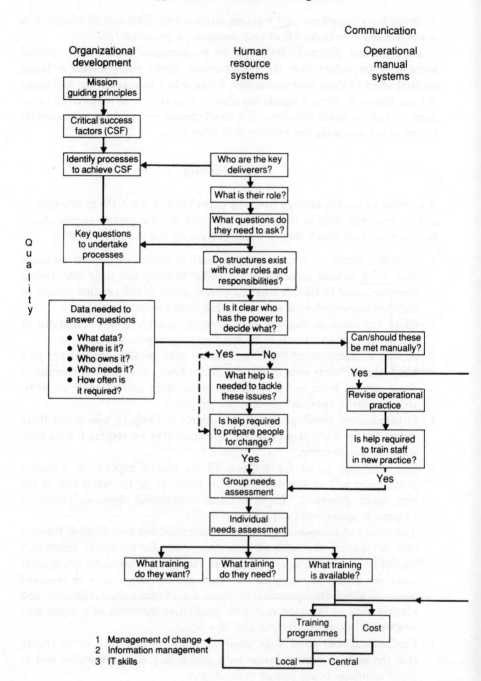

Computer systems   Computer
hardware

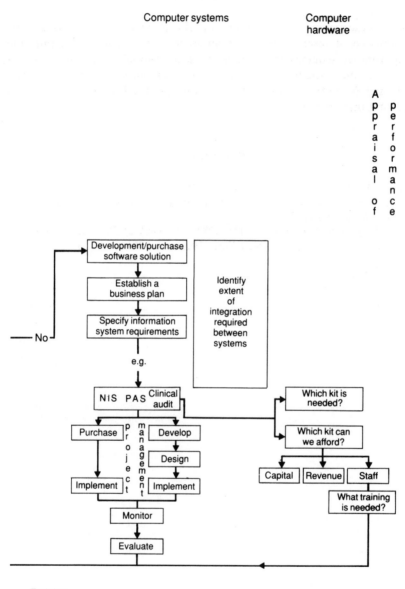

Training

FIGURE 13.2
Activities involved in resource management in the NHS

The Way Forward

Based on the experience of handling the change process associated with the introduction of resource management in the NHS, figure 13.2 puts into an appropriate sequence the actions which need to take place in developing the organization, the people who work in the organization, the systems that they operate and the information technology needed to assist them in operating these systems.

References

Buxton, M., Packwood, T. and Keen, J. (1991) *Final Report of the Brunel University Evaluation of Resource Management.* Uxbridge: Health Economics Research Group, Research Report no. 10.

Peters, T. J. and Waterman, R. H. (1982) *In Search of Excellence: lessons from America's best-run companies.* New York: Harper and Row.

New Approaches to Resource Management: Reflections

Stephen Harrison and Christopher Pollitt

There is a lot of common ground between the four preceding chapters. In particular, all four authors, in their different ways, demonstrate that it is misguided for either managers or politicians to think that reforms in resource management can be separated off and dealt with as some kind of self-contained technical exercise. On the contrary, the histories of resource management in the NHS and the universities, FMI in Whitehall and LMS in schools all show how intimately seemingly technical matters of budgetary rules are linked to wider issues of organization and political purpose.

The examples which illustrate this are numerous. LMS alters and enhances the role of head teacher. Resource management in universities reshapes the head of department position and raises questions of heads' training needs and job incentives. Decentralized resource management in social services implies (at the top) changed behaviour on the part of local politicians as well as ('on the street') negotiations between care managers and service users to reconcile the latter's wishes with budgetary realities. Resource management in the NHS raises sensitive questions concerning the ability of clinicians to commit and hold their peers to agreed courses of action. FMI reminds us, in the opinion of Gray and Jenkins, of the 'inevitable' tensions between political management and resource management. In other words, the application of models of rational, executive management to public service organizations always encounters an existing structure of power and interest, and one likely to offer some resistance to the pure budgetary logic favoured by some management accountants.

A second observation which is common to most of the chapters in this section flows from the first: it is that the reform of systems for managing resources always takes longer than the protagonists originally thought it would. Once the interconnections between technical, organizational and political issues is fully acknowledged this should come as no surprise. Resource allocation and the accountability for those allocations are inevitably issues which touch the heart of an organization's power structure and dominant culture. Even if budgetary change *were* purely technical it would still be a complicated, time-consuming exercise. When shifts in power relations and cultural assumptions are also involved then years may slip by before the full fruits of change are available for inspection.

The FMI is a good example: begun in 1982, Gray and Jenkins indicate that by the end of the eighties it had 'yet to fulfil the accountable management ideal'. Resource management in hospitals tells a similar tale. After earlier NHS experiments with management budgeting had been widely recognized as being in difficulty, the resource management initiative was launched in 1986. The Brunel team's evaluation report of 1991 concluded that 'the original timescale . . . was unrealistic' and that 'RM cannot yet be said to have produced a way of working that has demonstrated its ability to achieve significant measurable patient benefits' (Buxton et al., 1991, pp. 17 and 18). In universities some of the recommendations made in the seminal 1985 Jarratt Report have only slowly been implemented or, where implemented, have as yet put down only shallow cultural roots. It is one of the paradoxes of public services management that so many of the 'rational' management reforms of the 1980s were actually undertaken on the basis of an almost religious faith in a set of fairly untested (and perhaps untestable) assumptions. Resource management is not a 'quick fix'; it is a long haul involving work under all of McKinsey's '7S' headings. 'Top-down' approaches may succeed in getting new committee structures and computer systems in place relatively quickly. But the kind of 'bottom-up' work referred to as necessary by all five of our contributors takes time, patience, resources and a strategic plan. It is to be hoped that those coming slightly later to the joys of decentralized resource management (schools and, more particularly, social services) will take this on board.

A final reflection concerns the point of it all – the delivery of more effective, high quality public services. While many managers believe that this has already resulted from the resource management reforms described herein, it may be salutary to pause over the judgements made by our knowledgeable contributors. Levacic is concerned that the considerable theoretical advantages of LMS will be obscured and lost if general pressures on local authority expenditure lead to reduced educational funding in real terms. Sizer identifies comparative quality judgements as an essential but as yet unavailable component of the new system for universities. Without it the forces of competition may focus themselves exclusively on important but ultimately narrow questions of numbers and costs. Indeed, there are signs that this has already begun to happen. Gray and Jenkins believe that, in practice, FMI has tended to generate 'judgements dominated by input and financial criteria rather than by efficiency and effectiveness'. Symes, while optimistic that lessons can be learned from the experience of hospital resource management thus far, nevertheless warns that some of the pilot sites found it difficult to move beyond technical issues in order to address the scope for providing better and more cost-effective care. Warner graphically describes the revolution in information systems that will be needed in most social services departments before they can even know where they are in terms of quality and effectiveness.

It seems, therefore, that the central obstacle to rational management – the difficulty of linking resource decisions to measures of service outcomes, impacts or effects – has by no means yet been overcome. After a decade or more of effort most public services are still some way from being able to demonstrate their effectiveness. Effectiveness measures, as we saw in the first section of the *Handbook*, are conceptually challenging and politically sensitive. Yet, until public service management demonstrates its willingness to accept these challenges it is likely to continue to lack both public legitimacy and full acceptance from professional 'insiders'. Its mission will continue to appear, however unjustly, to be principally one of penny-pinching economy, internal discipline and the massage of the organization's public persona. If management is going to define and claim a distinctive space between those already occupied by the politicians and the professional service deliverers it must surely be this – the orchestration of organizational resources to produce the music of effectiveness. Thus, consideration of the technical apparatus of resource management eventually leads us back to a reappraisal of the ethics and purposes of management itself.

Part IV

Strategic Management

14

Organizational Design and Development: the Civil Service in the 1980s

Kate Jenkins

The Background to Change in the British Civil Service: the 1960s and 1970s

The Fulton Report on the civil service, published in 1968, considered the organization and structure of the civil service and the people in it, and recommended a wide range of changes. Throughout the 1970s, sensible and useful improvements were made. Building on the Fulton recommendations, training was improved, the Civil Service College and the Civil Service Department were established, new grading structures, recruitment and development systems were introduced. In the 1970s governments introduced new methods of improving policy analysis and central co-ordination. The Central Policy Review Staff (CPRS) was set up to improve the quality of central policy-making and decision-taking. The programme analysis and review system (PAR) was an innovation aimed at systematizing the process of major policy development.

Large departments were formed and reformed and alternative managerial structures were introduced; for example, in the Department of Employment, where activities not directly related to policy-making were hived off into statutory bodies. The Advisory, Conciliation and Arbitration Service (ACAS), the Employment Service, and finally the Manpower Services Commission (MSC), with its nationwide structure and vast budget, showed how much potential there might be in organizations freed from the immediate shackles of Whitehall.

The 1980s

At the start of the 1980s, in spite of Fulton, the civil service was still recognizably that of Northcote Trevelyan. There had been many cosmetic changes, names, organizations and structures had been altered, but the basic working method remained essentially that of the administrator, structured by rule books and organized by notes and minutes. Business was conducted in writing. In the early 1980s, all but the most junior of the senior grades of the civil service predated the Fulton changes in recruitment and training.

During this period there was considerable pressure on the civil service from a Conservative government which was strongly committed to the view that bureaucracy was inherently bad and the civil service far too large. The tensions this produced were compounded by the government's commitment to new and radical policies, whose development and implementation needed a substantial contribution from the civil servants.

Whitehall will always respond readily to clear direction combined with sustained pressure. The size of the civil service was reduced substantially, even in the face of rising demands for activity. Political pressure was a major spur, but two other factors were important. The first was the introduction of a new approach to reviewing the work of the civil service, which was pioneered by the Prime Minister's adviser on management, Lord Rayner. The second was, for the first time, a serious attempt to introduce systems to provide basic management information to monitor and, more significantly, to control the relationship between expenditure and output.

The Efficiency Strategy

The efficiency strategy was developed by Lord Rayner and a small team, with the enthusiastic support of the Prime Minister. The 'scrutiny process' was designed to push the civil service to review its methods of working, to challenge assumptions about the necessity, the cost and the effectiveness of areas of activity. The first studies were of relatively small areas of administrative work, but the process was extended rapidly to look at major expenditure programmes such as the unemployment benefit system.

The 'Rayner scrutiny' was a tool which could be used by Whitehall to achieve the targets the government had set for reductions in the size of the civil service. Indeed, for several years the key indicators kept by the Rayner Unit as a measure of effectiveness included the reductions in staff numbers, as well as the amount of public expenditure saved.

The principles of the scrutiny process were straightforward: look at what is being done, challenge assumptions about its necessity and its importance, find out how much it costs, assess its effectiveness, recommend any necessary changes and, critically, implement the recommendations briskly. The prescription was simple, comprehensible, and, used intelligently, proved a powerful way of getting to the root of an issue. Problems could arise if the system was not used with clarity and honesty. It was easy to lose sight of the requirement to find better ways of doing things and concentrate simply on finding cheaper ways. The drive for real efficiency, especially in the earlier years of the 1980s, when the pressure for crude reductions in numbers was strongest, tended to be associated with cuts in staff, reductions in service levels and a general atmosphere of gloom.

The methodology of scrutinies was simple. They were usually carried out by a small team of civil servants who understood the system but were not part of the line management. Their task, above all, was to go and find out for themselves what actually happened on the ground. It was the antithesis of the traditional desk-bound Whitehall review of paper evidence. Within the Efficiency Unit itself there were, initially, no files, no structures and very few procedures. The scrutiny was presented as a review by insiders of what actually went on. Its recommendations were designed to be radical, based firmly on factual evidence and, if the work was done effectively, they would be supported and implemented. This process, which was followed where possible with full publication of the review, was designed to ensure that the principles of radical administrative change were widespread, public and were given high-level ministerial support. The scrutiny process also, especially after the Efficiency Unit's own review of implementation, *Making Things Happen* (HMSO, 1987), placed particular emphasis on ensuring that the agreed recommendations for change actually happened.

The scrutiny programme produced results. The financial benefits were solid. By 1986, the National Audit Office, in their study of 'Raynerism', estimated that £1.5 billion had been cut from inefficient procedures and ineffective policies over the previous six years. More significantly, in the longer term, new approaches to organization and management emerged from the process of analysis and recommendation, followed up by action plans and reports on implementation. During the 1980s the scrutiny process itself was used on some 300 major areas of policy and operations and on subjects ranging from the maintenance of castles in Scotland to the magistrates' courts service and the taxation of unemployment benefits.

Within two years of its inception, efficiency had gained the status of a formal government policy, and a White Paper, *Efficiency in Government*, was produced in 1982 as a precursor to the introduction of the financial management initiative – the first systematic attempt to introduce modern management techniques on a widespread basis in Whitehall.

The Financial Management Initiative

As with the scrutiny process, the development of the financial management initiative (the FMI) was the responsibility of a small unit of senior people from inside and outside the civil service. They were responsible for ensuring that basic management systems were installed in government departments during the first three years of development.

The Unit's task was to see that departments had adequate systems of management information, that lines of accountability were clear, that responsibility was placed at the level at which decisions could be taken most effectively, and that there was a systematic process of delegated budgeting. It was a long and difficult process. The members of the Unit set a new style of centralized support and help, rather than the traditional process of central direction for departments which were dealing, in many cases for the first time, with the intricacies of management information theory and practice.

One of the most significant long-term effects of the new systems was the discovery by many senior civil servants of the value and potential of management information. The systems developed by the FMI gave senior managers detailed, quantified information about resource management, in many cases for the first time. Until the early 1980s, management information systems were primitive or non-existent, and there was little cross-referencing of expenditure against specific outputs. As detailed information became available, the opportunities for managing more effectively were more easily identified.

There was a developing recognition that targets, performance indicators, outputs and prices have a role to play in the management of modern organizations. The public expenditure White Papers of the 1980s chart this process clearly. The information systems were relentlessly showing the defects of old management habits. Ineffective use of resources, expensive processes and unnecessary bureaucracy became much more glaring when cost centres were established and unit costings produced. The most influential force on Whitehall, the public expenditure system, itself began to shift its focus to cover outputs as well as inputs and to record targets and results. The tension in this situation was self evident. There was a continuous downward pressure on costs and, in particular, on the running costs of departments, at a time when the external pressure for improved performance was mounting.

The 'Next Steps' Initiative

In 1986 the Efficiency Unit, the successor to Lord Rayner's unit, was asked to review the effectiveness of the government's management reforms for the Civil Service. Its report, *Improving Management in Government: the next steps*, was published in 1988. Its recommendations proposed new organizational structures which would clarify responsibility for policy and management and give departments a structure which forced them to think clearly about the relationship between policy and the resources and management needed to realize it.

At the heart of the executive agency process is the development of 'frameworks' or contracts to define the operating relationship between a department and its agencies. These contracts have to set out the results the sponsoring department wants to achieve from its policies, the resources necessary to achieve those results and the method of evaluation. No other process has pushed administrators into that most difficult of tasks: the specification of policy in practical operational terms.

It was this gap in the policy-making process which the *Next Steps* report identified as the long-standing weakness in civil service management. The publication of agency frameworks is showing, for the first time, the structures, the resources and the objectives of the main government operations in a way which can be publicly measured.

The agencies could not have been set up without the earlier development of information and computer systems to generate an adequate information base. It is now possible to develop realistic policies which can be interpreted in operational terms with clear statements of budgets and results. The traditional bureaucrat drafted an instruction which covered every possible event except the result. The new frameworks should be specific about the result and leave the route to the ingenuity of the manager.

The government's implementation of the *Next Steps* report concentrated on the recommendation that executive agencies should be set up to carry out the major operational tasks of central government. The executive agency concept emphasized the need for a structure designed to be appropriate for the job that was to be done. The concept is not, in itself, particularly innovative, but the changes in behaviour and organization which it is designed to achieve are far more fundamental. The development of a flexible system to cope with the different organizational needs and pressures of the civil service – from running a royal palace to running the economy, a military installation or a ministerial office – is a major shift from the long-standing assumption that the similarities within the systems of the civil service are more significant that the differences in the tasks.

Accountability

The executive agency concept has raised a further issue about which there has been a great deal of debate: the responsibility and public accountability of those working within agency structures. For agencies, as for government contracts with suppliers, the route of accountability is simple: the executive is accountable to the minister and the minister is accountable to Parliament. The significant change is that, whereas for an external contract, the nature and limits of that accountability are clearly set out in a legal contract document, the activities of much of government have hitherto been based on largely unwritten lore and assumption supported by detailed, complex but frequently unread instructions.

The framework document was designed to replace many departmental rules, both implied and explicit, with a clear statement of responsibility and accountability. Frameworks are, usually, public documents and chief executives public people, who will need the distinct skills of management and not only the skills of public administration. A crucial difference should be that both the agency and the department should understand the role and function of the manager, and the need to balance the flexibility which produced effective results with responsiveness to the public interest of both the clients and the customers of the agency. The department has the difficult task of specifying the service, monitoring its effective supply and ensuring that the agency has enough freedom and resources to deliver the optimum results. A department is therefore responsible and accountable for the effectiveness with which it manages its agencies; an agency is accountable for the way it carries out the responsibilities set out in its 'framework' document.

The question of the political accountability for executive agencies is a further dimension of this debate. Traditional accountability, the personal responsibility of a minister for the executive in detail, has waned as the complexity of government operations has grown. The framework document should be a clear statement of resources and an understanding about quality, service and internal management. The minister or his or her civil service surrogate remains responsible for the contract with the agency, and the executive head of the agency is responsible for the management of the contract. Policy and managerial success and failures can now be monitored and the minister or chief executive held accountable. Parliament, and ministerial colleagues, will hold the minister accountable. The process is more open and the critical responsibilities more precisely defined.

Human Resource Management

The current state of organizational development has implications for people working in the civil service. There are changes in roles; agencies are being set up for internal management, and the privatization of substantial public utilities has removed the need for detailed control over major areas of the economy, replacing it with the regulatory functions which are developing to control the new private monopolies. The development of new management systems is causing the public service to view its direct executive functions in a new light. The development of people who are expert at managing systems and organizations, as a consequence of the needs of the executive agencies, may change the Civil Service's view of the kind of people it needs to recruit and develop. A further consequence of the development of agencies may be the restating and restructuring of the role of departments as they become smaller and more focused on policy.

The increase in the need for specialists may mean that specialist jobs have to be carried out by people brought in on consultancy or personal contract from outside the civil service. If these contracts develop in a way that focuses, not on skills to be bought, but the results to be achieved, this will inevitably mean that the civil service has to be much more precise and prescriptive about the results it is expecting to see. A similar increase in the focus on results rather than process can be seen developing in those areas of the public service where the privatization or contracting out of activities has already taken place.

The scope for changing the structure of the civil service career as a consequence of these changes is extensive. The administrative structure is developing as a leading employer of a relatively untapped market – the highly trained woman with a young family. There are now, in the early 1990s, relatively speaking, substantial numbers of senior civil servants who work part-time, both women and men. An organization of a size to provide this kind of flexibility can retain the services of its staff for longer than it might otherwise do. This change is producing shifts in patterns of work which may be more far-reaching than simply a short-term acceptance of part-time parents, and they are putting the civil service in the lead as an employer using innovative approaches to working patterns.

The civil service is also moving down a more inventive path in the development of new, and rapidly evolving, proposals for merit and performance pay, which are given impetus from the developments in chief executive contracts, which have public statements of performance pay levels – a development which would have been unthinkable a decade ago.

The civil service's great strength does lie in its size and the variety of its work. It can afford to experiment with new working patterns, new structures and reward systems. As the structure of the labour market alters, the pressures and constraints of the 1980s may well have put the civil service into a position where it can benefit both from the changes already in place and from its newly acquired flexibility to develop further and continuously.

References

Gray, A. and Jenkins, W. I. (1985) *Administrative Politics in British Government*. Brighton: Wheatsheaf.

Metcalfe, L. and Richards, S. (1990) *Improving Public Management*. Second edition. London: Sage.

15

Organizing for Strategic Management: the Personal Social Services

Gerald Wistow

Social services departments are still relatively recent additions to the structure of local government. While based on earlier child care, health and welfare departments, they were established only in 1971 as an organizational response to a somewhat diverse range of issues and problems. Since then, they have been subject to what has sometimes seemed an almost continuous process of restructuring and reorganization, the bulk of it locally inspired rather than the product of legislative requirements. Twenty years later, however, and under the direct influence of the Children Act (1989) and the National Health Service and Community Care Act (1990), they stand on the threshold of fundamental change in their role and organization. Yet, throughout this somewhat turbulent history, a number of key themes and issues have posed dilemmas for organizational design which have, thus far, appeared to evade lasting resolution. Broadly speaking, they may be expressed in terms of the tension between genericism and specialization; centralization and decentralization; professionalism and participation.

These dilemmas have begun to resurface, albeit sometimes in modified guises, in the change agendas currently confronting social services departments. However, they have been overlain by a further set of considerations about the appropriate balance between direct service provision, on the one hand, and managing a greater diversity of supply, on the other. How and where that balance is struck over the next four or five years will necessarily have profound implications for the structure, organization and, perhaps, the continuing existence of social-service departments as separate entities. What is striking about this new role, however, is the extent to which aspects of it were prefigured almost a quarter of a century ago in the Seebohm Report (1968) which led to the foundation of local authority personal social services as we now know them. Indeed, the search for appropriate organizational forms continues to reflect unresolved tensions within that report, as well as aspirations which have since proved stubbornly resistant to realization.

The environment has been both demanding and turbulent. Initial government plans for double digit growth over a decade could not be sustained for more than two or three years (Webb and Wistow, 1983; Wistow, 1987). Since the mid-seventies, therefore, and despite growth rates well in excess of those for local government as a whole, departments have struggled to keep pace with the growth of demand. Increases in the number of frail elderly people and those suffering from mental health problems associated with age, growing numbers of children in care and families in difficulties, new legislative requirements and new problems (such as HIV/AIDS and child sex abuse), the faster rate of discharge from long-stay and acute hospital beds, together with increased expectations and assertiveness among users, have all been prominent among pressures which social services departments have faced since 1971. Examples of scandal and policy failure in residential care of elderly people and, most especially, services to children and families, have further added to the complexities and political sensitivities inherent in managing the personal social services. In such circumstances, relationships with members have not always been easy and the attrition rate among senior managers has been high. If the intensity of such pressures has grown over the last two decades, they are not entirely new ones. Indeed, social services departments were in part created to provide a stronger institutional base for responding to them. In practice, however, the initial internal structures of the immediate post-Seebohm departments proved insufficiently robust to meet the demands placed upon them.

Origins of Social Services Departments

The case for creating the personal social services as defined by the Seebohm Report (1968) was essentially one for the structural unification of social work and related social care services. The committee's report catalogued a wide range of shortcomings, including inadequacies in provision, poor co-ordination, difficult client access and insufficient responsiveness to need. As Hall (1976, pp. 60, 77) noted, this analysis of underlying problems led almost inevitably to the solution of a unified department large enough to win resources, plan the development of services in relation to need and overcome the problems of co-ordination inherent in the existing set of fragmented responsibilities. Such considerations combined to produce two key principles underpinning the committee's recommendations: first, the need for social work to establish a stronger organizational base and one which was, moreover, independent of medicine; and second, the importance of providing a single door through which users would be able to access integrated and localized services.

The client group specialisms around which existing departments were organized had been seen as a barrier to the realization of both principles. Thus, the unified departments founded in the wake of Seebohm were explicitly organized around two different principles: geography and function. Indeed, the two main organizational models which initially emerged were distinguished by which of those two principles provided the primary basis for organizational subdivisions within the new departments. Thus, a Brunel University study (BIOSS, 1974) identified two models of departmental organization: model A departments, which were subdivided first according to function (fieldwork, residential and day care, finance and support services, for example) and secondly according to geographic area; and model B departments in which those two principles were reversed, with geographic divisions taking precedence over functional ones. In the latter departments, therefore, senior members of the management team were responsible for all functions within a defined geographical subdivision of the local authority, while, in the former, they were responsible for defined functions across the authority as a whole.

As Challis (1990) notes, these two basic models have subsequently been replaced by a much more diverse pattern of organizational form. Thus, for example, Challis reports that of 65 departments which supplied information about their structures, 55 had introduced fundamental reorganizations since 1986 and 40 of them since 1988. To some extent, those reorganizations will have reflected or anticipated the major legislative changes now beginning to take effect in the personal social services, together with the broader pressures outlined above. At the same time, however, this apparently widespread interest in internal reorganization provides evidence of a continuing failure to resolve some of the organizational dilemmas identified at the beginning of this chapter.

Genericism and Specialization

The unification of the social work profession within social services departments represented the triumph of genericism. Practitioners who had hitherto worked with departments specializing in the care of children and families, mental health and the welfare of elderly or physically handicapped people were brought together in generic teams responsible for providing social work support to these and all other client groups. In addition, the principle of genericism was extended from the work-load of teams to the case-load of individual practitioners. Thus, the great majority of social workers found themselves dealing with all kinds of cases, instead of being restricted to those in which they had hitherto specialized and for which they had been trained.

This radical reorganization of social work practice was, in fact, based upon a fundamental misunderstanding of what was intended by Seebohm. As Hall (1976, p. 129) has pointed out, the report had suggested only that 'one social worker should have primary responsibility for each case not that every social worker should be able to deal with every eventuality'. Seen in this light, genericism was less concerned with broadening the knowledge base and responsibilities of individual social workers than with ensuring that social work interventions were effectively co-ordinated at the level of individual users. In practice, however, the former interpretation was pre-dominant. Hall argued that the 'zeal' with which the integration of case-loads was pursued caused a loss of morale within social work, accompanied by criticism from other professional groups about an apparent drop in standards.

Almost since their creation, therefore, internal and external pressures have existed to reintroduce specialization to social services departments. One such pressure has followed the recognition that so-called genericism effectively resulted in the case-load of qualified staff being dominated by work with children and families (Stevenson and Parsloe, 1978; Black et al., 1983). Statutory requirements, together with the exposed nature of such work in the wake of repeated child abuse scandals, help to explain this ordering of priorities. However, other factors located deep within the culture of the social work profession have been no less important. In a study of social work with elderly people, for example, Black and his colleagues (1983, p. 224) found that, so far as trained social workers were concerned, 'the skills they wished to exercise and the satisfactions they sought were more readily realised in cases involving children and families'. Other groups appeared professionally less interesting, received correspondingly lower priority and were more likely to be the province of less qualified and trained staff.

The National Development Team for mentally handicapped people (1982, p. 30) made a similar point and, in the early eighties, a number of studies reported families with mentally handicapped children expressing dissatisfaction with both social workers' lack of specialized knowledge of their client group and the minimal contact they had with social workers of any kind (see for example Barclay, 1982, p. 37 and Ayer and Alasewski, 1983). Paradoxically, therefore, one consequence of genericism proved to be, in effect, an increasing specialization in work with children and families.

The response to these criticisms has been the return of client group specialisms through the creation of specialist posts and specialist teams. These developments have not been comprehensively mapped, though a national survey of community mental handicap teams found that their numbers had increased from two in 1975 to 348 in 1987, with 92 per cent of these teams containing social work representation (Griffiths and Brown, 1988).

The progressive re-emergence of client group specialization has had two purposes therefore: first, to secure a stock of expert skills and knowledge for client groups other than child care; and, second, to ring-fence for those client groups fieldwork resources which would otherwise have been diluted in quality and quantity by the demands of work with children. Client groups are not, however, the only dimension of specialization currently evident. Others include:

- the type of intervention, for example one-to-one casework, group work or community social work;
- the period of intervention, including intake, short-term and long-term casework;
- the function, such as intermediate treatment, fostering and adoption, registration and inspection, medical social work;
- the age group – children and adults.

It should be emphasized, however, that each of these dimensions (like the wider debate about genericism and specialization) has primarily been related to the organization and deployment of social work resources rather than those of social services departments as a whole. Even when the commitment to genericism was at its height, residential and day-care services continued to be – and still are – organized on a client group basis. Despite comprising only some 12 per cent of the workforce throughout the last decade (Department of Health, 1991, p. 37), social work has been the dominant influence on the organization of social services departments, as is also indicated by the following discussion of decentralization.

Centralization and Decentralization

From the late seventies onwards, decentralization came to occupy the same status as a guiding organizational principle that genericism had held a decade earlier. The Seebohm Report had given emphasis to what were, in effect, two dimensions of decentralization: community development and the localization of service delivery. The latter was expressed through the organization of social workers in area teams serving populations of around 50,000 people. While potentially increasing the accessibility of services to users, this development had no necessary relationship to the decentralization of authority within social services departments. Indeed, concern about a perceived increase in centralization became a strong theme in the personal social services towards the end of the first post-Seebohm decade. A former general secretary of the British Association of Social Work has noted that, following the tenth anniversary of Seebohm and 'with more than a little irony', the Association's 1978 annual general meeting 'resolved that "the present organizational structure of social services departments is harmful to the practice of social work"' (Cypher, 1979, p. 1). The background to this concern was the growing scale of social services departments and what was perceived to be an accompanying growth in bureaucracy, remoteness and unresponsiveness.

The solution that emerged at the beginning of the eighties was the 'patch' system of community-oriented social work. This centred on populations of 5,000–10,000 served by teams expected to be better informed about the needs and resources of such areas. The expectation was that they would thus be better able to engage in preventive work and also to harness community resources to the meeting of need. As such, the patch model was consistent with the growing priority attached to the policy of promoting care by the community and the attendant imperative to stimulate and support the provision of informal care by families, friends and neighbours. The first Thatcher administration urged social services committees to examine whether 'the harnessing of voluntary and community resources was central to their own objectives' and directors were asked to ascertain whether fieldwork staff were 'ensuring that their clients [were] making the fullest possible use of caring resources available in their local communities' (Jenkin, 1980a). Not surprisingly, therefore, the patch system was commended by the first Conservative secretary of state for social services (Jenkin, 1980b) and received quasi-official endorsement through the Barclay Report's (1982) advocacy of community social work.

Such community-oriented and patch approaches were, however, also a manifestation of a broader trend towards decentralization in local government, which had diverse origins and objectives. Notwithstanding that diversity, Willmott (1987, p. 2) suggests that the initiatives which followed could be divided into two broad categories: those which attempted 'to improve services to council consumers through local delivery' and those which attempted 'to move towards a more participative style of democracy'. Patch and community social work tended towards the former and, in some respects, more limited objective, as did a further dimension of decentralization in the personal social services, its potential contribution to functional integration. Both 'model A' and 'model B' departments were characterized by substantial degrees of functional management, with crossover points between fieldwork and other services generally being above the area level and not infrequently being found only at headquarters level. This fragmentation of responsibilities impeded the development of a balanced pattern of provision related to local needs and also formed a barrier to the integration of services for individual users. In such circumstances, the decentralization of functional responsibilities to a level closer to the user appeared to offer the possibility of more integrated service delivery systems, responsive to individual need. Consequently, many departments were restructured on the basis of a flatter hierarchy in which area directors were responsible for all residential, day, domiciliary and fieldwork services.

In practice, decentralization has not been a self-evident success. Challis's (1990, pp. 95–7) account provides a range of explanations for this outcome:

1 administrative upheaval led to the dislocation of services;
2 functional decentralization was only partial, focused primarily on fieldwork and thus had little impact on problems of co-ordination;
3 decentralization stopped short of devolving substantial responsibilities for the control of budgets and deployment of staff;
4 the increase in access points to services was not matched by changes to professional practices and procedures, with the consequence that the balance of power between professionals and users remained much the same;
5 inconsistencies in levels and standards of services between different parts of decentralized structures were difficult to resolve.

In short, decentralization programmes have tended to be imperfectly conceived and executed, not least because of a tendency to give insufficient weight to the management systems and processes necessary to underpin decentralized structures. Perhaps the key exemplar of those weaknesses has been the reluctance or inability to devolve budgets, together with the absence of financial and other management information systems necessary to support such a move. Another example is the failure sufficiently to recognize that decentralization is not an alternative to hierarchy but creates the need for different kinds and degrees of control from the centre. It remains necessary to make explicit the limits of decentralized authority, to set standards, monitor performance and exercise accountability.

Participation and Professionalism

A further and, in many respects, related tension in the organization of social services departments has been that between professionalism and participation. Again, its roots lie in the Seebohm Report which, as Hadley and McGrath (1981) noted, 'offered two different directions for development . . . one was towards greater . . . professionalism . . . the other was towards greater community involvement'. Hadley and McGrath further pointed out that the report failed to recognize the incompatibility of those two approaches and that, by 'favouring large area teams on the grounds of the needs of social workers rather than the much smaller areas related to the requirements of the community', professionalism became the predominant force. While this conclusion was broadly accurate at the time they were writing (1981), there has since been a growing range of initiatives aimed at increasing involvement in the personal social services. Indeed, based on a national survey conducted in the second half of 1988, Beresford and Croft (1990, p. 18) have argued that 'user involvement has got beyond the stage of a few high profile development projects or pilot schemes . . . it is beginning to be routine and it is ingrained in the operation of some agencies.'

At the same time, however, a major criticism of personal social services provision during the last decade has been the continuing dominance of professional definitions of needs and solutions, combined with the assessment of individuals in relation to the limited range of services professionals are able to offer, rather than the tailoring of care packages to their needs (see, for example, Audit Commission, 1986). Reflecting this critique, user involvement in both assessment and care packaging processes is an objective of the White Paper *Caring for People* (Secretary of State for Health and others, 1989). Whether this development will lead to user empowerment must, however, be doubtful, especially in view of the absence in the White Paper of an unambiguous commitment to the concept of independent advocacy. In such circumstances, there are real dangers of involvement being cosmetic or ritualistic. Effectively leaving participation to the definitions and assumed disinterest of professionals is an improbable strategy for fundamentally shifting the balance towards users and away from those professionals. The more probable outcome is the more sensitive gearing of professionally led services to the needs and preferences of users, rather than the empowerment of either the latter or wider community interests.

Providing or Enabling

As was noted above, a notion of social services departments as mobilizers of community resources was to be found in the Seebohm Report and underpinned the patch/community social work models. These models of social work practice have since been extended into the concept of an enabling role for the statutory personal social services as a whole. First articulated in this form by Norman Fowler (1984), it envisaged a strategic role for social services departments in relation to all sources of care within their boundaries, accompanied by recognition that the direct provision of services was and should be only one element in that total pattern. Sir Roy Griffiths

(1988, paragraph 1.3.4) took up this theme in his recommendation that local social services authorities should act 'as the designers, organisers and purchasers of non-health care services, and not primarily as direct providers'. Griffiths further recommended that this strategic role should be complemented and paralleled at the micro-level of individual users by care managers with responsibility for identifying and assessing individual needs and ensuring the delivery of integrated care packages tailored to those needs.

The separation of responsibility for purchase and provision is a fundamental element of the community care White Paper. However, it poses a number of organizational dilemmas which have, as yet, barely begun to be addressed. In essence, they revolve around two issues: the balance to be struck between statutory and various forms of non-statutory provision; and the organizational arrangements necessary to underpin the enabling role. Considerations affecting the first of these issues include: the extent to which the retention of public provision is necessary to ensure choice, competition and the implementation of 'break' clauses in contracts with independent providers whose performance fails to meet specifications; and the extent to which independent sector providers operate across the full range of services, the assumption being that they may be more reluctant to provide for the most dependent or stigmatized groups.

Further questions need to be addressed in respect of the organizational arrangements through which the purchaser/provider split is effected. Key issues include:

- the level at which such responsibilities are disaggregated; the nature of contracts/service agreements (block or cost and volume, for example);
- the extent to which purchasing decisions are decentralized;
- the arrangements for performance monitoring, together with their relationship to the 'arm's length' inspection units; and
- the implications for committee and sub-committee structures.

Perhaps the core issue concerns the relationship between departmental purchasing strategies as a whole and those of individual care managers: what level of budgetary decentralization will operate; what degree of purchasing autonomy will care managers possess; how far will they be restricted to a limited menu of options derived from central bulk-purchasing strategies; and how far they will be expected to create more flexible and less formal services based on the resources of local communities? It is at this point that the care manager as resource allocator (and rationer) interacts with the softer concept of community social work as the enabler and mobilizer of such resources. Whether such roles are compatible remains to be seen, but two outcomes seem likely: first, that the tasks of resource management and community development call for very different sets of skills and expertise; and second, that a profession which has generally found community social work less attractive and satisfying than face-to-face casework (in Baldock and Prior, 1981; Black et al., 1983) is likely to be even less comfortable with a resource management role.

A further tension between enabling and providing relates to the long-standing concern to improve service integration. Generic social work was originally conceived as the route to that objective. Subsequently, the way forward was seen in terms of combining functional responsibilities closer to the point of service delivery. However, the principle of separating out responsibility for purchase and provision is, by definition, incompatible with the creation of such integrated structures at any point below that of the director of social services. Moreover, not only does it imply the dis-aggregation of responsibilities for needs assessment, the design of care packages and the delivery of service elements specified within those packages, but it does so in a context where provision is to be further diversified through the extension of a mixed economy of care. Against that background, the task of service integration falls to care managers operating at the level of individual users. The demands which those tasks and responsibilities impose upon such front-line staff should not be under-estimated, particularly as care packages will frequently depend on multi-agency contributions while care managers will control budgets from at best only their own agency. As with so many other aspects of the community care White Paper, its implementation will be considerably more problematic than its authors allow (see Wistow and Henwood, 1991).

Moreover, and just as the enabling role implies the disaggregation of functions which were being integrated within decentralized structures, so the new legislation implies further degrees of fragmentation. Many depart-ments appear to be responding to the somewhat separate demands of the children's and community care legislation by restructuring into child care and community care (or adult) divisions. This specialization by age group is emerging as the primary principle in the internal organization of depart-ments. Assuming sufficient social workers can be found to occupy the care manager posts in adult divisions (and there is an expectation that some will be filled by domiciliary services officers who have experience of managing budgets), this principle should help to safeguard fieldwork resources for adult groups from the pressure of child care work. However, it is ironic that the wheel has almost turned full circle and the possibility of separate child care and community care departments was apparently considered by Griffiths.

Conclusion

Looking across the two decades of their existence, there is a considerable degree of continuity in the issues to which social services departments have sought to provide organizational responses. Taken together, they represent a continuing search for a framework through which departments can enable users to secure ready access to a full range of local services; services which are, moreover, both responsive to their needs and preferences and also integrated at the point of service delivery. Potential solutions have varied: genericism was followed by decentralization which shaded into strategies for customer consciousness or user empowerment. Currently, a mixed economy and care management are the favoured solutions. Nonetheless, two themes have recurred in the process of implementing all of the above approaches.

First, they have tended to be conceived or implemented as though the organization of social work could be equated with that of social services departments as a whole. To some extent, access to locally integrated services has been confused with decentralized models of social work in which the devolution of budgetary and other resource-allocating responsibilities has played little, if any part. The Kent Community Care Project and its derivatives provide a rare exception to that general pattern but, even in those cases, financial decentralization is largely in the form of 'shadow' rather than 'real' budgets (Davies and Challis, 1986). Paradoxically, the purchaser/provider split is compatible with an organizational model (care management) focused around the boundaries of social work and other front-line professions. It is, however, a model incompatible with the values and skills of social work as currently constructed and its implementation will require substantial behavioural change within the profession.

A second recurrent theme has been the tendency to design and implement structural solutions in isolation from process and systems change. As a response to service fragmentation, for example, genericism was less appropriate than a key worker system. Similarly, decentralization was only rarely supported by the financial, information and monitoring systems necessary for meeting its objectives. Such decentralized systems are, moreover, essential preconditions to user participation in decision-making about assessment and service packaging. In their absence, users will inevitably become disillusioned about the inability of front-line workers to respond to them quickly and authoritatively. In this context, it is particularly significant that the two key elements of the community care changes are essentially driven by process rather than structure. The separation of purchase from provision revolves around processes of contract specification, negotiation and agreement, without which the two functions cannot be brought into any meaningful kind of relationship. Significantly, national guidance on purchasing and contracting is focused very largely on such processes rather than on structural solutions to the purchaser/provider split (Department of Health, 1990). Similarly, care management is essentially organized around a systematic process of assessment, prescription, intervention and evaluation. Again, the fact that it is concerned with a systematic process of working, as much as the reshaping of professional and organizational structures, is being given prominence.

Both of the above developments are strongly dependent, however, upon the creation of decentralized information systems of a kind whose absence was the subject of a typically terse and acerbic comment by Griffiths (1988, paragraph 28): 'The present lack of refined information systems and management accounting within any of the authorities to whom one might look centrally or locally to be responsible for providing care would plunge most organisations in the private sector into a quick and merciful liquidation.' Against this background, it is clear that there is still much to do before the personal social services are capable of constructing organizational frameworks which will realize the objectives both Griffiths and Seebohm have set for them over the course of the past 25 years.

Some progress is being made in process and systems design through the development programme associated with the National Health Service and the Community Care Act. For example, the Department of Health supported financially a partnership between the Association of Directors of Social Services and the Chartered Institute of Public Finance and Accountancy to produce guidance and training materials on information strategies and financial management, including devolved budgeting. Practice guidance on planning, purchasing and care management are also being prepared by the Department as further elements of what is a wide-ranging strategy to equip personnel at all levels in the personal social services for the new roles implied by the post-Griffiths changes.

It remains to be seen, however, whether such developments will prove sufficient to secure the breadth and depth of behavioural change demanded by the enabling role. As our earlier analysis has indicated, that role and its organizational implications are broadly incompatible with the organization and practice of what has continued to be the dominant mode of social work, a model of face-to-face casework which is at best relatively innocent of, and at worst unsympathetic to, resource management disciplines. By contrast, the enabling role not only implies the consolidation of a community-oriented model of working but also its operation within a framework of devolved budgeting. Bayley and his colleagues (1989, p. 160) concluded that the development of a community-oriented approach was 'likely to take a long time'. Wistow and Wray (1987) showed that a developmental model, in some respects akin to the enabling role, was being practised in the Nottinghamshire Community Mental Handicap Teams (see also Vincent et al., 1989). The underlying elements of that success lay in a remit for team members which specifically excluded them from day-to-day crisis-oriented work with clients. Even so, there was a tendency for some team members to 'regress' to the professional casework model with which they felt most comfortable, in which their skills were perceived to lie and whose continuing practice was seen to be essential to career progression (Wistow and Wray, 1987, pp. 10–12).

It remains uncertain whether the current reorganization of social services departments will succeed in shifting the balance between different social work models. The provision of better information about costs and consequences of professional decision-making may prove to be a necessary, but not a sufficient, condition for behavioural change by social workers. The production of detailed practice guidance on systems design and operation offers a more systematic basis for the implementation of change than has accompanied previous major organizational restructurings in the personal social services. The creation of a case manager route to career progression also provides organizational and individual incentives outside, and in addition to, the traditional casework route. Lastly, the Department of Health training support grant was extended in 1991 to provide additional post-qualifying training. Taken together, these initiatives represent a multifaceted strategy for professional change. There remains the impression, however, that in may departments change is managerially led and has yet to penetrate to fieldwork levels. Unless practitioners are convinced that new models of working not only offer opportunities for their own advancement but also provide better outcomes for their clients, change at the level of service delivery may lag considerably behind the policy and organizational rhetorics.

References

Audit Commission (1986) *Making a Reality of Community Care*. London: HMSO.

Ayer, S. and Alaszewski, A. (1983) *Community Care and the Mentally Handicapped*. Beckenham: Croom Helm.

Baldock, J. and Prior, D. (1981) The roots of professional practice, *Community Care*, 19 March, 17–18.

Barclay, P. M. (1982) *Social Workers, their Roles and Tasks: report of a working party*. London: Bedford Square Press.

Bayley, M., Sayed, R. and Tennant, A. (1989) *Local Health and Welfare: is Partnership possible?* Aldershot: Gower.

Beresford, P. and Croft, S. (1990) Opportunity knocks, *Insight*, 18 July, 18–19.

Black, J., Bowl, R., Burns, D., Critcher, C., Grant, D. and Stockford, D. (1983) *Social Work in Context*. London: Tavistock.

Brunel Institute of Social Service (1974) *Social Services Departments: developing patterns of work and organisation*. London: Heinemann.

Challis, L. (1990) *Organising Public Social Services*. London: Longman.

Cypher, J. (1979) *Seebohm across Three Decades*. Brighton: British Association of Social Workers.

Davies, B. and Challis, D. (1986) *Matching Resources to Needs*. Farnborough: Gower.

Department of Health (1990) *Community Care in the Next Decade and Beyond: policy guidance*. London: HMSO.

Department of Health and Office of Population Census and Surveys (1991) *Annual Report* (Cm. 1513). London: HMSO.

Fowler, N. (1984) *The Enmabling Role of Social Services Departments* (a speech to the Joint Social Services Annual Conference, Buxton, 27 September: mimeograph).

Griffiths, R. (1988) *Community Care: agenda for action*. London: HMSO.

Griffiths, T. and Brown, S. (1988) *National Survey of Community Mental Handicap Teams*. Loughborough: Centre for Research in Social Policy.

Hadley, R. and McGrath, M. (1981) Patch systems in SSDs: more than a passing fashion, *Social Work Service*, no. 26, May, 10–12.

Hall, P. (1976) *Reforming the Welfare*. London: Heinemann.

Jenkin, P. (1980a) Speech to the Association of Directors of Social Services, April (mimeograph).

— (1980b) Speech to the 'Patch Workshop', National Institute of Social Work, 15 September (mimeograph).

National Development Team for the Mentally Handicapped (1982) *Third Report 1980–81*. London: Department of Health and Social Security.

Secretary of State for Health et al. (1989) *Caring for People* (Cm. 849). London: HMSO.

Seebohm, F. (1968) *Report of the Committee on Local Authority and Allied Personal Social Services* (Cmnd. 3703). London: HMSO.

Stevenson, O. and Parsloe, P. (1978) *Social Service Teams: the practitioner's view*. London: DHSS.

Vincent, J., Webb, A., Wistow, G. and Wray, K. (1989) *Community Mental Handicap Teams: an evaluation in Nottinghamshire*. Loughborough: Centre for Research in Social Policy.

Webb, A. and Wistow, G. (1983) Public expenditure and policy implementation: the case of community care, *Public Administration*, 63, 21–44.

Willmott, P. (1987) Introduction. In P. Willmott (ed.), *Local Foremost Decentralisation and Community*. London: Policy Studies Institute.

Wistow, G. (1987) Personal social services. In M. Parkinson, *Restructuring Local Government*. Newbury and New York: Policy Journals and Transaction Books, 77–97.

Wistow, G. and Henwood, M. (1991) Caring for people: elegant concept or flawed design? In N. Manning (ed.), *Social Policy Review 1990–1991*, London: Longman, 78–100.

Wistow, G. and Wray, K. (1987) CMHTs, service delivery and service development: the Nottinghamshire approach. In G. Grant, S. Humphreys and M. McGrath (eds), *Community Mental Handicap Team: theory and practice*. Kidderminster: British Institute of Mental Handicap, 1–20.

16

Strategic Management in Local Government and the NHS

Rodney Brooke

Introduction: The Impact of Thatcherism

The concept of strategic management in the public sector has undergone a transformation over the last few years, propelled by the massive legislation pushed through by the Conservative government. A major platform of the government has been to play down the importance of the public sector. The first two terms of the government were marked by a general reduction in the role of the public sector, a lessening of its importance and the search for additional controls on non-subordinate agencies like local government or quasi-independent agencies like District Health Authorities. The government's third term has seen a much more sophisticated approach, based not only on shifting the private/public sector boundary but also on changing the culture of the remainder of the public sector. Underlying the changes is a firm commitment to undermine corporate bureaucratic power and rationality, to replace the struggles for order and to thrust aside the propositions of the Enlightenment.

The government certainly seems to have succeeded in changing the culture. Paradoxically, the changes have shifted the emphasis from efficiency and economy to the third and neglected 'E', effectiveness. As a result the concept of strategic management has moved from an introspective view of the organization to a holistic view of the surrounding environment, an ironic consequence in view of the government's distrust of bureaucratic planning.

Market Democracy v. Representative Democracy

The government has shown its scepticism of the validity of subordinate forms of representative democracy. It has been firmly committed to the view that the market is better able to determine needs than a local council or a quasi-representative body like a health authority. Change is exemplified in the new education system, with its blend of centralization and decentralization, where the rights of parents to choose their children's school has been solidified and where they are to be given better information on which to base informed decisions. At the same time schools themselves are given independent budgets by their local authority to be spent as they think fit. Parent power has been increased on governing bodies. Schools can opt out of local authority control by seeking grant-maintained status. City technology colleges provide parents with a further alternative. Bureaucratic planning in inner London has been swept away by the abolition of the Inner London Education Authority. Co-ordination of further education, thought by professionals to be essential in the conurbation and highly segmented by ILEA, will be replaced by a market free-for-all. Colleges will be able to compete for students without the restrictions imposed on them by a central bureaucratic planning authority.

Ironically, the decentralization of power from the local education authority to schools, colleges and parents has been accompanied by a further removal of powers in favour of central government, diminishing the responsiveness which the government allegedly seeks. The imposition of a national curriculum, national testing procedures and the removal of the polytechnics and colleges of further education from local authority control are the most significant examples of the loss of powers upwards.

These moves have been heavily criticized. In the absence of bureaucratic protection, it is feared that specialist further education courses will collapse because of wasteful and uneconomic provision; that the option for grant-maintained status is a back-door way of recreating grammar schools and secondary modern schools; that unpopular schools which cannot be closed because they provide essential capacity will become unviable and unable to offer a full range of options; that sixth forms and non-vocational adult education will be jeopardized; and that sink schools will result. The citizen exercises responsibility, but the consumer shows egotism, it is argued. Parent governors will have only a short-term view of their school's needs, limited by the time horizons of their children's stay. The search for individual good will replace the search for collective good. The articulate will benefit and the inarticulate suffer.

Competition v. the Public Service Ethic

The government distrusts the public-service (and professional) ethic as a dissimulation of inefficient cartels and an abuse of monopoly power. As the private sector uses monopolistic powers to increase profits so, it is argued, the public sector uses monopolies to reduce throughput or increase professional satisfaction at the expense of users.

Competition is the answer chosen by the government. If no genuine market exists, then a simulated internal market must be created. There may be no realistic alternative in large areas of the National Health Service, but managers must behave as if there is. It is, as Adam Smith has pointed out, not the entry of a competitor in the market which changes behaviour, but the possible entry of a competitor. If organizations are uncompetitive then eventually a competitor will arrive. The change is propelling public-sector agencies into their own market simulation by the spread of service-level agreements in local government. Direct service organizations compelled to compete seek freedom themselves to enter the market for support services or, if this is seen to undermine corporate culture too far, to specify the service they receive from central support departments whose overheads might otherwise undermine their competitiveness.

There is an assumption that the public sector will tend to lose competitive battles. Certainly this has been true in the past; municipal wash-houses were wiped out by the launderette. Only in the areas where free provision (like libraries) or subsidized provision (like leisure centres) was made did local government succeed. But local government managers seem to have imbibed the competitive culture. They are fighting to compete. So far the overwhelming majority have competed successfully.

Local authorities have to compete on a front wider than compulsory competitive tendering alone, in areas like education and housing. Interestingly, the National Health Service has reacted entirely differently to the proposed creation of National Health Service Trusts. Local managers and many district health authorities have been committed to encouraging their local hospitals to opt out of their control. The top managers have been attracted to the trusts rather than to the new style district health authorities. Resolutions passed by district health authorities opposing the setting up of trusts seem to have had no effect. Certainly there seems to be no intention to consult consumers systematically about the proposals.

Compulsory competitive tendering – or more precisely the specification of services required – provides an opportunity for differentiation of service supply, and in particular, the opportunity for consumers to pay an additional charge for a higher level of service. Geographic differentiation is an option which politicians can also choose in the Health Service. The introduction of an accounting system whereby money will follow patients gives the theoretical incentive to hospitals to compete, though opponents argue that spare capacity in the Health Service does not exist except as a result of underfunding. While local authority direct service organizations are heavily restricted in the ways in which they can compete, hospitals will have *carte blanche*. Already business plans are being prepared with a view to attracting patients, followed by funds which will enable hospitals to improve their equipment or extend their services.

The Purchaser/Provider Split

The purchaser/provider split is a concept which underpins government thinking on the public sector. The introduction of an independent regulator is a variant where the split does not comfortably give adequate controls. National Health Service Trusts and self-governing units have been separated from the direct management of the health authority. In local government schools, transport operations, airport operations and direct service organizations function at arm's length from the local authority. Local authorities themselves have not been slow to pick up the message. A combination of financial stringency, lack of statutory powers and the need to overcome bureaucratic constraints has prompted more than half the local authorities in the country to set up their own companies. They are being propelled to put these at arm's length by the Local Government and Housing Act, 1989, or otherwise their companies would come within the ambit of the local authority's own financial systems and their expenditure would count against the local authority's own capital allocation. Local authorities are increasingly working through a whole medley of partnerships with the private sector or by contracts or understandings with voluntary bodies.

A major consequence is the freeing of the time of members of district health authorities and councillors from the routine processing of administrative business. Their agenda need not be circumscribed by the bureaucratic needs of the service department with which their committee was associated. Managers are freed from the routine management of their departments, which so often took away the opportunity for strategic thought. This freedom from routine creates time to look not only at alternative means of delivery of services for which members and officers are statutorily responsible, but also for a scan of wider horizons.

Health Service chiefs concerned to cut down demands on their services will wish to address the correlation between social and economic conditions and their patients' problems. They are seeking to influence the policy of the local authority. The local authority will address issues in which its statutory services play only a part. One feature of the much reviled poll tax is the interest which it has aroused in local government elections. In some London boroughs turnout was at the level of a general election. As a result, local authorities will become even more conscious of the concerns of their electorates and will wish to address those concerns.

The fragmentation of agencies created as a result of the government's dislike of centralized bureaucratic planning nevertheless requires something beyond policy-making. This fragmentation gives local authorities an opportunity – even a necessity – to assume the mantle of co-ordination. The Audit Commission has canvassed the idea of regeneration audits in the inner cities, audits in which all actors will be involved by the local authority in order to establish a common agenda of concern and a concerted plan of action.

Thus, derogation from local government corporatism may paradoxically increase the local authority's role, though at the expense of the direct supply of services. Cordial relationships have been established in areas where a few years ago there was only hostility. In the classic case of Sheffield, an era of hostility between the Chamber of Commerce and the council ended when the chairman of the one and the leader of the other discovered that they had more in common than in conflict. A partnership was concluded which has made the new Sheffield a byword for such a relationship. Throughout the country, local authorities are increasingly engaged in relationships with bodies whose efforts can complement their own. With an enlarged vision of their role they will seek to influence agencies which touch areas in which they have concerns, like the environment. In turn the private sector has become aware of its own need to influence and work with the local authority as a key to economic success. It needs the thrust of the local authority in areas like planning, education and environmental improvement.

The Network of Influence

The strategy of coalition building has caught on in local government. Allies are sought in unlikely places. The disliked Urban Development Corporations and the encroaching Training and Enterprise Councils have been colonized or regarded pragmatically as partners. The Audit Commission is now perceived as a benefit rather than a burden. Its comparative statistics are being increasingly used by local authorities; and its value-for-money studies consistently highlight the frustrations and inefficiencies caused by central government meddling and the distortions caused by government financial systems. Academic institutions and think-tanks of the right and left are now on the local government agenda. The major local authorities and regions seek European partners with common interests to besiege the European Commission with requests for money or friendly policies. The Commission itself is seen as a major ally on the side of local government against central government.

Competition has goaded the existing trend towards consumer responsiveness. Competition will prompt marketing initiatives towards consumers and further develop the local authority's closeness to its residents. The growing preparedness of the public to take collective protective action will prompt authorities to accept further involvement of a constructive nature.

In the field of the environment pressure groups will be seen as an agent to accomplish objectives rather than an obstruction to progress. Local authorities will try increasingly to involve the public in the actual delivery of services. Concern for carers is a vital part of the new community care regime. Indeed, this major new responsibility for local authorities will prompt a whole raft of new relationships, requiring careful networking with health authorities, general practitioners, residential home proprietors, the Department of Social Security – as well as other local authority departments like education, leisure and housing.

But the new systems of working will create new tensions and conflicts. Purchasers and providers do not necessarily have the same interests. Purchasers will actively seek to restrict the market as a means of rationing, since demand for free collective goods is limitless. Providers, on the other hand, have a vested interest in marketing their services. It is easy to see a National Health Service Trust propagating demand for medical treatment – especially that involving expensive new equipment not currently available in the locality – while the District Health Authority tries to restrict the market by pooh-poohing the need for new treatments. District Health Authorities will certainly examine critically clinical audit returns to see whether treatment is effective, in the forlorn hope of stanching the exponential growth of spending on the acute services at the expense of community care.

Developments in services will take aback the inventors of the system. Budget-holding general practitioners, for example, may find it both cost-effective and attractive to their patients to bus in consultants for local surgeries. General practitioners' purchasing consortia can bypass the District Health Authority middleman and defeat the concept of strategic health promotion. General practitioners may find taking over uneconomic cottage hospitals a cheaper and more popular way of providing treatment than using high technology National Health Service Trust establishments. Schools opting for grant-maintained status may do so to avoid reorganizations or closure.

Within an organization rigid purchaser/provider splits may undermine corporate values as units determinedly avoid the maximum use of various specialists. Costing systems may perversely lead to inefficiencies if, for example, departments fail to seek legal advice for fear of incurring costs. Lawyers make their living from clients who failed to seek timely advice or to recognise its desirability. Informal chats with solicitors were encouraged before the days of time-clock charging. Public relations departments, now treated as profit centres, may miss out on key stages of new proposals as service units try to economize.

If the purchaser/provider split does lead to incongruities of this sort, then at least the retention of central co-ordination does give politicians and managers the opportunity of overall analysis of budget programmes which contribute to corporate objectives, such as the problems of poverty or the environment. Central control retains the possibility of action to overcome the shortcomings of subordinate agencies and to ensure that they contribute to a corporate goal.

New approaches to issues will not be confined to direct action of this sort. Public sector strategists will establish a range of mechanisms to influence strategic allies and to seek synergy. The diminished scale of operational management on the purchasing side will create an opportunity for greater co-ordination and synthesis of influence. Planning and development control powers will be used to achieve a variety of organizational objectives. Purchasing will be used in a more pointed manner. As well as working through contract and agreement, local authorities will seek to use their own land holdings constructively. They will be prepared to volunteer consultancy expertise in appropriate cases and inject judicious supplies of finance into appropriate organizations. Public relations will be used more skilfully and more purposefully.

The imaginative deployment of resources in these ways calls for the concentration by local authorities of resources at the boundaries of the organization, looking outwards. Traditionally a role of the chief executive in his ambassadorial capacity, responsibilities must in future be spread more widely. Providers, of course, will be under constant scrutiny by the purchasing agencies. Programmed monitoring systems will highlight any deficiency in their provision. Networked systems like those between community care managers, the Health Service, general practitioners and other local authority services will also be monitored, both in terms of finance (where budgets will increasingly be pooled) and in terms of output. There will be a constant need to monitor the attitudes of consumers and their needs. Ephemeral shifts in public taste will have to be recognized if not catered for. The public will have to be kept on-side.

The use of information technology for consumer interface has hardly been developed in this country, but over the next ten years it will make a major impact on the delivery of local government services. Local authorities will use the possibilities of information technology for interactive exchanges as well as for disseminating information.

New purchaser requirements will also require new linkages: community care workers will need an effective online interchange with their various providers. Monitoring of clinical outcomes requires exchange of data between consultants and GPs. Decentralized budget holders will need to communicate regularly with the centre. The new health management regime will require the recording, gathering and syndication of data in a much more systematic way. In this field local government enjoys an enormous advantage because of its already comprehensive database. Once the potential for the use of that base is realized through improved communications, then the influence of the local authority as data possessor can be used to great advantage. Selective data exchange with key participants can greatly change the latter's perception of their responsibilities. For example, communication by the police to the local authority of crime statistics broken down by geographical location and type of crime can have a marked effect on a local authority's own programmes.

Indeed, the police force has been one of the first organizations to perceive the benefits of syndicated knowledge, the procurement of allies and the harnessing of public opinion. Capitalizing on the favourable public opinion of the police, they have used these attitudes to harness public support towards crime prevention (or at least prevention of the fear of crime, which they properly identify as being almost as great a problem).

How Durable is the Concept of Strategic Management?

The new concept of public sector management has attracted passionate adherence. Will it survive? All revolutionary fervour dies down when the revolution has been accomplished. The idealism and commitment fade with the growth in desire for televisions and Toyotas, dishwashers and dachas in the country. Mao Ze Dong, with the nostalgia of the old revolutionary for the days of privation and the Long March, deliberately rekindled the revolution, but out of its time. Bourgeoisification had set in too deeply.

So with most management ideas. The ghosts of management by objectives and planning, programming, budgeting systems (PPBS) will no doubt be joined shortly by abandoned and derelict mission statements. The process of management renovation itself serves a vital purpose in shaking up the organisation, but the revolution is incapable of perpetuation indefinitely. The bureaucracy ticks over; comfort dominates until the next leader becomes committed to the need for a further shake-up. Every system becomes obsolete and must be changed before it ossifies.

The attraction of the purchaser/provider split is that, in theory, it avoids these recurrent traumas, but builds in a constant re-examination of activities. With purchasers divorced from providers the vested interest in bureaucratic comfort is eliminated. A core of purchasing strategists, with alternative sources of provision theoretically at their summons, can maximize their own comfort by constant pressure on providers, as the purchasers react to financial stringency, political and consumer pressures. Each round of contract negotiations imposes an implied duty on the purchasers to improve on the last in terms of cost effectiveness, quality, differentiation and responsiveness. Even when competition is largely non-existent, as in much of the Health Service, the annual round of negotiation will automatically prompt a re-examination of the delivery of service.

As well as concentration on the increase of output and effectiveness, there will be a growing concentration on quality. Already in the National Health Service the level of debate on quality is high and it is growing in local government. In the Health Service regular consumer surveys, monitoring of waiting times and assessment of the hotel services are being extended into medical audit. This systematic concentration on outputs in the Health Service threatens the role of the professional and will prompt changes in professional attitudes. The automatic plea of professional judgement may prove empty as professions find themselves second-guessed through statistical analysis of outcomes.

Pressures will come most immediately through attempts to find the most cost- and clinically-effective measures and to require the purpose and expected result of treatment to be stated, followed by monitoring of the outcome. Following the introduction of data sets as recommended by the Körner Reports (Steering Group, 1982), some comparisons have become evident and the incursion of the Audit Commission into the Health Service can be expected to sharpen these up. Decentralization of budgets and transfer of responsibility to clinical resource directors will accentuate peer pressure. Clinical resource directors trying to make explicit rationing decisions will be in a position to rebut professional pleas from colleagues. Cost-limited community care managers will be in the same position in relation to their case managers. The purchasers can be expected to keep up a relentless pressure.

The providers will also have a regular incentive to review their own activities – partly because of the pressure on them by purchasers, but also because of the incentive of keeping financial gains within their own organization. For the private provider these will result in increased profits. For the public sector provider they could produce increases in performance-related pay or free cash for development.

The specification of outputs should in theory move the debate away from the narrow concepts of efficiency and economy into effectiveness. It should sharpen the debate on the measurement of outputs and, in theory, on the definition of the true objectives of a service. The core of planners should constantly re-examine the needs of their consumers and consider alternative strategies to meet those needs. In some cases these strategies could dispense with the need for service delivery altogether. Purchasers should be led towards marketing strategies which change the perceived needs so as to avoid expensive service delivery. They will try to engineer changes in social behaviour, following the example of crime prevention, anti-drugs and anti-litter campaigns.

Such at least is the theory of the brave new world. It has certainly gripped the imagination of managers in the Health Service and local government, who have gulped large draughts of the conventional wisdom. The purchaser/provider split gives managers a new precision in objectives which public sector bureaucrats have always craved. It frees the time of strategists for conceptual thinking and releases them from day-to-day management concerns which were inseparable from a chief officer's responsibility for service delivery. The incompatibility of professional training with ultimate management responsibilities has always been a theme of critics of the professional base of local authorities. The reciprocal divorce of clinicians from management in the Health Service has attracted equal criticism. The new approach tries to address both problems.

The purchaser/provider split is probably politically robust, though it is inconvenient to politicians to have to choose clear priorities and set precise targets. Every decision in a period of contraction is certain to upset someone. The element of compulsory competition is unacceptable to Labour politicians in local government. The Labour Party sees the element of competition in the Health Service as inappropriate and likely to cause severe distortions in service – at least in those areas where competition might be a reality. They paint a picture of National Health Service managers trying to keep unfinanced capacity by undercutting adjacent hospitals, causing illogical and unplanned bed losses.

Against this is the advantage of bringing the professions to accountability. The systematic monitoring of outcomes and the comparison of different treatments and stays in hospital seem universally welcomed. So is the involvement of clinicians in the budgetary process, on the assumption that they will shoulder explicit responsibility for rationing. Nevertheless, making such decisions explicit will inevitably increase the pressure for greater spending in the Health Service – and in some local government services too. Not only managers but also politicians will be made more accountable. The system will sharpen the democratic process. Such explicitness in decision-taking will also increase the potential for judicial review, as formerly imperceptible decisions are exposed and become capable of challenge.

The Role of Local Government

It is ironic that greater accountability is to be introduced into the National Health Service at the same time as the accountability of the health authorities themselves is to be diminished. Attempts to depoliticize the National Health Service will be unsuccessful. The public articulation of decisions on rationing will prompt a demand for direct accountability. The case for local government control of the Health Service is greatly increased by the present changes, not least as a result of the grey boundary area between social and medical community care. There is certainly an inconsistency in Labour Party proposals to create an elected regional tier which will administer the health service while relying on an appointed district tier which will be coterminous with its local authority.

It is likely that local authorities will take a greater interest in the activities of their local health authority, impinging as it does on so many of their programmes and on their holistic view of the welfare of the area. Other sector-scything issues will present themselves to local authorities. They cannot neglect the impact of new forms of service delivery and information technology on their own staff. The retraining of workers to survive the next industrial revolution is a key topic. Local authorities must address corporately the demographic time bomb, decreasing the number of 16- to 19-year-olds by a quarter in less than a decade and multiplying the incidence of the very old even more sharply. The new phenomenon of the third age must be addressed.

Both bureaucratic planning and decentralized management have equity as a goal. The market does not, and in the next decade equity will surely resurface as an issue. Its re-emergence will emphasize the importance of local government in being able to assemble anti-poverty strategies which span not only their own services but also straddle those of other agencies.

One of the most striking examples of the new role of local authorities is their re-examination of the role of the city. Industrial restructuring and the removal of geographical constraints have compelled local authorities to redefine the *raison d'être* of their cities and to begin to transform them into centres of entertainment, culture, consumption and professional services. Acutely aware that they are competing with other European cities, an attractive image has been sought. Cultural flagships have been launched, like the Alhambra in Bradford, the Glasgow Opera House and the Manchester Royal Exchange. Birmingham has produced its Exhibition Centre and Gateshead its Metrocentre. Transitory events like the Sheffield student games, and the Liverpool (and succeeding) garden festivals have been sought. Heritage areas like the Albert Docks and Covent Garden have been created. A museum is launched in England every two or three weeks. Improvement of the environment is being seen as a key element in competition, as well as having an impact on the quality of life of residents.

Local authorities have been compelled to take these actions to maintain the city as an entity, since information technology has removed the constant need for interaction. The restructuring of industry and commuting has removed the need for concentrations of housing adjacent to labour-intensive industry. It remains to be seen whether these spectacular developments will generate wealth which can impact on the problems of poverty, homelessness, education and health – or whether adequate financial mechanisms will be in place to enable local authorities to tap that wealth.

Since issues such as these permeate the community, it can be expected that local authorities will react corporately as they go through the stages of assessment, planning, securing action, monitoring and regulating. As a result local government will reschedule its service committees away from the delivery of services and towards strategic objectives, such as its strategies on the local economy, the environment, demographic change, service quality and equality of opportunity. There is an urgent need for local authorities to address the concept of differentiated services. What does consumer choice mean in the delivery of service? Can the elderly choose from a menu of community care services? Can the resident choose the standard of refuse collection, perhaps paying more for an improved service? The National Health Service has begun to involve patients in their care plans. How can these developments be replicated in local government?

An exciting new generation of members (of all parties) and chief executives has assimilated this agenda. They have moved away from the Fordist concept of corporate power into the manipulation of a diaspora of influence. They see the local authority's role as much more than a machine for the direct delivery of a uniform set of services to a homogenous population. The council should be the focus of community government. Such a concept requires a strategic capacity. Even the government now concede that some co-ordination is necessary. Having published their own strategy for Greater London they perceive the need for this to be reflected in SERPLAN's strategy for the south-east as a whole.

Conclusion

In this shifting scene of strategic management there will be some pain and discomfort for the managers of the public sector. Those members who feel a special affiliation to service delivery will feel betrayed. Officers who have perforce been associated with the agenda of and the delivery of Fordist solutions will find it difficult to adjust to the delivery of responsive and variable services. But the overall consequence of a post-Fordist role for the public sector may result in the strengthening (not the demolition) of local authority influence, as consumers seek a locally responsive body capable not only of the sensitive delivery of collective goods, but also of preserving and improving their living environment.

As local government throws off paternalism and moves towards the differentiation of services with equity in access and delivery, hands-off municipal control can step in to cater for those whom the market neglects. Local government can secure the public services which the market cannot provide.

References

Steering Group on Health Services Information (1982) *First Report to the Secretary of State*. London: HMSO. (The chairman of the group was Mrs E. Körner.)

17

The Organizational Structure of the Police

Roy Wilkie

The present organizational structure of the police force in the United Kingdom was endorsed – implicitly, if not explicitly – by the Royal Commission on the Police in 1962. The recommendations of the Commission were designed to secure three objectives: a system of control over the police which would achieve the maximum efficiency and the best use of manpower, adequate means of bringing the police to account and proper arrangements for dealing with complaints. The first two of these objectives were not, in the Commission's judgement, adequately secured, and there was even some dissatisfaction expressed with regard to the third but, nonetheless, the objectives were capable of being secured in the Commission's words, 'without any fundamental disturbance of the present police system'. The recommendations of the Royal Commission were broadly encapsulated in the Police Act, 1964, and the Police (Scotland) Act, 1967.

The system that was to be left undisturbed was one easily identified. First of all, the police forces were divided by ranks – probationary constable, constable, sergeant, inspector, chief inspector, superintendent, chief superintendent, assistant chief constable, deputy chief constable, chief constable. And, secondly, the police had tended to group their activities under some rational order. In most forces in Britain, there would be the main activities of operations (sometimes referred to as uniform), criminal investigation and traffic. Traffic, for example, would contain road safety and vehicle maintenance, while the criminal investigation department would contain the fraud squad and the special branch. The structure was largely a function of piecemeal adaptation.

Backing these primary functions, most forces would have had administrative, personnel, training and support service functions. Again, under these would have been placed, in some rational fashion, sub-functions. Support services may have the dog branch, the mounted branch, com-

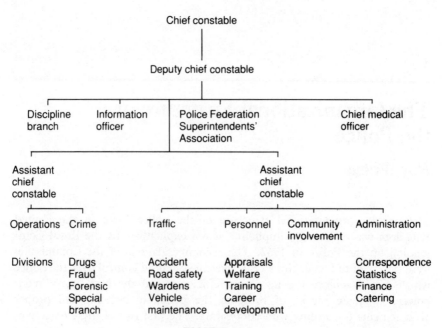

FIGURE 17.1
Typical organization of an urban police force

munications. Personnel may have training, welfare, appraisal. Administration may have finance, accounts, statistics, licensing. Whatever the
particular arrangements of these sub-functions, many forces in Britain
would have had the organizational structure shown in figure 17.1.

These two points of rank and function suggest that the formal organization of the police is quite straightforward. Now, in Weber's view (1947),
everything about an organization should aid in the pursuit of its goals and
objectives so that it is a mechanism for their rational, efficient accom-
plishment. The fully developed bureaucratic mechanism, he suggested,
compares with other organizations exactly as does the machine with non-
mechanical modes of production. Precision, speed, unambiguity, continuity,
discretion, unity – these were raised, he considered, to the optimum point
in a strictly bureaucratic administration.

In its most rational form, bureaucracy, to Weber, had the following
defining characteristics:

1   The staff members are personally free, observing only the impersonal
    duties of their offices.

2　There is a clear hierarchy of offices.

3　The functions of the offices are clearly specified.

4　Officials are appointed on the basis of a contract.

5　They are selected on the basis of a professional qualification, ideally substantiated by a diploma gained through examination.

6　They have a money salary and usually pension rights. The salary is graded according to position in the hierarchy. The official can always leave his post, and under certain circumstances it may also be terminated.

7　The official's post is his sole or major occupation.

8　There is a career structure, and promotion is possible either by seniority or merit, according to the judgement of superiors.

9　The official may appropriate neither the post nor the resources which go with it.

10　He or she is subject to a unified control and disciplinary system.

The fifth characteristic – selection on the basis of a professional qualification – would not be true in this case. Recruitment and selection to the British police has not entailed holding any professional qualification, although 'professionalization' can be seen to be intruding at the margins with an HNC in police studies established in Scotland in 1968, sponsorships to universities coming on stream in the 1970s and a few higher institutions offering a degree in police or criminal justice studies. Doubts could also reasonably be expressed about the third characteristic: some officers would complain that their functions are not clearly specified. Nevertheless, in addition to functional specialization and the hierarchy of offices, the police service in Britain would comfortably meet these remaining Weberian characteristics of a bureaucratic organization.

Changes Since the 1962 Commission

The Police Act, 1964, and the Police (Scotland) Act, 1967, on the basis of the Royal Commission's recommendations, established how this bureaucratic organization would be controlled. The local authorities had the power to appoint their chief constable and to determine the number of persons for each rank, and, after consulting with the chief constable, to appoint the deputy and assistant chief constable, subject to the authority of the secretary of state. They were charged with securing the maintenance of an adequate and efficient police force and keeping themselves informed about how complaints made by members of the public against members of the police force are dealt with by the chief constable. The chief constable had the power to appoint, promote and discipline all officers up to the rank of chief superintendent. Each police force was under the 'direction and control' of its chief constable. The third party to this arrangement – central government – paid 50 per cent (changed in 1986 to 51 per cent) of the cost of each force, could require a police authority to call upon its chief constable to retire in the interests of efficiency, could order a local enquiry into any matter connected with the policing of an area, could make regulations about the government, administration and conditions of service of police forces and could direct a chief constable to provide mutual aid to another force.

A great many changes have gone on since the Commission and the two Acts. First of all, the number of forces has changed. In 1962, there were 124 police forces in England and Wales and 33 in Scotland. Now, there are 43 police forces in England and Wales and eight in Scotland. Of the 43 in England and Wales, 25 each have an authorized establishment of under 2,000 officers, and of the eight in Scotland, four have under 1,000 police officers.

Secondly, the numbers of police officers have changed. In 1962 there were 75,600 in England and Wales and 9,000 in Scotland. Now, there are about 124,000 and 14,000. Moreover, the distribution of these numbers throughout the ranks has changed. For example, in Scotland in 1962, there were 33 chief constables and five assistant chief constables. Now there are eight chief constables, eight deputy chief constables and 12 assistant chief constables. In 1962 there were 76 superintendents. Now there are 146.

A third change has been the increased recruitment and varied employment of female police officers. In 1962, there were 2,420 female officers in England and Wales and 313 in Scotland. Two county forces in Scotland had no policewomen. Up until the 1970s, policewomen tended to work in their own sections, carrying out their specialized duties for 90 per cent of the pay of their male colleagues. They did not work night shifts, and, if called out during the night, it was generally on overtime. Then the Equal Pay Act of 1970, the Employment Protection Act of 1975 and the Sex Discrimination Act of 1975 became law. From 1975, 'policewomen' no longer existed. In 1988, these numbers were 14,800 and 1,158. What research there has been into the employment of female police officers suggests that their assimilation has not yet been completed and that older and senior male officers still have reservations about their effective 'equality'.

A fourth change was in the employment of civilians. In 1962, there were 8,091 civilians employed in England and Wales and 1,162 in Scotland. Now there are 39,201 civilian full-time staff as well as the equivalent of 3,149 more full-time staff as part-time employees in England and Wales and 2,800 in Scotland. Moreover, the jobs done by these civilians have also been changed. Whereas they would once have been janitors and cleaners, now they are van drivers and turnkeys. A civilian has held the position equivalent to assistant chief constable in the Devon and Cornwall and in West Yorkshire forces. The station officers in operational divisions in the Lothians and Borders police are now civilians.

The number of traffic wardens in 1962 in England and Wales was 1,800 and there were none in Scotland. Today there are 4,644 in England and Wales and 573 in Scotland. The number of special constables in 1962 in England and Wales was 47,600 with 7,000 in Scotland. Today these figures are 15,788 and 1,747.

All these changes – fewer forces, more police officers, more female police officers, more civilian staff, more traffic wardens and fewer special constables – helped to create the development of the personnel function in police forces. For example, there were very few formal staff appraisal systems prior to 1970. Then the question of staff appraisal was considered by an *ad hoc* working group representative of the local authorities and police associations. This group recognized that staff appraisal had become an established part of the system of man-management in the armed forces, civil service and industry and a formal system of staff appraisal was now desirable. Their report formed Home Office Circular 227/1970, *Staff Appraisal in the Police Service*, which was approved by the Police Advisory Board for England and Wales at its meeting of 20 October 1970 and then circulated to police authorities, chief officers of police and police representative associations. In 1971 the circular was considered by the Police Advisory Board for Scotland, which acknowledged the importance of staff appraisal and its likely increasing importance with the forth-coming re-organization of local government. Since then, police forces have adopted some systems of appraisal which have had various degrees of acceptance by police officers.

Sixth, another characteristic of the organizational structure of the police is that, over the last 20 to 30 years, it has created a number of *ad hoc* units or departments or functions which have been simply tacked on to the other two structural factors of rank and function. These 'additional' units range from hard-nosed ones to soft-nosed elements.

An example of the former changes might be that of the police response to drugs. As a policing issue, drugs did not appear on the police agenda throughout the sixties and the early part of the seventies. Then, throughout the remainder of the seventies and into the eighties, drugs specialization was built up in the Criminal Investigation Departments of many forces. In October 1985, the National Drugs Intelligence Unit came into operation, based in New Scotland Yard. Its main objective was to collate all information on drug trafficking in the United Kingdom and to identify criminal activity involved. The unit was staffed with a mixture of Customs and

Excise officers and officers drawn from police forces throughout the United Kingdom. In 1986, drug wings were attached to existing Regional Crime Squads in England and Wales. The Scottish Crime Squad drugs wing was set up in October 1986, with a detective chief inspector, based in Glasgow, given operational control for two wings in Glasgow and Edinburgh with ten officers at each office. The officers were selected from the eight Scottish police forces. In April 1989, an additional Scottish Crime Squad drugs wing was set up in Stonehaven in the Grampian Region. An example of a softer-nosed unit might be public relations. Most forces now have a public relations officer or unit or department.

So, over the years, a number of organizational units had come into existence and, as might be expected, not many have gone out of existence. Regional Crime Squads, the Scottish Crime Squad, the Serious Crime Squad, community involvement units – these, and other 'extra' units, often giving the impression of simply being bolted on to the existing police structures, create all sorts of problems – for example, who fills them, who controls them and where are they to be located. Community relations or, as they sometimes called, community involvement officers, for example, usually have an ambiguous role within operating divisions.

Some conscious attempts at reorganization have gone on. For example, the Northamptonshire police force, which was among the first to dabble with 'policing by objectives', reorganized its sub-divisions, which became semi-autonomous and under the direct control of an officer of the rank of superintendent, and redefined the traditional, commanding role of chief superintendent with an inspectorate as opposed to an operational function. 'Policing by objectives' can easily be described as the most innovative design change in the last two or three decades but, to be fair, it hasn't had a lot of competition. In 1989 the Metropolitan Police introduced a programme to increase public confidence by improving the level of service provided to the people of London. The protagonists claimed that it was not an 'image' issue but a programme that would bring about a whole cultural shift, changing attitudes and behaviour, with everyone in the organization examining what they could do to improve service to the public and to each other and with the whole organization pulling together as one unit. By the end of 1990 disquiet was being expressed about the middle management's lack of enthusiasm and dragging of feet.

A seventh organizational characteristic of the police has been its peculiar use of technology. In 1962, transistorized equipment with its lower battery consumption was beginning to dispense with the need to use large-capacity batteries and heavy duty dynamos on police vehicles. Trials of small-pack sets for use by the beat constables were in progress. Panda cars came into prominence with unit beat policing in the 1967/8 period. A police national computer, which contains information about wanted suspect persons, missing persons and stolen cars, was established in 1970. A Criminal Records Data Bank was established in Scotland in 1987/8. But, by and large, technological innovation has been an extremely haphazard affair, with many forces often 'doing their own thing' without considering the broader implications of their decisions. For example, at the Lockerbie disaster in December 1988, the police cars of the different forces involved (at least five initially) could not communicate directly with one another by phone, nor was the hardware needed for the Home Office Large Major Enquiry System (HOLMES) common to all the forces. Lothian and Borders officers had to adapt to the Strathclyde hardware system.

All of these changes suggest an *ad hoc*, piecemeal response of the British police forces to the changing social conditions of the country. The police forces have not undertaken any fundamental review of their organizational structures. By and large, they have bureaucratized their problems. The structure is held together by an immense apparatus of procedures, codified as 'standing orders' which, in its detail, specifies how everything should be done and, equally, that some other, usually more efficient way will be pursued. Meanwhile, these changes were taking place within a changing political, social and economic environment which made the conditions of the fifties, from which the Commission's members drew their wisdom, seem more and more remote and irrelevant to the problems of policing.

What kinds of changes would make one judge that the police ought to have undertaken such a review? One example might have been the amount of legislation that the police forces were being asked to enforce. There has been an enormous amount of new legislation placed on the statute books since 1962. The index to the current *Scottish Police Training Manual* contains reference to 226 main statutes, excluding road traffic legislation, over 60 per cent of which dates from 1960. This legislation ranges from measures reflecting social changes (for example, the Child Abduction Act, 1984) and changing social attitudes (for example, the Licensing (Scotland) Act, 1976) to legislation meeting identifiable risks and combating dangerous behaviour (for example, the Prevention of Terrorism (temporary provisions) Act, 1980). Some of it bears directly upon police and police practices. The Criminal Justice (Scotland) Act became law in 1980, the Police and Criminal Evidence Act came into effect in 1984 and the Public Order Act became law in 1986.

Another example might have been the actual behaviour of police officers. There were bribery and corruption scandals of the 1970s and 1980s, notably within the Metropolitan Police. In 1988, the West Midlands Crime squad was disbanded, following complaints of alleged corruption. Related in many people's minds to these facts was the evidence that some police officers did not consider the law good enough for them or thought that the law was an instrument for their exclusive use. For example, the three boys convicted in 1972 of the murder of Maxwell Confait were exonerated in 1979, and the official inquiry established that the boys' rights had been violated and that some police officers did not seem to know the proper procedures for interrogation. These criticisms were amplified in recent cases, in which the Court of Appeal dismissed long-standing terrorist convictions against the Guildford Four in 1989 and the Birmingham Six in 1991.

There has also been some evidence that the conventional police strategy of minimal force enshrined in the Royal Commission's thinking was being eroded, and a clearer trend to harder-line policing of political and industrial conflict could be discerned. Throughout the eighties, the country witnessed the paramilitary style of the use of force by the police at urban rioting, political demonstrations and industrial disputes – Bristol in 1980, Brixton and Toxteth in 1981 (the first use in England of CS gas was in July 1981), Grunwick in 1983, the miners' dispute in 1984–5, Handsworth, the Broadwater Farm estate, and Manchester students in 1985, Wapping in 1986/7 and Stonehenge in 1987.

Allied to these cases was the accompanying suggestion that the importance attached to the notion of policing as a social service was in decline. For example, research in Devon and Cornwall and Greater Manchester police forces claimed that police officers viewed that kind of work as 'rubbish work', even though the public regarded it as worthwhile. A similar observation in another piece of research was made about crime prevention work.

Another example of the kind of change that might have occasioned a fundamental rethinking of police organization is, of course, in the field of law enforcement. What evidence there is suggests that the actions of police forces in controlling crime and public disorder are becoming less and less effective. In 1962, there were about 1 million crimes and offences known to the police. In 1988, the figures were over 4 million. Moreover, in the 1980s, a newly established British Crime Survey estimated that total crime exceeded recorded crime in a ratio of 3 or 4 to 1. Not only did it appear that crime and offences were on the increase but the clear-up rate was falling. For example, from 1971 to 1988 the clear-up rate for all crimes fell in England and Wales from 45 per cent to 35 per cent and in Scotland from 38 per cent to 34 per cent.

A final illustration of change that might have warranted organizational rethinking would be the cost of policing. Policing cost £4,177 million in 1988, increasing at 8 per cent per annum. In the 1980s, the central government focused on the efficiency and effectiveness issues as part of its general campaign to control public expenditure. Circulars were sent to chief constables, alerting them to the government's decision not to create any additional posts without guarantees that the police's existing resources were already being used to the best advantage. Were the police clear about what they were doing? Did they have their priorities sorted out properly? Could more civilian staff and technical support be brought into employment? Were the police management systems adequate for coping with changes in the nature of police work? These and other questions edged police forces towards organizational initiatives like Northamptonshire's adoption of 'policing by objectives', a version of which most forces took on by the middle and later 1980s.

Now, as might be expected from the recounting of these bare facts about personnel, structural and technological changes inside the police forces and the volume of legislation, the actual behaviours of police officers, the increasing and different criminal activities and the increasing costs, the fairly limp or belated knee-jerk response by the police force would vindicate its description as a highly bureaucratic organization. Certainly, it suffers all the usual complaints about bureaucracies – rigidity, impersonality, goal displacement, departmentalism, empire-building, the cost of control and the creation of stress and anxiety. Interestingly, there is a column called 'Dogberry' in the Police Federation's monthly journal, *Police*, full of stories of bureaucratic dysfunction which fleshes out the usual human expressions of bureaucratic pathology – character corruption, moral poverty, mania for promotion, obsequiousness towards the bosses upon whom promotion depends, arrogance towards people in lower ranks and servility towards those in higher ones. It is generally regarded as essential reading for all police officers, especially senior ones (if only to find out if they are mentioned!) and ought to be so for students of police affairs.

The Future of the Structure

What is likely to happen after these improvised organizational responses to the increasing turbulence of the police environment? One obvious answer is the demand for a national police force. The issue of a completely integrated national force answerable only to a new Ministry of Justice has been lurking about since Dr A. L. Goodhart's 'memorandum of dissent' to the 1962 Royal Commission, where he pointed out that, according to the principles of public administration, the police should be under the control of central government. Central government already controlled pay, conditions of service and rules of discipline. The Police Federation was organized on a national basis. Goodhart proposed a single police force for England and Wales and a separate police force for Scotland. The Home Secretary and the Secretary of State for Scotland would be responsible to Parliament for the proper maintenance and administration of the police forces. They must therefore be given the ultimate control in regard to all police matters as, in his view, there can be no responsibility without the power to control and direct.

That the ideas of this minority report are now back on the table can be seen in a number of ways. For example, in the summer of 1989, Sir Peter Imbert suggested in a speech to the Police Federation that elements of the 43 national forces, nine Regional Crime Squads, customs and immigration services, along with legal, computer and accountancy experts might be organized along the lines of the American FBI. Competing enforcement agencies, he claimed, could only benefit the criminal. Douglas Hurd, then the Home Secretary, responded by saying that he was willing to listen to Imbert's ideas. In the interim, Hurd promised to make money available to the Association of Chief Police Officers so that it could extend its London-based secretariat and look into better arrangements for forces to share intelligence and investigations. Another example is the *Operating Policing Review*, 1990, a special report which is the first major research programme to be commissioned by the Joint Consultative Committee of representatives from the Police Federation of England and Wales, the Police Superintendents' Association of England and Wales and the Association of Chief Police Officers. The report, arguing that the fear of crime, particularly drug, international and terrorist-related crime, and the best use of resources will ensure that fundamental questions of organization will be raised, goes on to assess the various scenarios of the status quo, a national structure, a regional structure, a semi-national/semi-local structure (maintaining the existing local operational framework but at the same time increasing central control and introducing new specialist national agencies). My own bet would be on a version of regionalization, for the other scenarios take too much away from the chief constables.

Another item which is looming over the horizon concerns the quality of top management in the police. How are we going to ensure that the police forces have good quality managers? One solution comes from the Home Affairs Committee report, *Higher Police Training and the Police Staff College*, in the spring of 1989 which, acknowledging the importance of the quality of management towards the success of the organization, came out with the bureaucratic solution that, from 1993 onwards, attendance on the senior command course at the Bramshill Police College should be a compulsory requirement for all officers applying for posts at the ranks of chief constable and deputy chief constable. Another idea floated in the columns of the quality newspapers in the spring of 1990 was a two-tiered management system which could include the shoehorning in of outside managers into the higher levels of the police forces.

Much the most fundamental issue of the 1990s, however, will be the creation of a new Royal Commission, generally now acknowledged by most interested parties (only the police group of the Conservative Party seems opposed) as essential towards resolving the extraordinary heterogeneity and mishmash of ideas about policing. The real issue for the 1990s is that the police are asked to pursue a number of goals – the maintenance of law and order, the protection of persons and property, the prevention of crime, the detection of criminals, the control of traffic, and so on – any one of which, taken singly, is open to a wide range of interpretation and, if combined with any other or others, can lead through goal collisions to bureaucratic conflict. Only through such a device as a Royal Commission could we ensure that the structures of the British police and their organizational practices were brought more into line with the problems that the police forces are, and will be, facing.

References

Bradley, D., Walker, N. and Wilkie, R. (1986) *Managing the Police: Law, Organisation and Democracy*. Brighton: Wheatsheaf.

Jefferson, T. and Grimshaw, R. (1984) *Controlling the Constable*. London: Muller.

Langworthy, R.H. (1986) *The Structure of Police Organisations*. London: Praeger.

Morgan, R. and Smith, D.J. (1989) *Coming to Terms with Policing*. London: Routledge.

Reiner, R. (1985) *The Politics of the Police*. Brighton: Harvester.

Royal Commission on the Police (1962) *Report* (Cmnd. 1728). London: HMSO.

Weber, M. (1947) *The Theory of Social and Economic Organisation*, trans. A. M. Henderson and T. Parsons. New York: Free Press.

18

Strategic Management in the Prison Service

Chris J. Train and Christine Stewart

This chapter sets out the process of strategic management in the prison service of England and Wales. It begins with a description of the organization itself – its current structure, constitutional position and relationship with other organizations – and of the setting in which it operates. Against this background it describes the systems which have been developed in recent years to improve management control and to enable strategic planning to take place and the strategy to be delivered. What is presented is a picture of an organization in a state of change. Some of the systems described are more developed than others, which are still evolving, so this is simply a snapshot of the prison service in its current state of development.

The Nature and Task of the Prison Service

The prison service is a large and geographically dispersed organization. Its task is to keep in custody all those committed by the courts, either on remand or under sentence, in England and Wales (separate services exist in Scotland and Northern Ireland). In order to fulfil this task it employs some 33,750 staff to manage the system and to run the 124 establishments which make up the current prison estate. In 1990/1 the service looked after an average of 45,000 inmates each day at an annual cost of £1.3 billion.

Constitutionally the service is part of the Home Office and falls within the responsibilities of the Home Secretary. Its day-to-day management is the responsibility of the director general of the prison service. A review of the organization and location of the service above establishment level, which took place in 1989, led to a major reorganization with effect from September 1990. This involved the abolition of the previous regional structure and the creation of more operational and policy directorates, designed to bring about a closer integration of headquarters and the field.

The three operational directors, along with three directors of services (building, personnel, finance and medical), form the top management of the prison service. All are members of the Prisons Board, which is chaired by the director general, and which has on it two non-executive directors from the private sector.

Influences on the Prison Service

The prison service is an integral part of the criminal justice system and has links with the other criminal justice agencies, i.e. the police, the Crown Prosecution Service, the courts, and the probation service. Each of these agencies operates independently and has its own functions to perform which impact differently on the prison service. The prison service is the last link in the chain and has to accept all those who, having passed through the hands of the other agencies, are remanded or sentenced to custody. It controls neither the numbers which it receives nor the length of time for which it must hold them. Its task is, within the finite resources available to it, to keep all those it receives in secure but humane conditions during the currency of their sentence; to occupy and, where appropriate, educate them; and to prepare them, so far as possible, for release back into the community.

In its performance of this task the service is accountable to ministers and, through them, to Parliament. But penal policy is a sensitive and controversial area which attracts the interest of a wide range of people and organizations, including pressure groups, trades unions, the media, Parliament, and the public at large. Each may have different and possibly incompatible, albeit legitimate, concerns and expectations. The pressures which are placed upon it are many and varied and there is a risk that in seeking to respond to them the prison service could become an entirely reactive organization, constantly changing direction to meet the needs of the moment and without a longer-term vision.

This risk can be aggravated by the need for the service to cope with sudden surges in the number of inmates which cannot immediately be matched by increases in accommodation. As the size of the population varies markedly from year to year, projecting the prison population is fraught with difficulties. Many different factors influence the commission, detection and punishment of crime, including, for example, social, educational and economic circumstances, the resources available to, and the policies of, individual police forces, and the view taken by the judiciary of the appropriate response to different types of offence. Demographic trends may also have an effect. It is extremely difficult to assess what has been the significance of each of these factors and of their relationship to each other and to attempt to project them all in a statistical model of the prison population.

The prison service has adopted a fairly pragmatic approach in which the starting-point is a projection of trends in the two factors which have the most direct bearing on the size of the prison population – the number of persons received into custody and the length of time served. The approach assumes the continuation of past trends and current policies except where planned changes can be quantified. It allows certain other assumptions to be built in – the severity of custodial sentencing and demographic factors, for example, are taken into account subjectively. The projections are used as a guide for planning purposes. In the nature of things they cannot be relied upon to predict with complete accuracy the demand which the service may have to face. And variations which may seem marginal can have a major impact. Three or four hundred prisoners more or less is the equivalent of one whole prison.

The reality is that the service has to operate in an uncertain environment. Although that environment can be influenced to a certain extent, many of the relevant factors cannot be controlled by the prison service. A surge in the population of the sort which was experienced in the mid to late 1980s, leading to serious overcrowding, can place the service under severe pressure as, of course, can major disturbances such as those which occurred in a number of prisons in April 1990.

Against this sort of background the task for senior management is to devise a means of running the service which provides a sense of stability and coherence and which allows it to make progress towards the long-term and long established aims of improving conditions for prisoners to live in and staff to work in, rather than being constantly blown off course by short term crises and pressures. It will never be possible to devise a planning system which will cope with all eventualities – this is perhaps particularly true in the case of the prison service which, as indicated, is subject to variable pressures and to sudden unforseeable crises. But it is possible to devise a system which provides a stable framework within which such crises and pressures can be managed. The prison disturbances in 1990 put this proposition to the test in the case of the system which has been developed in the prison service.

An Integrated Approach

It is a truism, but no less important for that, that a key element in successful management is a clear sense of purpose and of objectives, which is shared by all those in the management chain. This sense of purpose, and commitment to the aims of the organization, needs to be constantly reinforced through communication up and down the line – that must be two way, involving all levels of management, and must be iterative in an organization which is operating in a changing environment.

Prison service management has developed an integrated system for directing activity within an overall strategic framework. This system has grown out of day-to-day management needs and has then been refined, rather than having been planned in its entirety at the outset. The advantage of this approach is that it responds to the world as it is, not as some planner in an ivory tower thinks it should be. It is seen to be pragmatic and to reflect the management needs of the service. It also means that each of the elements of the system has had an opportunity to bed down and to become accepted by staff before new initiatives have been taken. A potential disadvantage, of course, is that the system grows up piecemeal, contains too many inconsistencies and lacks an overall shape. This is clearly a danger, but one which we have sought to avoid by a process of review and refinement, and more recently by attempting, with the help of the University of Strathclyde Business School, to produce a computer model of the system which, because of the logical rigour required in its construction, tests the linkages between the various elements and enables any inconsistencies to be identified. In this way a system has been produced which meets the needs of ministers and senior managers, while at the same time providing useful tools for management down the line.

The system can best be envisaged as a series of wheels. Each wheel starts to turn at different times of the year and the period covered by each of the planning cycles varies, thus allowing each part of the process both to drive and to be driven at different times by other parts. The following diagram illustrates the cyclical nature of the processes and the importance of the linkages, which are sometimes direct and sometimes indirect (the processes referred to in it will be discussed later).

Statement of Purpose

As already indicated, an essential ingredient for the successful management of an organization which is operating against a background of uncertainty and of sometimes conflicting pressures is a clear sense of purpose. It is, of course, impossible for an organization such as the prison service to be completely proactive and, indeed, it would be wrong for it to set itself rigid targets which might constrain it and prevent it from responding flexibly to fluctuating demands and changing public and political pressures.

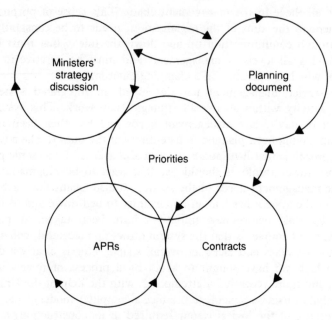

FIGURE 18.1
The prison service management system

Nevertheless, if it is to avoid being constantly in the business of short-term crisis management, it must have a clear sense of what, ultimately, it exists to do. Without that sense, which itself gives direction, staff morale is likely to suffer, because they will have no confidence that managers know where they are going, and the service will lack credibility in the eyes of the public, who are entitled to the reassurance that those whom the courts have decided need to be removed from society are being safely and securely contained.

This much seems obvious. But devising statements of purpose is by no means easy. Anyone with experience of large organizations will know that staff at different levels tend to have quite different perceptions of the organization in which they work. And the task is further complicated by the fact that those viewing the organization from outside have differing expectations of it. Over-elaboration can lead to controversy and thence to confusion and lack of impact. One has to catch the essence of the organization in a simple and direct statement of what it is there to do and how it should do it, which can be accepted and understood by staff and which provides a point of reference against which to judge its activities. The prison service adopted the following statement of purpose in 1988: 'Her Majesty's Prison Service serves the public by keeping in custody those committed by the courts. Our duty is to look after them with humanity and

to help them lead law abiding and useful lives in custody and after release.'
This statement is displayed publicly at every prison service establishment
in the country and is reproduced on the back of the identity card carried by
all members of the service. In the short time since it was introduced it has
become accepted as part of the culture of the service and it helps to shape
the way in which members of staff at all levels approach and think about
their work; in short, it has fostered a sense of corporate identity in the
service.

The Ministerial Dimension

The service's relationship with ministers is a crucial one. The Home
Secretary is responsible not only for the prison service but also for general
policy on law and order. He takes a broad view across the whole of the
criminal justice system and has to see the aims of the prison service against
that wider canvas. The articulation of the statement of purpose, which
has the specific endorsement of ministers, is helpful in this context since
it helps to develop in all concerned – ministers and officials – a shared
understanding of the nature of the prison service and of its role. This
provides a starting-point for the essential process of strategic planning.

That process, which is repeated annually, begins with a day-long meeting
of ministers and senior officials drawn from the whole of the Home Office
in the autumn of each year. The meeting takes place away from the Office
and provides an opportunity to review strategic progress over the year and
to consider priorities for the future. As other parts of the Home Office have
responsibilities for different elements of the criminal justice system, an
occasion of this sort gives time for reflection upon the linkages between
policies that are developing or changes that are occurring in the various
parts of the system. In this forum the prison service is able to play some
part in shaping the environment in which it operates and, to that extent,
in reducing some of the uncertainty referred to earlier. More directly, this
meeting conditions the developing policies and the priorities of the service
for the coming year and beyond. No formal and detailed programme of
work emerges. The issues which are raised are fed back into the relevant
parts of the Home Office and into the more formal process of strategic
planning which then takes place.

The Prison Service Planning Document

The vehicle for this is the prison service annual planning document. This is
written in March. It covers a five-year period (the current year, the year just
about to begin, and the three forward years which will be the subject of the

public expenditure survey). It formally sets out the framework of plans within which the service is and will be operating, by bringing together in one place at the start of each financial year the results of the various planning exercises relating to that year which have taken place on both the financial and the policy side. All of these exercises are conditioned by the statement of purpose (which is set out at the beginning of the document) and by a statement of the longer term goals of the service:

- to accommodate prisoners remanded or sentenced to custody in secure, safe, decent and uncrowded conditions;
- to treat men fairly and humanely;
- to provide positive regimes; and
- to use with maximum efficiency and in accordance with best management practice the resources of staff, money and plant available.

These goals, and the strategic objectives which flow from them are, in effect, the signposts setting out the general direction for the service to follow in the medium to long term. They are cast in broad terms but are accompanied by a set of specific indicators of success which help to measure progress towards their achievement. They are reviewed with ministers as part of the annual planning exercise but, given that they set the longer-term framework, they are not subject to frequent change.

Beneath this set of strategic objectives is a set of short-term objectives relating to specific activities which are planned to take place during the course of the year in futherance of the service's goals. Delivery of these is specifically attributed to named officials who are responsible for ensuring that the underlying programme of work is completed, and progress against them is monitored by the Prisons Board in the autumn and the spring, when they are reviewed as part of the annual revision and updating of the planning document. Taken together, these elements make up the prison service's current and forward programme.

As well as setting out the policy objectives of the service, the planning document provides a means of matching the service's objectives to the available resources. It contains, in effect, a budget statement for the coming year and a statement of resource needs for the three following years which will be the focus of the annual public expenditure survey (PES). So the planning document serves a number of purposes:

1 It provides an opportunity to review progress in delivery of the service's programme which has been achieved during the year just ending.
2 It enables senior officials and ministers to focus on detailed plans for the coming year and to ensure that they are consistent with the long-term goals.

3 It provides a focus for considering longer term plans.
4 It acts as a starting-point for discussions with the Treasury at ministerial level about the future resource needs of the service.

It also fulfils a more general purpose. Mere statements of intent, even when shaped by a clear view of the longer-term aims of the organization, must be made a reality by managerial commitment to them. The planning document is one of the means of securing that commitment. It is submitted to, and agreed with, ministers and, in effect, forms the service's contract with them. It helps to condition the relationship between ministers and officials, since it sets the parameters within which both will be working, providing a sense of continuity and avoiding the otherwise strong tendency to focus on immediate issues at the expense of longer-term strategic thinking. It gives practical and detailed effect to the guidance on strategy that flows from the autumn meeting referred to earlier. And it is an explicit statement of the framework for the service's work for the year ahead at divisional, regional and establishment level.

Annual Priorities

The planning document is a top level planning tool – a sort of corporate plan for the prison service. While it is an essential mechanism for re-viewing, co-ordinating and planning progress at the aggregate level, it is not sufficiently focused on day-to-day issues to enable it to be used very far down the management chain in setting work programmes for headquarters units and for establishments.

In order to provide this clear focus the Prisons Board has instituted the practice of setting priorities for the service for the coming year. These priorities are formulated having regard to the goals and long-term pro-gramme of the service as contained in the planning document. They are limited in number – three in 1991/2 – so as to ensure that the efforts of the service are not dissipated. They are set out in a letter which the director general personally sends to all governors and heads of headquarters units. The letter also contains a list of all the initiatives, deriving from the service's forward programme, which are planned to take place during the coming year and which will have an impact on the work of establishments, in order to enable governors to plan their work programmes for the year in the knowledge of the demands which are likely to be placed upon them.

This practice of setting annual priorities was introduced in January 1989, but it is already an integral part of the management system and has proved effective in directing the work of the service towards the strategically key issues and in delivering progress towards them. Much management effort has gone into securing its acceptance. It has been widely publicized throughout the service by means of *Prison Service News* (the service's newspaper) and *Briefing* (a management bulletin issued regularly to all members of staff) and senior managers review progress when visiting establishments. This clear indication of management commitment has been an indispensable element in the process as, indeed, it is in relation to each of the other planning processes.

Contracts

The way in which the programme is translated into action in establishments relies upon a system of management by contract. As explained above, the planning document is a form of high-level contract between ministers and the prison service as a whole. On a more detailed level are the contracts which are drawn up annually between governors of establishments and their respective line managers.

This system has been operated for the last four years and has its origin in a circular instruction to the service which was issued by the Prisons Board to all establishments in 1984, setting out a statement of the task and functions of the prison service and clarifying management responsibilities. The circular instruction emphasized the key relationship between governors and their line managers – a relationship which needed emphasizing in a service in which governors had traditionally acted fairly independently, running their own establishments in their own way and with little central managerial direction. It also introduced the concept of a contract between the governor and the line manager which has to be agreed annually and has to set out clearly the functions of the individual establishments, the level of service to be provided in respect of them, how this is to be met within the resources available and any objectives for change in respect of local or national (i.e. strategic) priorities that are required in the year ahead. When it was introduced this contract setting process, which takes place in February/ March, was the first building block in the management structure which is designed to ensure that the service as a whole delivers its task and functions. It now provides the means of feeding the annual (strategic) priorities into the system and of ensuring that they are firmly embedded at establishment level. It also provides a formal opportunity each year for a discussion of plans and performance between the governor, his senior staff and his line managers, and it gives all concerned a means of monitoring and measuring progress in the year.

In a similar way, but a little earlier in the year, headquarters units produce annual performance reviews (APRs) which identify the purpose and functions of the particular unit, set out the objectives for the year and review performance against the objectives set in the previous round. These APRs are, in effect, the contracts between heads of units and their respective directors. They are also used by the director general as the basis for an annual discussion of progress and plans in the first half of each year with every head of unit and in this way enable issues to be raised which can be fed back into the planning process at the top level, so completing the planning loop.

Summary

This chapter has described the systems for strategic management in the prison service of England and Wales. Each of the elements described is used in its own right, as well as being part of a broader strategic system. But the system works as an integrated whole, because each of the elements, as well as fulfilling a specific need and therefore having a life of its own, makes its own contribution to the development and delivery of the service's strategy. The different elements have not been forced to fit into some intellectually elegant and predetermined structure. Rather the system has developed organically, with each element being planted firmly in the management culture, the linkages being intentionally loose and the whole being held together by a well established process of communication at each level of the management chain.

The advantage of a system of this sort is that it provides a basis for continuity in a changing and demanding environment. By identifying at the appropriate level key issues and tasks, within an overarching and steady commitment of purpose and function, it helps to provide a clear sense of direction for management at all levels and the means by which they can judge their success as managers. It serves above all to produce both the sense and the reality of coherence in the organization.

19

Strategic Management in Social Service

Norman Tutt, Jean Neale and William Warburton

Shortly after the publication of the government White Paper on community care, *Caring for People*, the Yorkshire Regional Health Authority produced an excellent video to explain the proposed changes to staff. As you would expect, the video had a 'health' slant, with a health service interpretation of the pattern of community care in Britain in the 1990s. Leeds Social Service Department for a variety of reasons, primarily related to resources, did not produce such a video for its own staff. We were content to use the RHA video to show to council members and our staff, despite the importance of the White Paper to the work of the social services department in the city. We will be the 'lead authority' in community care and yet the health authority was already setting the pace and establishing its position in the partnership relationship prescribed in the White Paper. A minor incident perhaps, but one which encapsulates the notion of strategic management. In periods of rapid change, those organizations wishing to survive and prosper must learn to manage their environment and their relationships with the other organizations active within it. This is the dilemma, or, more positively, the challenge facing social services departments and other public service organizations as they move into the 1990s.

Within a local government setting, social services departments are in the business of helping with a wide range of social and personal problems. We have specified statutory responsibilities to provide services for certain groups of people like children and the elderly, but wide discretion as to the nature of these services and how they are delivered. When offering welfare services, we are frequently concerned with encouraging and supporting change in the lives of our clients or customers. Social work staff may spend hours talking to people with problems, assessing needs, looking at options, devising action plans to encourage clients to take responsibility for their own lives and future. Social services departments have been slow to adopt this approach in their own development as organizations. We have tradi-tionally played a passive role, reacting to local and central government policies and to scandal and crises. Our external environment, like the outside world of many of our clients, can be harsh, unfriendly and full of uncertainty.

Why Strategic Management?

Social services departments are striving to come to terms with fundamental changes in their external environment. Some of these changes mirror the management revolution in the private sector, inspired by the now familiar ideas of excellent service to customers, cost effectiveness, leadership and enterprise. This has meant a change in the nature of public services in general and the relationship between central and local government in the past decade. Successive financial crises of the 1970s, sparked off by oil price rises, raised question marks over the continuation of long-term planning and development of public services as practised in the 1960s. Restraints on local government expenditure, together with a host of ideological and other changes, set the seeds for what the Audit Commission called 'the local government revolution'. Local authorities had now to learn to adapt to the introduction of radical principles of restraint on local government spending, the new community charge, competition in providing services, privatization and consumerism. Social services were subject to these changes too, and were forced to look at the provision of services very differently. The Griffiths Report on community care in 1988, for example, focused the debate about services for the elderly not on how many residential places and home helps were needed but on what type of services were required and who should provide them. Ideas of joint planning and collaboration with other agencies began to develop. Social services departments are now emerging, like many other local departments and local councils themselves, with a new and predominantly 'enabling role', no longer the sole or even the main provider of services. More traditional methods of management based on a reactive, *ad-hoc* approach, with autonomous decision-making by social work professionals, are no longer sufficient to cope with this speed of change in the environment. Management experts suggest that in this situation organizations require a strategic management approach. Social services departments are no exception.

What is Strategic Management?

Strategic management is associated with the setting, planning and meeting of the primary goals of the organization. It requires the formulation of strategies to cope with a wide range of variables. It should enable departments to abandon the familiar role of passive victim at the mercy of conflicting pressures, uncertain political and economic climates and other competing organizations. It requires a clear vision of the future and of the future goals of the organization and a willingness to take risks. At a more concrete level, strategic management depends on flexible structures, a different management style and a new range of organizational processes. These include strategic, medium-term, planning functions based on research and analysis, with effective budgetary control systems and performance monitoring.

The key to the understanding of the strategic management approach is the way in which organizations manage the external environment in which they operate. The introductory section indicates two broad categories of environment, one that concentrates on the other organizations with which the local organization transacts and another that emphasises macro-level forces, such as the economic climate or demography. How the public services manage this environment will vary from the methods used by other types of organization. Social services departments cannot, for example, in their strategic management approach, weigh up the key variables, consider the competition from other organizations and then decide to change the product or withdraw from the market altogether. They are obliged to provide services within an imposed statutory framework and meet their legal responsibilities. Social services departments must, therefore, concentrate on controlling or influencing the other institutions active within their environment, but also forecasting and responding to the macro-level variables. Social services departments cannot operate or develop without reference to central government, particularly the Department of Health, including the Social Services Inspectorate, the Home Office, increasingly the Audit Commission and the Department of the Environment, with its responsibilities for the capital programme. The arrival of 1992 may also see a European dimension, as the work of social services departments is affected by directives and regulations from Brussels. At a local level, social services departments work within a long established local government framework of committees, elected members, annual budgets and other municipal departments. Also at a local level, these departments interact with other statutory bodies, particularly local health authorities, the police and courts at a planning and operational level. The voluntary organizations, non-profit agencies and private companies, which together make up the non-statutory sector, are now poised to become more significant figures in the external environment. Then there is the client or consumer, whose views are actively sought anywhere along the continuum from customer satisfaction with services to participation in the planning of services. On the fringe of the network, but ever ready to publicize a scandal or expose a shortcoming, are the media.

This complex pattern of relationships does not operate in isolation. It is shaped and affected by changes in a wider context. The present political commitment to controlling inflation and reducing public expenditure by the economic strategies of high interest rates and low public sector pay awards is bound to affect social services departments. The longer-term political and economic climate, however, is not easy to predict, dependent as it is on a range of national and international variables. The use of public expenditure controls as one of the major economic levers makes financial planning difficult for local authorities. An excellent illustration was provided in April 1990 when a number of local authorities found themselves 'charge capped' by government after the start of the financial year. Consideration of these variables and the complex pattern of relationships in the external environment and the extent to which they can be managed, controlled, influenced or predicted forms the basis of this contribution on strategic management in social services.

Managing the Key Relationships

Analysing the social services environment is a difficult task, where words like 'dynamic' and 'volatile' are barely sufficient to describe the process of change. A review of the network of relationships within any of the client groups and services can soon become out of date. Not only are social services departments changing, but the organizations they interact with are changing too, as is their relative importance within the framework. Reference to the planning process for community care will highlight some of the key points in the analysis. Here, more than anywhere else, it is clear that social services departments are entering a new, even more complex era. It would be foolhardy to speak for all departments in this analysis, but our experience in Leeds is probably typical of many others.

In more slow-moving times, our department offered a traditional range of services to a large multicultural population with a vast array of different social services needs. Services were planned and delivered within budget constraints without much regard to the work of other organizations, either statutory or non-statutory, or even the wishes of the consumer. Our contact with the private sector, for example, was confined to the inspection and monitoring of homes for older people. During the 1980s, changes in local government and in the development of the concept of community care beyond that of the mentally ill began to be reflected in services for other client groups, particularly the elderly. Inter-agency collaboration and experimental joint projects usually supported by joint social services and health authority finance, appeared with a commitment to avoid duplication of services. Joint strategies, objectives and annual targets become familiar language in social services departments, as they adapted to a changing situation.

The publication of the White Paper on community care and the 1990 National Health Service and Community Care Act confirmed the introduction of the concept of the 'enabling authority' into social services. This piece of 'strategic' legislation has set the framework for the care of the elderly and other client groups for at least this decade. Community care will be based on social services departments taking a leading but enabling role, in partnership with the health authorities and other statutory organizations, together with the non-statutory agencies, to provide a 'mixed' economy of care. Clients and carers too are to be involved in care planning. Hence our carefully worded mission statement confirms that we are in the business 'of ensuring the provision of a choice of high quality social services for the people of Leeds'.

These proposals have had a dramatic impact on social services departments' environment, particularly in the care of the elderly. Managers at a planning and operational level now have to handle a complex network of relationships to ensure the provision of services, with constant reference to external factors. Hence the need for a strategic management approach.

The nature of the relationships between social services departments and other key organizations within the context of the community care planning process can be plotted along a continuum. They range from those who control and regulate social services departments, through to those who partially control them or who work in roughly equal partnership with them, to those organizations whom social services departments support, influence or control themselves. Their position along this continuum influences the degree to which they can be 'managed' or manipulated by social services departments, which is one of the underlying themes of strategic management.

Social services departments' relationship with central government in the shape of the Department of Health, via the Social Services Inspectorate and increasingly, the Department of the Environment, is clearly at one end. The Department of Health sets the regulatory framework for social services departments and our statutory responsibilities. The Social Services Inspectorate implements the Department of Health's policy and inspects, as the name indicates, local social services departments to improve effectiveness and efficiency.

The relationship between the Department of Health, the Social Services Inspectorate and social services departments is complex and often misunderstood by those working in or offering advice to the public sector. Indeed, we believe Sir Roy Griffiths failed to understand this relationship in his report on community care, and the subsequent White Paper has compounded the misunderstandings. The Social Services Inspectorate is a regionally based service which acts on behalf of the Secretary of State in inspecting local authority services, reporting to and advising the Secretary of State on those issues. It is only comparatively recently that reports of the Social Services Inspectorate have been published.

A director of social services is appointed by a statutorily elected committee of the local authority. In the past the Secretary of State for Health reserved the right through the Social Services Inspectorate to vet short lists of possible directors. This process has long been abandoned but is still a crucial definer of the relationship for other chief officers, most notably chief constables and the Home Office. Sir Roy Griffiths proposed a Minister of Community Care and seemed to assume that there would be a chain of command as in the Health Service, from the Secretary of State through regional managers to district managers in local authorities, namely from the new Minister of Community Care through to directors of social services. This totally misunderstands the constitutional position of local authorities. The community care White Paper follows this misconception, demanding that community care plans (which are required to show how the local authority intends to stimulate the development of the independent sector) shall be submitted to the Social Services Inspectorate for the approved of the Secretary of State. This poses major strategic management problems for directors of social services, since the objectives defined by the Secretary of State for the 'mixed' economy of care may be quite different from those defined by the locally elected council, which has the statutory responsibility for the delivery and partial funding of the service. The requirement for the director, therefore, is to produce a strategic plan which is acceptable to his/her direct employer, the local authority, and acceptable to a Secretary of State in a government which has a quite different set of political objectives. In this tense position, the Social Services Inspectorate attempts to hold the ring by ensuring that the plan meets appropriate 'professional' rather than political objectives.

Part of strategic management is the management of these conflicts, so attempts are made to influence the situation through various routes. These might include regular meetings between the regional Social Services Inspectorate and the regional branch of the Association of Directors of Social Services, at which directors would inform and hopefully influence the Social Services Inspectorate on the current position and likely future problems, in order that this information can be fed to central administrators to brief the Secretary of State. The Association of Directors of Social Services offers

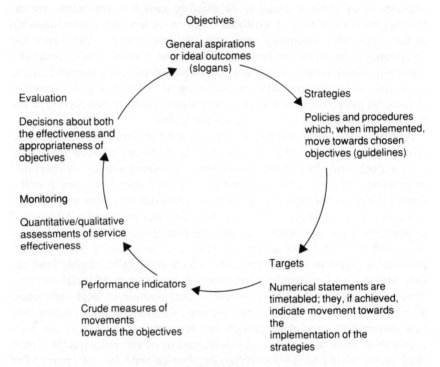

FIGURE 19.1
Strategic management model

advisors to the Association of Metropolitan Authorities and the Association of County Councils and through those means can inform local government members who, in turn, will be negotiating with ministers and senior officials in the annual setting of public expenditure and other vital forces.

Other means of influence, possibly the most influential, are the development, monitoring and publicizing of models of good practice. Much policy is influenced by small-scale pioneering practice projects, for example, Kent's case manager programme is clearly discernible in its influence on the community care White Paper. Alternatively, the influence of Lancaster University and later social information systems monitoring and research on juvenile justice is widely acknowledged in the move away from the use of custody for young people. If this process is so influential, then an important part of strategic management is the promotion of pilot or pioneering projects, evaluation and publicity.

It would be an understatement to describe the introduction of community care as either a pilot or a pioneering project in the social welfare field, but the development of an effective planning process to turn community care into a reality has certainly demanded this type of approach. As such, it also provides a topical and lively case study of strategic management in action. Key stages in a strategic management cycle (Figure 19.1) include defining objectives, devising strategies, setting targets, monitoring progress, evaluation and back again to redefining objectives.

The Background to Community Care

At the national level, just as the uncertainty surrounding its introduction and timing is illustrative of the macro-level forces making strategic management so challenging, community care planning was part of the Conservative government's legislative programme for 1990, with a three-year phased implementation starting in 1991–2. Social services departments were required to produce plans for most client groups by April 1991 for approval by the Department of Health. As the planning process got underway, the Government announced that the implementation would be delayed, largely because of the political necessity of reducing its impact on the poll tax. Keen to avoid any loss of momentum and the corresponding staff disillusionment, Leeds chose to carry on planning for Community Care. Despite the start-stop background to the production of community care plans, the significance accorded to them by the Department of Health has directed the attention of social services departments to adopting a more strategic approach.

Questions of Fitness

Social Services Departments can assess their fitness for community care planning. Below is a list of questions to test whether they and their partners in planning are prepared (or fit) to 'plan'. The more yes answers the fitter they are to begin the process.

1 Does the planning focus on need, inputs, outputs, processes, outcomes and cost effectiveness?
2 Is the planning for local use rather than an exercise to satisfy central government?
3 Does the planning take account of the needs of localities? (Note: what tensions exist between local authority-wide planning and locality planning?)
4 In terms of joint planning – and in particular the mental illness specific grant (MISG) – are problems of coterminosity resolved?

5 Are joint information bases used in the planning process? If information systems are not joint, then are they at least compatible?

6 Are joint planning structures in place? (Can the joint consultative committee/joint care planning team structure be used to help the work on community care plans and the MISG?)

7 Do all agencies define terms such as learning difficulty, mental illness, mental health, disability and so on, in similar ways?

8 Are all agencies agreed on general philosophies and principles of community care? If not, are all parties clear on areas where there is disagreement, and are there systems or processes in place to handle any resulting conflicts?

9 Do all groups trust each other? In particular, do social services departments and district health authorities trust each other in respect of the MISG? (For example, some district health authorities feel that social services departments will spend the money on, say, children's services; whilst some social services departments feel district health authorities will use the MISG as an excuse to cut back on other joint ventures.)

10 Does the current or intended community care planning process genuinely extend beyond the social services department and the district health authority to other partners?

11 Is the involvement of user and carer groups as partners more than a token one? (Have steps been taken to empower or build up effective community/user/carer contributions to the planning process?)

12 Do all agencies have the necessary resources to cope with planning processes for staff, finance and information systems?

13 Does the planning process integrate services planning with financial planning?

14 Does the planning process accommodate aspirations at the same time as it recognizes political realities and financial constraints?

15 Does the planning process integrate revenue with capital considerations? (Note: for no good reason, both local authority and central government financial planning tends to split revenue planning from capital programme planning).

Aims and Objectives of Planning (Questions 1–3)

Social services departments have been comforted to realize that some of the work demanded by community care planning has been done already. All departments have some sort of strategic planning mechanism, based on a conceptual model of service to the main client groups. This preparation of departmental annual plans for services across an authority and for specific neighbourhoods or communities has given staff an initial focus for the plans. The most useful annual plans will have concentrated on needs, outputs, inputs etc., as question 1 suggests.

Working with Partners (Questions 4–11)

Most social services departments will already have established some working relationships with their other partners in the planning process. In Leeds, for example, working with the district health authorities and the voluntary sector to develop joint strategies on mental health and mental handicap has provided a model for the new community care relationship and a foundation for the content of the plans themselves.

Questions of coterminosity, joint information systems, common terminology, philosophies, understanding and, indeed, mutual trust will present a greater challenge. Joint consultative committees and joint consultative planning teams can provide the foundations for new structures; but extending the partnership to include other council departments or user and carer groups is less familiar territory.

Assessing Resources (Questions 12–15)

Staff, finance and information systems all represent key elements in the planning process. Leeds Social Services Department is of the view that involvement in planning should extend to all sections of the department. New conceptual approaches are required to cope not only with the new aspects of community care, but also with the planning and consultation process itself. A skills analysis amongst staff may well expose shortages in certain areas, necessitating new training packages or speedy recruitment programmes. Morale amongst staff faced with new legislation, a new planning approach and, in some cases, the threat posed by community care itself may cause further concern. The planning process does not happen in isolation, for most staff will continue to have operational responsibilities. The ability of departments to manage both processes will be an interesting test of the flexibility of new management structures. The planning process too will have major financial implications. The service plans cannot develop in isolation but must feed into traditional financial planning mechanisms, acknowledging a whole host of financial and political constraints on the way.

There are in addition some more hidden planning costs. These are likely to be extra staff for both administration and planning, stationery and photocopying costs and others associated with the translation of the plans into other languages and Braille to facilitate the consultation process. There are implications too for management information systems, and these also need to be assessed against the demands of the planning process. Peter Drucker, the management guru handing down hints for handling the 1990s, urges managers to give up managing by walking around as there is not enough time. 'Manage,' he advises, 'by taking responsibility for your information needs.' In Leeds the newly expanded planning and monitoring division is working to produce high quality information and statistical analyses on current service provision. They are also working on key out-come measures, input and output and assessment of need, as well as ad-vising on the general format and content of plans. The contextual statistical information collected by the division will be different from that previously collected. Such changes will have implications for the IT functions and capacity of the department, as well as for the current work-load of the planning section staff. The division has also taken the lead responsibility for co-ordinating and monitoring the process itself.

Devising Strategies

Devising strategies to meet the objective of producing a community care plan is the second and perhaps the most important stage in the strategic management cycle. Division of the work-load into meaningful and man-ageable chunks is obviously a key issue. Leeds has set up working groups to cover the three broad bands of service users and to cover organization changes, contract specification and inspection and monitoring. The service user groups have since been subdivided to ensure that all services have been covered adequately. Their first task has been to define the scope of the plan, a common format and a realistic timetable. Assembling the information to conduct a detailed assessment of need and a review of current provision can then begin.

Community care is a corporate enterprise involving not only social services, but also housing, leisure, environment and education departments. Accordingly, the plans need to reflect a corporate approach. In Leeds it has been agreed that the social services department and district health auth-orities should produce a jointly agreed strategic approach to community care and a single joint operational plan for each service-user group. Hence the two Leeds District Health Authorities have nominated planners and consultants to join the working groups. The task of co-ordinating the plans will be undertaken by senior staff from each organization. The appropriate planning relationship with the regional health authority and the self-governing hospital trusts is also under review. The voluntary and inde-pendent sectors, together with consumers and carers, will be involved formally with planning at the consultative stage. Most departments would prefer to take account of their views at a much earlier stage. Strategies to build new working relationships will be needed here to address the problems of planning with a range of organizations, each with specific goals and working to different aims and objectives.

The quality of the relationships forged between all the partners in planning will be reflected in the ease with which they can then agree priorities within and between the service-user groups. Political and professional compromises and trade-offs will feature in the planning process, wherever resources are scarce.

Setting Targets

Once devised, planning strategies have to be set against agreed targets and a realistic timetable. This has to take into account social services departments' internal service and financial planning cycles and those of its partners. The process must also match the local political and financial cycle to allow elected members to consider and approve the draft plans. The whole process has to be completed by March, to ensure that locally approved plans can be forwarded to the Department of Health for inspection and comment.

Monitoring Progress

The great size of the task of community care planning and the tightness of the current timetable make an effective monitoring system essential. Whilst everyone involved has a responsibility to see the completion of the task, it is clearly a management function to monitor progress and maintain momentum. Monitoring, however, is not just confined to meeting deadlines. Plans must also be of high quality as well as ready on time. Many social services departments will have been reorganized to meet the challenge of community care. Their ability to monitor and control the process of preparing plans will be another test of the appropriateness of some new management structures. Senior managers must have at their disposal the right staff at the right time to ensure that the planning process is efficient and effective and is not completed at the expense of operational duties.

Evaluating the Process

No cyclical process, whether training, learning or planning, is complete without a final evaluation stage. The community care plans will include sections on key outcome measures. These will be needed to assess the success or otherwise of the planning process. Strengths and weaknesses can then be identified and the lessons learnt should be incorporated into next year's planning cycle.

This analysis of the planning process should leave little doubt about the challenges facing social service departments in a period of rapid change. Leeds Social Services, like many others, has adopted this strategic planning approach to ensure the continuation of high quality services to local people and our survival as an organization in a hostile and uncertain world. This means, as far as community care is concerned, turning the legal status of social services as the 'lead authority' into a *de facto* position of first amongst equals in its development.

In social work parlance, it is important that departments move away from their helpless victim role, seize the initiative and take full responsibility for their future development. In this analogy strategic management then becomes akin to social work. This has the power to turn the client's (or department's) view of the future into a reality by setting a series of achievable goals and then keeping the client on course for independence, prosperity or success.

Strategic Management: Reflections

Stephen Harrison and Christopher Pollitt

The variations in approach in this final section of the *Handbook* are perhaps more noticeable than in the preceding section on resource management. This may reflect the different circumstances of the different services represented, or a certain vagueness in the very concept of strategic management, or (most probably) some mixture of the two. Clearly there is a difference, for example, between a centralized, national service such as the prison service and a local, networking operation such as community care. Equally, there is a range of models of strategic management, some highly participative and 'bottom up', others essentially hierarchical, with other stake-holders being brought in only on terms set by the management of the focal organization. There is also a certain amount of terminological juggling between the overlapping concepts of 'strategic management' and 'strategic planning'. In the ideological climate of the 1980s the former title was often preferred because of its association with the (virtuous) private sector while the latter was regarded with suspicion because the term 'planning' had bureaucratic connotations.

Indeed, one of the ironic features of the 1980s was the way in which 'planning', at first scorned by the market purists of the new right, crept back in. By the late 1980s, as several of our contributors make clear, 'strategies' were firmly back in fashion. Yet, despite the insistence that strategic management is now the way forward, it is too soon to be sure what its prerequisites may be, how effectively it can be applied within the public services sector, or even what its essential components are (Pollitt, 1990, pp. 156–64). The chapters by Wistow, Brooke, Wilkie and Tutt, Neale and Warburton all indicate that we are nearer the start than the finish of the process of implementing strategic management. The very last chapter provides a useful checklist of 15 questions by which local authorities can assess their preparedness to embark on the strategic management of community care. It does not take too much imagination to adapt that list for application to other areas of the public services, and we suspect that, when this is done, many readers will admit that there are plenty of questions still to be addressed in their own organizations.

Two fundamental issues which seem common across several of the services examined here are, first, the compatibility of strategic management and internal markets and, second, the problems of assuring service integration whilst simultaneously pursuing radical decentralization.

The very existence of large private sector corporations testifies to the fact that markets and plans are not fundamentally incompatible. Yet the *kind* of planning that is feasible may depend heavily on the structure of the markets in which a given corporation operates (Pollitt, 1991). Local monopolies and oligopolies can plan and manage in ways that organizations in more fiercely competitive and uncertain circumstances cannot. In a public service context there is the question of how far a purchasing or strategic management authority can assume that the population of potential suppliers is fairly stable or how far it may face problems of discontinuity of supply. In so far as supply is organized through a series of contracts or quasi-contracts this question partly resolves itself into a practical problem of how risk and uncertainty is distributed between the two parties to each contract. Whether the overall result is increased efficiency and quality or fragmentation and rising costs remains indeterminate (Bartlett, 1991). With such high stakes the need for managers to learn strategic skills is indeed an urgent one. Perhaps Brooke puts the matter in a suitably two-edged way when he writes that 'Developments in services will take aback the inventors of the system.'

Even where a majority of service providers are to be found within a single organizational hierarchy (as is likely at first to be the case for the prison service, the police and many district health authorities and local education authorities) there is still the problem of finding the right balance between decentralization and integration. The contributions from Jenkins, Wistow and Train and Stewart all address this problem. Agency managers, care managers, prison governors and others will each need discretion, backed up by information systems and budgetary flexibility, to enable them to make good use of that discretion. Yet they will also be actors within some larger strategy. How is that strategy to be communicated to them without it becoming a bureaucratic restraint upon their managerial creativity? Can 'results' actually be specified with a precision that will leave such local managers free to find their own 'best way' (as Jenkins suggests)? Or will there still need to be extensive regulation of the *means* which they are allowed to use? The experience of both LMS and the first few months of the NHS internal market suggests that it will be difficult to resist the temptations, political and bureaucratic, to festoon local discretion with a web of procedural rules and prohibitions. Brooke puts the other side of this argument when he points out that 'central control retains the possibility of action to overcome suboptimization by subordinate agencies and to ensure that they contribute to a corporate goal'. The alternative term for 'suboptimization' is, of course, 'local optimization'!

Inevitably, therefore, the *Handbook* concludes on a note of uncertainty. In this final section we have dealt with the most demanding and difficult part of the manager's role. Strategic management requires a holistic view, plus an ability to combine structural change, cultural change, the introduction of new systems and the design of new processes. That this is not a straightforward matter is hardly surprising. Perhaps an appropriate final observation would be that such a feat cannot be accomplished by management alone. Heroic strategic management, parachuted in by charismatic chief executives, is also likely to be poor strategic management. For if strategic management is anything it is relational; that is, it requires the creation and nurture of relationships of trust and respect between different levels and groups within an institution, and between the institution and other key actors in its environment. This takes time and effort from senior managers, but it also involves many other categories of staff. Management, one might say, is too important to be left exclusively to the managers.

References

Bartlett, W. (1991) *Quasi-markets and contracts: a market and hierarchies perspective on NHS reform.* Bristol, School for Advanced Urban Studies. Studies in Decentralization and Quasi-Markets no. 3.

Pollitt, C. (1990) *Managerialism and the Public Services: the Anglo-American experience.* Oxford: Blackwell.

— (1991) Plans and markets. In *Managing public services*, B887, Block 2, Part A (MBA course), Milton Keynes: Open University.

Index